D0553934

The publisher and the University of California Press Foundation gratefully acknowledge the generous support of the George Gund Foundation Imprint in African American Studies.

Blue Eyes, Brown Eyes

Blue Eyes, Brown Eyes

A CAUTIONARY TALE OF RACE AND BRUTALITY

Stephen G. Bloom

UNIVERSITY OF CALIFORNIA PRESS

University of California Press
Oakland, California

Library of Congress Cataloging-in-Publication Data

Names: Bloom, Stephen G., author.
Title: Blue eyes, brown eyes : a cautionary tale of race and brutality / Stephen G. Bloom.
Description: Oakland, California : University of California Press, [2021] | Includes index.
Identifiers: LCCN 2020058497 (print) | LCCN 2020058498 (ebook) | ISBN 9780520382268 (cloth) | ISBN 9780520382275 (epub)
Subjects: LCSH: Elliott, Jane, 1933- | Racism—Study and teaching (Elementary)—Iowa—Riceville. | Prejudices in children—Study and teaching (Elementary)—Iowa—Riceville. | Racism—United States—Psychological aspects.
Classification: LCC LA2317.E44 B56 2021 (print) | LCC LA2317.E44 (ebook) | DDC 370.8909777/312—dc23
LC record available at https://lccn.loc.gov/2020058497
LC ebook record available at https://lccn.loc.gov/2020058498

Manufactured in the United States of America

30 29 28 27 26 25 24 23 22 21
10 9 8 7 6 5 4 3 2 1

For Iris, my brown-eyed girl

It was the whiteness of the whale that above all things appalled me.

HERMAN MELVILLE,
Moby Dick, 1851

CONTENTS

Illustrations follow page 133.

AUTHOR'S NOTE: THE SCAB

It started with a phone call.

"Is this Stephen Bloom?" an emphatic voice asked out of the blue one spring morning seventeen years ago.

Without waiting for a response, the caller sprinted ahead. "Well, this is Jane Elliott and I want to talk to you!"

I had never spoken with or met Elliott before and I had no idea why she'd be calling me. She seemed insistent and determined. The only thing I knew about Elliott was a provocative classroom experiment credited to her.

For a decade, Elliott, a teacher in a small, rural Iowa town, had separated her third-grade students, for two days, into two groups—those with blue eyes and those with brown eyes. On the first day, she told the blue-eyed children that they were genetically inferior to the brown-eyed children. She instructed the blue-eyed kids that they wouldn't be permitted to play on the junglegym or swings. They'd have to use paper cups if they wanted to drink from the water fountain. They wouldn't be allowed second lunch helpings. The next day, Elliott switched the students' roles. The brown-eyed kids would now be considered inferior. The experiment was Elliott's way of showing eight- and nine-year-old white children what it was like to be Black in America. Starting in the mid-1980s and for the next thirty-five years, Elliott would increase the experiment's voltage by trying it out on adults in thousands of workshops worldwide.

I asked Elliott why she had called me, and without hesitation, she responded, "Because I want you to write a book about me."

At the time, a decade in Iowa had taught me that Iowans generally follow protocol, spoken and unspoken. Many Iowans are reserved and deferential, especially those from the rural part of the state (which is pretty much all of Iowa). Blustery or brazen isn't part of most Iowans' DNA.

I was alternately put off and intrigued by Elliott's entreaty. I got the sense that she had set out to find a kindred spirit, perhaps someone who might crack open for her the world of publishing. You can't be conferred global-icon status until you write a book about yourself—or better, until someone writes a book about you.

Elliott's moxie piqued my curiosity, and as soon as I got off the phone, I set out to learn more.

Years before the Black Lives Matter movement or the killing of George Floyd by a Minneapolis police officer in the summer of 2020, Elliott, a white woman from out-of-the-way Iowa, had transformed herself into an international authority on all issues of racism and bias. An award-winning network TV documentary had aired about her, followed by a starring role at a headline-sparking White House conference on education. By 1984, Elliott had left her public school teacher's job in Riceville, Iowa (population: 806), sixteen miles from the Wisconsin state line, and had taken the blue-eyes, brown-eyes experiment on the road. She tried it on tens of thousands of adults, not just in the United States and Canada, but also in Europe, the Middle East, and Australia. She traveled to conferences and corporate workshops. She took the experiment to prisons, schools, and military bases. She appeared on *Oprah* five times. Elliott became a standing-room-only speaker at hundreds of colleges and universities. In the process, she had turned herself into America's mother of diversity training.

Elliott was so successful at what she did that she was granted membership in the historic pantheon of the West's most revered educators: Plato, Aristotle, Horace Mann, Booker T. Washington, John Dewey, Maria Montessori, Jean Piaget, and Paulo Freire. In 2004, the American publishing giant, McGraw Hill, created a multipanel poster suitable for classroom display that included Elliott along with the other venerated thinkers and teachers.[1]

In *Psychology and Life,* a one-and-a-half-inch-thick standard textbook that hundreds of thousands of undergraduates are assigned, Elliott's experiment would be praised as "one of the most effective demonstrations of how easily prejudiced attitudes may be formed, and how arbitrary and illogical they can be." The textbook's author, Stanford professor Philip G. Zimbardo, described Elliott's classroom activity as "a remarkable experiment, more compelling than many done by professional psychologists."[2]

That Zimbardo had been so struck with Elliott made sense. In 1971, when Elliott was pitting blue-eyed students against their brown-eyed classmates, Zimbardo was running his own experiment, the Stanford Prison Experiment, to ostensibly show how easy it was to make thugs out of college students once they were given an overdose of power.[3] Like Elliott, Zimbardo had become an expert when it came to pushing and pulling levers to reveal humanity's nastiest urges.

In nearly every announcement of her appearances on the lecture circuit, Elliott would tout an endorsement from famed child psychiatrist Robert Coles, a Harvard professor, MacArthur Foundation Award recipient, US Medal of Freedom honoree, and Pulitzer Prize winner. Coles's heralded commendation—calling the experiment "the greatest thing to come out of American education in a hundred years"—carried certainty and gravitas.[4] It said Elliott was the real thing.

All of the above drew me in, and a week after that first phone call, I found myself driving the one-hundred-and-fifty miles from Iowa City to Mitchell County to meet Elliott. On a cloudless day set against a robin's-egg blue sky, she ushered me onto her porch and offered me iced tea in a Ball mason jar while patting the well-worn cushion of a bamboo chair.

I started out all wrong by calling the famous classroom lesson an "experiment."

"It never was an *experiment*!" Elliott scolded me, an index finger shooting within inches of my face. "I didn't experiment on children! I was their teacher! I was giving a child an experience for the purpose of changing their brain and that is exactly what it does every time I do it. It was an *exercise*!"

At the time, I let the semantics slide, even though the wiggly distinction troubled me. What Elliott had done to eight- and nine-year-olds *wasn't* an exercise. To me, a journalist, classroom *exercises* were trying out innovative writing assignments or singing musical scales. There was something fun and transitory about them. They might carry educational import, but their impact would not last a lifetime. An *experiment* was something different. It implied unproven and uncertain consequences. To me, Elliott's separation of students based on their eye color seemed like a risky experiment that raised all kinds of ethical issues. In fact, as I was to learn, the experiment had been inspired by Nazis, as Elliott would be the first to admit. She had lied to impressionable children who trusted her. She had told them that half of the class was less intelligent because of their eye color, because of their genetics. The experiment became so real that fistfights erupted on the Riceville Elementary School playground. That seemed bad enough. But Elliott did nothing to stop the fights. She encouraged them, based on the children's newly granted superiority or inferiority. That was part of duping the children into thinking that the experiment was real.

Elliott had constructed a gut-wrenching, true-life nightmare in order to make an indelible point that would stay with her students for the rest of their lives. In essence, she tried to induce a dose of racism into the minds of the third graders.

I visited Riceville four more times after that first meeting, both to interview Elliott and to visit with residents to find out what they thought about her and the experiment. This wouldn't be my first time descending into rural Iowa. I had written one book about a small farming commuity in the state with several more to come, and knew that a stranger asking pesky, personal questions was a violation of the most basic covenant that undergirds such insular places. I knew an even bigger lapse would be for the locals to confide in me. And here I was, poking my nose into what I found Riceville residents hated most: "the experiment," as everyone in town called it.

Fifty years is an eternity, but the people in Riceville remembered what Elliott did to their children—and to them—as though it had happened yesterday. Even if they weren't alive when Elliott presided over the experiment, or they lived somewhere else, they *still* remembered it. Any stranger picking at a scab like that was bound to draw blood.

Word travels fast in small towns, and when I called on retired teachers in Riceville, a half dozen flatly refused to talk about Elliott. Just about everyone I approached ran the other way. Some wouldn't answer their phones. When I knocked on doors, no one welcomed me. The few who consented to meet did their best to evade my questions. They looked at the floor or straight through me. Several heard me out, then quietly asked me to leave. Avon and Mary Kay vendors get more respect.

It was during those initial trips to Riceville when I got word that a pair of retired teachers would talk—but only on the condition that I not use their names and that we drive in separate cars to Charles City, the neighboring county seat of eight thousand residents, thirty miles south. Just as I was about to embark on this Deep Throat rendezvous, the teachers pulled out.

"I've been under her clutches before and I know what it's like," one of the teachers told me. When I asked her to elaborate, she hung up.

It wasn't until I met former mayor Walt Gabelmann, the eighty-three-year-old owner of the Riceville Livestock Pavilion (the downtown barn where cattle are auctioned) that I began to get somewhere. Gabelmann, a jolly man who wrote a column in the weekly *Riceville Recorder* called "Bullshipping with Walt," wasn't put off by much. He volunteered that Elliott had been "a kind of cult leader." Gabelmann labeled her "the devil" and added, "she could get kids to do anything. She actually had them hypnotized."[5]

Meeting Gabelmann proved to be a watershed. Once he opened up, others began to drop their guard while looking over their shoulders. They accused Elliott of all sorts of things. Using innocent Riceville children as guinea pigs. Lying to them. Egging them on. Inventing a tall tale about genetics, about who's superior because of the pigmentation in their eyes. Without asking parents. Pitting children against each other. Then traveling the world, making herself an authority on race, all the while turning her back on Riceville and becoming a millionaire. About the only credit anyone would allow was that Elliott *might* have been a good teacher. A few went as far as saying that Elliott might be considered a visionary—but that was only if you didn't mind the cruelty she had inflicted on hundreds of children of Riceville. Then there was the issue of her "ego." *My oh my*, they said.

I stopped short in undertaking the book Elliott had enlisted me to write. Instead I wrote a magazine article in which I laid out the black-and-white of Elliott and the experiment.[6] Nothing more, nothing less. My own take on Elliott and the negative reaction to her never fully made it into print. The story portrayed Elliott as a heroine who against all odds had done something good.

Flash forward a dozen years.

While walking home from my university office in Iowa City one early September evening, I noticed the red-lettered marquee of the local theater promoting an appearance by Elliott. On a whim, an hour before showtime, I joined the line snaking outside. Parents had brought their young children, adults stood with their aging parents. Three hundred people stood patiently in an orderly queue.

The moment Elliott walked onstage, the almost all-white audience exploded in thunderous applause, rising as one in a rapturous ovation that lasted a full five minutes. Excitement and anticipation, mixed with a sense of history, ricocheted like supercharged ions inside the Englert Theatre that evening. Elliott, compact and robust, wearing a white sweatshirt, black pants, and sneakers, raised her hands like an Alpha Warrior, then exhorted the crowd to take their seats. Emblazoned on the sweatshirt was a quote in black letters that read "Prejudice is an emotional commitment to ignorance," along with the name of the epigram's author, Nathan Rutstein.[7]

"Will every white person in this room who'd like to spend the rest of his or her life being treated as we treat people of color, please stand?" Elliott started.

Seven hundred people and no one stood.

"Do you know what you just admitted?" Elliott asked, her voice turning from a TED Talk to a cultural barn-raising. "That you know racism is real, that you know it's ugly, and that you know you don't want it for yourself or your family. So, why are you so willing to accept it for others?"

The question, I was to realize, was vintage Elliott. The evening would be an exercise in how Elliott played to crowds. She had no use for dissenters or outliers. There was no middle ground. You were with her or you were the enemy.

Everyone in the audience seemed to nod in unison. Spontaneous applause erupted. Some people openly sobbed. Boxes of Kleenex appeared and made the rounds from row to row to row. Elliott was riding an emotional tidal wave. She had unlocked a kind of elemental wellspring. At the end of the evening, the audience wouldn't let her leave.

Elliott's hallelujah performance had once again piqued my interest, and the next weekend, I found myself bouncing along Iowa's washboard backroads, entering that wholly separate cosmos I had grown to know in what had become by then a quarter of a century of my living in Iowa. A makeshift billboard for the Scratch & Dent body shop on the north side of Cedar Rapids was my marker for leaving one world and entering another. Cyclones, fires, floods, and presidential wannabes converging on the local Chat 'n' Chew are what most Americans see of this fecund land in the middle. I was searching for something more—a revelatory portrait of a town that had risen up to eject one of its own. Why was there such a divide between the locals who knew Elliott and the rest of the world who lionized her?

I knew it would mean going down one rabbit hole to get to another and then another and another. It would mean visiting with Jim, who'd suggest I call on Dwight, Harold, or Elaine, who in turn might drop my name to Tom, who might (or might not) have something to say, but surely as soon as I left would call Mary, who'd mention a word or two to Debbie, who when she ran into Bruce and Cheryl at church would recall that some outsider had been asking all kinds of questions about the woman no one in town had forgotten or forgiven.

Just as during my first forays in Riceville, as soon as I mentioned Elliott's name, a transformation seemed to take over whomever I was talking to. It was so unmistakable that I came to expect it. Seemingly pleasant people would suddenly narrow their eyes into slits and glare. There'd be a moment of hesitation, then a display of sorrow or anguish, capped by frustration and anger. Some would shake their heads and frown, others would offer a silent prayer of contrition. Dropping Elliott's name in Riceville was like invoking a word of profanity.

She experimented on our children. She experimented on us. More than one resident told me, with no small amount of pain, "We need to pray for Jane."[8]

A leathery farmer in his eighties declared that, even after all these years, no one from the outside had ever gotten the Jane Elliott story right. Or even close to right. No one from "out there" had the wherewithal, interest, or grit to set the record straight. Certain bends in the truth were never going to get ironed out, and the twists and turns about Elliott and that experiment were about as crooked as they come. "And that's all I'm gonna say," he added, hurrying away as though I was a bill collector.

The locals had long ago convicted Elliott. As often happens in places small and large, there was a degree of contagion when it came to separating fact from fiction, and since nearly everyone in Riceville felt the same way about Elliott, whether based on truth, hearsay, speculation, rumor, or misinformation, there seemed to be no room for error.

Could an entire town be wrong? *That* wrong?

I got the sense that people in Riceville looked at Elliott as a "local girl" gone horribly rogue.

Let her regale and delight big-city folks who come knocking at America's pastoral back door. That's who she's been courting for five decades, crowing to convoys of big-city chroniclers who travel far and wide, notebooks open, tape recorders and cameras whirring. At your service.

Elliott had polished her story so that by now it shone like a snow moon on a clear, cold winter night.

Through persistence, diligence, and perhaps worst of all, in the eyes of Riceville, sheer ambition, Elliott had catapulted herself to immortality. Regarded, respected, revered. Outside Riceville, she was a visionary, a combination of Rosa Parks, Eleanor Roosevelt, maybe even Joan of Arc. Inside, she was a con artist.

Elliott was like a politician whose popularity was greatest with voters who least knew her. She was exalted in inverse proportion to her distance from Riceville. No way could Elliott be a prophet in her own land, but she could take an audience's breath away in places like San Francisco, New York, Glasgow, Melbourne, London, Amsterdam, or Berlin.

Back home, the locals seemed to view Elliott as Professor Howard Hill, the snake oil salesman from *The Music Man,* set in River City, but in reality,

Mason City, where author Meredith Wilson grew up, fifty miles west of Riceville. Like Professor Hill, Elliott had pulled the wool over everyone's eyes. That's what nearly everyone told me.

Truth be told, Elliott never cared much for the locals either. The handful of innovators tiny Riceville has ever known have faced censure and consequences. That's often the story with small-town America, despite any idealized hype to the contrary. Even before she tried out the experiment on Riceville children, Elliott had been skating on thin ice. After the experiment, she'd fallen through. And no one in town was about to come to her rescue. I got the impression that most would have preferred that she'd drowned.

Elliott had set out to see how much havoc she could stir by putting her thumb on the scale of human emotion and empathy. That was the heart and soul of the experiment. During the experiment she became the opposite of squeaky-clean Mister Rogers, a hero of the same generation, who gleefully sang to kids: *It's you I like. Every part of you. Your skin, your eyes, your feelings. It's you I like!*[9]

Elliott would have none of that. She hated the values that some Riceville parents had instilled in their children. Elliott seemed to know what these young children would grow up to become—unless she imprinted her wisdom on their squishy, developing brains. Elliott's mission was to administer a mind-altering social-experiment inoculation, even though neither the kids nor their parents had asked for such a vaccination.

To most Riceville locals, it was bad enough that Elliott had staged the experiment in the first place, but it was even worse that they had permitted it to flourish for the better part of ten years. How could they have stood by and just watched this "game" being played on their children? Rural Iowans ordinarily wouldn't question those paid to teach their children—that's a given. But this was an experiment inspired by Nazis. How could it have taken so long to stop Elliott? There seemed to be a collective sense of guilt, turned to anger, that Riceville residents now shared.

There also was the issue of how ruthless locals felt Elliott had been in steamrolling her way. Her ambition had been so sharp, people said, she could have sliced open a sow's ear with just a sideways glance. Anyone could have seen that.

Just who was Jane Elliott, born poor outside Riceville city limits, to wave her corrective wand to improve the lot of our children, not to mention all of humankind? Who was she to belittle and insult seemingly happy and contented children, and later, do the same with adults?

For a host of reasons, some serendipitous, others calculated, the experiment Elliott popularized in 1968 multiplied at dizzying, geometric speed. It spread to other teachers and school districts across the nation and around the world. Thousands of teachers and trainers would adopt the experiment and try it out on students young and old. During the dawning era of multiculturalism, hundreds of corporations used the experiment on their workers. For some who sat at Elliott's feet, it changed them for the good. The experiment exposed them to racism and its far-reaching impact. But for others, decades after being tormented by an experiment ostensibly designed to teach about racism, many of her subjects *still* feel the wallop of Elliott's smack-them-over-the-head method. For more than a few who experienced it, Elliott's self-proclaimed exercise turned into a monster experiment.

It surely was powerful, since the supposed simulation lasted only one or two days. Yet for many, its impact lurked in people's memories for a lifetime.

If Elliott's reach and influence had stopped in Riceville, her impact would have been felt but it also could have been contained, like a brushfire stopped from spreading by local firefighters, the town's trusted guardians. A case of limited damage, confined to one community and no more.

Elliott had to pay for the wildfire she had ignited, starting with Riceville's own children. The people of Riceville needed to do something, even though the blaze had by then spread far and wide. They needed to do *something*. They needed to transform Elliott into a kind of Tessie Hutchinson, the doomed housewife in Shirley Jackson's dystopian short story "The Lottery."[10]

But what was the truth? What *really* happened in Classroom No. 10, where Elliott tried out the experiment? What *really* transpired in the thousands of sessions she led around the world?

Maybe the locals had gotten Elliott wrong. Could a collective amnesia have corroded the memories of the townspeople, mutating what had happened into what never had happened? Shadings of the truth change over the course of fifty years.

Had Elliott been an unlikely, prescient ally to people of color, a white teacher from a remote recess of America, who pried open the eyes of white children whose lives had already been steeped in bigotry? Or was Elliott guilty of appropriating cultural oppression for her own personal and financial gain? Could Elliott have been, in essence, a race-baiting grifter?

It came as no surprise that my snooping around town would not sit well with Elliott. Word was bound to get back to her in a place as chatty as Riceville.

One Monday morning after yet another trip to Riceville, the message light on my office phone flickered insistently. A voice mail. As in our first conversation, Elliott was forceful and strident but this time there was an acid edge:

It won't be necessary for you to return this call and it won't be necessary for you to come up here at any time to interview me for any reason.... Your decision to vilify all the citizens of Riceville because of the behavior of a few is the worst form of discrimination. I won't tolerate it. I won't cooperate with it, and I do not choose to be a part of what will now be an unauthorized biography. If you insist on going ahead with this, I'm going to talk with my attorney ... just as quick as I get off of this telephone and find out what I can do to get you to stop *now*. Riceville is the home of my upbringing. My grandfathers, my great-grandfather was one of the first settlers there, and I do not choose to have that community vilified because of the idiocy of the lunatic fringe. Thanks, it's been nice knowing you. Goodbye.[11]

But I'm getting ahead of myself.

Prologue

THE LIGHTS. THEY WERE THE FIRST THING Elliott noticed. How could she not? They were *blinding*, so bright that her first impulse had been to shield her eyes with her hands. But she couldn't do that! She'd have come out from behind the curtain looking like she'd just awakened from a dream in the dead of night.

Elliott squinted as she moved left to right across the stage. Don't forget about the step, she kept repeating to herself. Remember the step. The step.

The thunderous applause from the cavernous studio theater was exhilarating. Striding toward the trim, slender funnyman and his enormous sidekick, Elliott flashed a smile and waved diffidently to the audience. Against the constellation of blazing lights, she could barely make out the forms of several people scattered in the front rows. They were nodding and clapping. Darald was out there somewhere, but these were strangers, at least the ones whose faces she could make out. And they were welcoming her! Elliott could see, hear, and feel that.

The raised platform ahead of her was a stage on a stage. That's where Johnny Carson, the most popular man in America, and second banana Ed McMahon were waiting for her.

All the while, Elliott could see out of the corner of her eye the neon audience APPLAUSE signs blinking maniacally. By the sound of the clapping, everyone was looking forward to the teacher from someplace somewhere about to say something. Everyone liked Johnny Carson, and who doesn't like teachers? A night with America's premier court jester and his special guest. This would be fun!

It turned out that Elliott didn't need to remember to step up to greet Carson. For the thirty feet she had to traverse across the TV studio stage, Elliott had the eerie sensation that she was *floating*.

She shook Carson's hand first, then McMahon's. Carson's felt like a slippery eel, McMahon's like an enormous mitten. Quick and business-like. A trio of nods and smiles. She got comfortable in the gray-upholstered chair to Carson's right. Shimmying a little, she tugged at the bottom of her dress so that the hem might drop a little closer to her knees. Was it *too* short?

As the applause died down, Carson opened by tossing a throwaway line about Elliott's trip to New York, a big-city rip to anyone from America's interior.

"I understand this is the first time you've flown?"

"On an airplane, it is," Elliott answered straight up, not missing a beat, which made for a ripple, then in a second or two a delayed reaction, and finally a wave of knee-slapping laughter from the audience.[1]

Elliott hadn't realized what it was she'd said or what it could possibly have meant. But that didn't make any difference. She had scored. This thirty-four-year-old teacher with the short brunette bob had a sense of humor. Carson and the hayseed from Iowa or Ohio or Indiana or wherever she was from ought to be good. Carson extracted the best from everyone, especially from civilians. When it came to non-Hollywood types, Carson's shtick could border on the cruel, but viewers loved it anyway.

With those five words, Elliott had already become a hit.

When she'd been in makeup earlier, while two young women in miniskirts applied pancake to her cheeks, *Tonight Show* producer John Carsey had welcomed Elliott this way: "Mrs. Elliott, the people who watch *The Tonight Show* don't want to think. They want to be entertained. So *please* don't say anything thought-provoking. And, *please*, don't say anything depressing. Got it?"

Elliott being Elliott wasn't going to let any of that go unanswered.

"I can't think of anything that *isn't* depressing about racism," she remembered shooting back.

"Don't worry," Carsey replied smoothly. "We're gonna punch it up."

Elliott wasn't quite sure how an experiment designed to show the impact of discrimination on third-grade children could be punched up, but she was willing to see what Carson and his merrymakers had in mind.

Carsey told Elliott that she'd be the show's first guest, the warm-up act to the night's main attraction, winsome actor James Garner, promoting his new movie, *How Sweet It Is!*, costarring bouncy ingénue Debbie Reynolds. The Box Tops, a Nashville band that had run the *Billboard* charts to No. 2 with their hit "Cry Like a Baby," would also be appearing. It sounded like a fun

Friday night, something for everyone. The beginning of the long Memorial Day weekend.

The show would start taping at six thirty and would be aired at eleven thirty on both coasts, ten thirty Central time. No one knows whose idea it had been to invite Elliott, but surely *Tonight Show* producer Rudy Tellez had approved of her appearance, and certainly Carson, compulsively hands-on, had signed off on the invitation. Carson wouldn't have personally called Elliott to invite her if he hadn't.

Carson and Elliott shared more than a little in common. Not only were they Midwesterners, but both were Iowa natives. Carson had been born in the southwestern corner of the state, in Corning. His family had lived in three other rural Iowa towns, Avoca, Clarinda, and Red Oak, before moving to Norfolk, Nebraska, when Carson was eight. If Carson ever were to be cast as mischievous Frank Hardy from the Hardy Boys, then Elliott would be intrepid Nancy Drew. Both were smart and inquisitive, pushing to make more of themselves than their Iowa roots nominally might allow. At this point in their respective careers, forty-three-year-old Carson's dream of fame had already been realized; Elliott's was about to start.

Carson had been intrigued by Elliott's classroom experiment. Despite an aversion to tackling provocative, topical issues, Carson was well read and politically aware. *Tonight* wasn't a political show, and if Carson ever turned it into one, his ratings would have tanked. If Americans wanted politics before they slid off to visit the sandman, Carson wasn't the man to deliver it. But every once in a while, Carson liked to surprise late-night TV viewers. Carson's version of a poke in the ribs, a way to say, "Don't go to sleep *yet*." Tonight would be one of those times.

Elliott wasn't politics, per se. She was a teacher from the middle of America who had done something extraordinary. No one outside of miniscule Riceville, Iowa, had yet heard about Elliott's little experiment. At this point, the only ink about Elliott and what she'd done had appeared in the *Riceville Recorder*. Why not have the spunky teacher explain the experiment to the rest of the nation?

Carson's people had banked on Elliott. That, though, would depend on her. She could talk in the opening slot for as long as she'd be entertaining. Within reason, of course. If she bombed, Carsey would give her the hook.

At least, the producers had been optimistic enough not to give Elliott the "death slot," the long minutes ticking to the show's close at one a.m., reserved for "serious conversation," when writers like Gore Vidal, Truman Capote, or

William Saroyan invaded the show and made night owl appearances. Elliott, the producers reasoned, could be a quirky, offbeat hit—a third-grade teacher from Flyover Country dropped into the mix with a gee-whiz story. There was room on the show every now and then for someone like that.

Upbeat. Breezy. Snappy. That was the key, as Carsey had advised Elliott in makeup. Don't be somber about whatever it was you did back wherever you came from. Make it light. We don't want serious. *The Tonight Show* is entertainment. We're here to *entertain*.

Certainly Elliott had an important story to impart, given Martin Luther King Jr.'s assassination seven weeks earlier and the endemic racism that continued to ravage the United States, which had escalated into violence and looting in dozens of cities at the time. *The Tonight Show* had to do *something* to pay homage to King. Maybe the schoolteacher and her offbeat story would be the ticket. It wouldn't be much, but Carson's people never intended it to be. A nod and no more. Fade to commercial.

Would she ramble? Would she freeze? Or would she go gaga, never getting anywhere except to mug to ten million viewers how awestruck she felt sitting in America's living room?

None of this would be bad for *The Tonight Show*, by the way. But in moderation. It was the reason civilians were asked to appear on the show in the first place. Nonprofessionals offered verbal miscues, pratfalls, and occasionally, yes, sincerity and insight. Every once in a while a visit from a non-Hollywood type actually worked. An everyday American who shared a nugget of wisdom with the folks back home. In moderation. If the guest turned out to be funny, that'd be even better. *Tonight* viewers liked Don Rickles and Buddy Hackett, but really, how much boozy Vegas humor could Carson's mainstream audience take? Viewers loved plain-folks heroes. Just as long as Elliott didn't turn serious.

Carson was Everyman—only smarter, quicker, funnier, richer, thinner, and handsomer. Americans valued what he said, and by extension, listened to what his guests had to say. Anyone who had a message wanted to get on *Tonight*. Getting on the Carson show was getting to America.

Carson veered toward the safe and comfortable. Night after night, he projected a reassuring presence that made him, for better or worse, a national bellwether. While he was uncontested as America's master of the come back one-liner, he also was the litmus test of all things American. For better or worse, Carson was the nation's prima facie spokesman. That *The Tonight Show* aired at a time when viewers were unwinding, about to sleep, stew, or frolic, also was an ingredient in the ninety-minute program's rat-a-tat-tat recipe. Carson was cool, as was the medium, per Marshall McLuhan's au courant observation. How many other middle-aged males could get away with being called "Johnny" if they weren't?

What those on the Studio 6B set seemed to worry about was whether Elliott would turn her once-in-a-lifetime opportunity into a guilt-tripping polemic about race. Yes, King had been murdered. Yes, American cities were going up in flames. But if Elliott went there, it'd be the kiss of death. Keep it simple. Answer Johnny's questions. Keep it light. *Banter.*

At exactly six thirty the show began, first with Paul Anka's upbeat instrumental, which had been Carson's signature since his first show in 1962, followed by sidekick McMahon's booming "And now—here's Johnny!"

Carson, looking a little lost, sauntered onstage, beaming like a dressed-up, buttoned-down version of Huck Finn. McMahon, at his perch, offered his signature greeting—fingertips joined, hands flattened, bowing in mock Buddhist benediction to sensei Carson. McMahon let fly a couple of *Hi-YOOOOOH*'s!, his bromantic cry to the boss. Band leader Doc Severinsen, clad in his usual eye-popping getup of a sequined shirt and shiny bell-bottoms, followed suit, bidding Carson a bemused smile as he raised the index finger of his right hand and twirled it from head to waist while bowing his head, his nightly trademark.

Dressed in a worsted-wool dark-brown Hart Schaffner and Marx suit that looked too snug, loose-limbed Carson began his monologue center stage.

There was a lot to make fun of that day. Carson started by zinging political candidates elbowing for the lead in the year's presidential primaries, which would culminate next week in winner-take-all California. A month earlier, President Johnson, in his slow, molasses-thick Texas drawl, had announced his decision not to seek a second term, leaving the Democrats scrambling to run against Republican front-runner, jowly Richard Nixon. Tenacious Bobby Kennedy was rising meteorically against antiwar candidate Minnesota senator Eugene McCarthy, while Johnson's heir apparent, Vice President Hubert Humphrey, was turning more and more pugnacious, fearing defeat.

Carson avoided in-the-trenches politics, but no way could he not lob a few grenades tonight, particularly at Nixon. Carson deadpanned three quick one-liners, broke into a puckish smile, then rolled his eyes skyward. Classic Carson. A few canned guffaws, followed by a round of eager applause from the audience. It was going to be a good night.

Carson touched his Windsor tie, pulled at his shirt cuffs, and leaned back on his heels. Playing the modest Midwesterner, acting as though he was embarrassed by all the attention, Carson cracked four more jokes, mimed his famous half golf swing, then broke for a commercial, intoning *The Tonight Show*'s groan-worthy stanza: "We'll be right back."

During the break, Carson moved left to greet McMahon at the desk and chair on the stage on a stage; the furniture set looked like it came from some discount wholesaler in the bowels of New Jersey. The two men feinted and dodged, exchanging warm-up patter, acting like teenage boys at a junior high dance. "Ten seconds," a man with a board suddenly shouted, and Carson on cue turned serious, tap-tapping out what seemed like Morse code with the pink eraser top of a yellow no. 2 pencil. Three, two, one.

Back on, Carson teased the appearance of tonight's headliner, nice-guy Garner, a wife-pleaser pajama-clad husbands could tolerate. But, in the meantime, Johnny had a special guest.

After another commercial break, producer Carsey, standing next to Elliott backstage, touched the small of her back. It was time.

As the show's rainbow curtains parted, Elliott squared her shoulders and inhaled. As Severinsen and his band struck up a folksy tune, America was introduced to Jane Elliott.

When the applause died down, Carson asked a setup about what had brought Elliott the thousand miles from Iowa—he first said she was from Ohio, then corrected himself—to New York. It was Elliott's prompt to present the classroom experiment.

This was her moment. And she went for broke.

Carefully, even meticulously, Elliott explained the experiment, how she had come up with the idea to split her third-grade class into two groups—one of children with blue eyes and the other, children with brown eyes. She explained how she gave privileges, such as extra time for lunch and recess, to the brown-eyed students just because of the color of their eyes. She said the blue-eyed students had to use paper cups if they wanted to drink from the water fountain. She slowed her speech, then nodded, for all this to sink in. Elliott was a teacher, after all.

She described how she had instructed the blue-eyed students not even to think about doing their homework because they were too dumb to get any of the answers right, and even if they managed to finish it, they were too lazy to remember to hand it in the next day. "That's just the way blue-eyed children are," she told Carson, who nervously cracked a joke about his own blue eyes, which nicely cut through what Elliott was saying before it began to sink in.

Elliott talked about fights breaking out on the playground between the blue-eyed and brown-eyed children. She mentioned how miserable and despondent the blue-eyed kids had become once their privileges had been stripped from them. She added that the next school day she switched the experiment, making the brown-eyed kids the superior group, and finally how she had explained to all the children that the two days had been a way to demonstrate something she called "discrimination." That word was a mouthful for third graders, but Elliott said eight- and nine-year-olds are smarter than most adults give them credit for.

This is how Black children feel *every* day, she told Carson, adding that her twenty-eight students, all of whom were white, felt absolutely terrible about what they had done to each other during the two-day experiment.

Elliott spoke passionately. She was forceful, articulate, and powerful. The way she explained it, her little experiment to import make-believe racism into a rural classroom made complete sense.

Elliott couldn't make out the audience's reaction to any of what she was saying. The lights were too bright, but she noticed how quiet they'd become. She had tried her best to transport the 465 members of the studio audience, and the viewers at home, to Room No. 10 in Riceville Elementary. That called for some concentration, as well as some interest on the part of those watching her. *Tonight Show* viewers were more accustomed to the Gabor sisters dishing about their ex-husbands than a teacher talking about racism.

But when the studio's APPLAUSE signs blinked on, the audience clapped appreciatively. They seemed receptive to what Elliott had said. Or maybe they were just being polite. As for the viewers at home, if they were about to fall asleep, Elliott had nudged them awake. What Elliott had said on national television was either heroic or crazy. Maybe it was both.

Carson prided himself on figuring out public reaction before the public could, and his first impression this evening was that Elliott was trouble. Choosing her as a guest had been way too ambitious, he now realized. Carson kept nodding at Elliott. No way could he break in and crack another joke. Not with this guest, not with what she was saying, not with the King assassination raw on everyone's mind.

What Elliott was talking about could blow up. End-of-the-week Friday audiences wanted to laugh, not hear a sermon. Guilt wasn't part of *The*

Tonight Show's repertoire. Minutes into Elliott's appearance, Carson's narrowed eyes shifted to the producer Carsey at the edge of the stage, just out of view from the TV audience.

Get her off the show. Now.

Talking about kids was fine. Not every night, but once in a while. Everyone loves kids. Art Linkletter had made a career out of them, but Linkletter's show didn't straddle the witching hour five nights a week. Carson's genius had been to create a hip variety show for adults. Next-day chatter around the office water cooler. His monologues, full of double entendres, along with the show's mix of eclectic guests—some famous, others nobodies—were conversation starters. They were part of the nation's cultural zeitgeist.

But pushing America's lifestyle guru to discuss issues of racism and discrimination, that bordered on the risky, even the fatal, more appropriate for *The David Susskind Show* than *The Tonight Show*.

Carson reflexively fidgeted with his tie. He picked up one of the sharpened pencils on his desk. Elliott had turned the tables on Carson. She was making *him* nervous.

Elliott's appearance on *The Tonight Show* had been an experiment in itself, and six minutes was as long as America would get to hear about it. She had been a chancy appetizer. If she went on too long, she'd ruin the whole meal.

Crouched just off camera, Carsey held up a big card that read, "Go to commercial."

Carson nodded knowingly. During the next commercial, Elliott was whisked off the set, a casualty of the American Condition losing to the People's Entertainment. It was a showdown Elliott had lost as soon as she had opened her mouth. Edgy political comedian Mort Sahl, whose fights with Carson were the stuff of legends, assessed the every-night intellectual voltage of *The Tonight Show* this way: "Carson's assumption is that the audience is dumb, so you mustn't do difficult things."[2]

Elliott had raised all kinds of issues that skewed terribly wrong for *The Tonight Show*. She had been intended as just another in a series of offbeat guests to spice up pre-summer ratings. The week before, a man who trained geese, chickens, and turkeys to ring a bell, which they did with alacrity, had appeared; the week after, another Iowan came on the show and shot a Coca-Cola vending machine with a rifle. If those guests weren't bizarre enough, the preceding Monday, Tiny Tim, without fiancée Miss Vicki, trilled "Tiptoe through the Tulips" in an ear-ringing falsetto while strumming an off-key ukulele.

Elliott was something very different. Her message of racial harmony achieved through an experiment of make-believe racism had managed to slip through America's public persona of feel-good TV during a pivotal moment in history. She appeared on the last evening in May during what would be a spring America would never forget.

Negroes, as Black Americans were politely called at the time, were treated as fifth-class citizens by whites, most of whom didn't have a clue about what "those people" could possibly want. That is, if whites even cared. Eradicating racism, discrimination, and prejudice started with teaching young white children the damage their parents inflict every day on Negroes. That was Elliott's message.

Of course, she couldn't get much of that out, sandwiched between Carson and McMahon, but her appearance on the show nonetheless was a milestone. Carson had given Elliott a megaphone, whether he or his viewers wanted to hear her or not.

Within minutes, the reaction to what Elliott had said hit home. NBC's switchboard lit up, as newspaper columnists and other commentators are wont to say, "like a Christmas tree." NBC logged an avalanche of callers who were aghast that this mild-mannered teacher could have devised such a brutal experiment. One woman called in to say, "How dare you try this horrible experiment out on white children! Black children grow up accustomed to such behavior, but white children, there's no way they could possibly understand it. It's cruel to white children and will cause them great psychological damage."[3]

Which was exactly Elliott's point.

Undaunted, Elliott basked in the dimming spotlight. She relished being the center of attention. For Elliott, the appearance would be a signature moment. *The Tonight Show* would change her to her very core.

Of course it did. How could it not?

To Elliott, her over-almost-before-it-started appearance had been a directive to right what was wrong with America. A white schoolteacher from Iowa champing at the bit to lead a movement to alter how white Americans view Black Americans, one child at a time. Her phosphorescent moment had been a personal invitation to participate in a compact of fairness and equality that Americans believed in. Or liked to think they believed in. Or maybe ought to believe in. Or perhaps just gave lip service to.

Fame is a strange thing. For some, it's ephemeral; for others, it's defining. For the next half century, Elliott would unceasingly remind people of her national debut on *The Tonight Show*, before dismissing the appearance as a fluke. Yet, when she looked out at the studio audience that last Friday evening in May, glaring spotlights blinding her, the nation's attention directed at her, she saw rows and rows of darkened gray silhouettes of faces, smiling, nodding, clapping.

Elliott's whole life was about to change. She would have it no other way.

ONE

The Corn

FOR MORE THAN A CENTURY, Iowa has produced more corn than any other place in the world, and in Jane Elliott's hometown of Riceville, corn reigns supreme. Thousands of acres of it encircle Riceville the way shimmering water surrounds a tiny Pacific atoll. Corn grows quickly, shooting from seedling to eight-foot stalk in less than fourteen weeks. So rapid is its growth that in July, if you happen onto an Iowa cornfield, you'll hear crunching, crackling sounds, a symphony of stretching and pulling as the nascent plants struggle to ascend toward the heavens.

Tucked within each husk, kernels have an exacting architectural precision. They're staggered in interlocking rows, each row containing an even number of kernels. Farmers plant corn seed with the same precise rigor, rows plumb with nary a squiggle of deviation. Ninety-nine percent of the state's crop is known as "field corn," not to be confused with the sweet stuff to be eaten on the cob, slathered with butter, sprinkled with salt. Field corn is used for livestock feed, ethanol production, and corn syrup. It's an entirely different species, with big ears and inside the husk, kernels that form dents as the corn dries. Most farms maintain a tiny plot of sweet corn, usually tended by children and sold on the side of the road from a pickup with its tailgate down. A dozen ears for five dollars is a fair price. The local version of Girl Scout Thin Mints.

The rows extend farther than the human eye can see, farther than most urban minds can fathom. On and on they go, seemingly forever. The glimmering fields have a way of insulating this pocket of rural America, buffering it from the rest of the nation's vitality and vulgarity. The corn cushions Riceville, as though whatever happens here is wholly contained in a separate and complete universe. With a gentle lilt from a summer breeze, the russet silk strands sprouting from the green-sheathed ears create an undulating carpet of red and gold hues as the sun begins its daily elliptical descent over the ordered maize.

Corn isn't the only harvest that defines Riceville. The confluence of pig and cattle manure is so sharp that the locals refer to Riceville as "Stinkville," even though everyone seems so used to the stench (a combination of ammonia and hydrogen sulfide) that most insist they don't smell anything. Iowa is the nation's leading producer of pigs. The state's population of three million is dwarfed by the multitude of hogs: at any given time, twenty-three million pigs call Iowa home, and on an annual basis, that amounts to almost fifty million swine, or about seventeen pigs per person. There's a one-in-three chance that the bacon strips next to your eggs and hash browns this morning came from Iowa.[1]

Corn, hogs, soybeans, and increasingly, wind-turbine energy are what define the state, along with the quadrennial Iowa caucuses, when itinerant presidential candidates show up in pressed denim and stiff leather boots, glad-handing anyone with a pulse. After 2020's bungled caucus, the nation's first presidential preference contest, with its arcane rules and unreliable returns, may never return. With Black residents making up only 4 percent of a statewide population of 3.1 million, how representative of the rest of America can Iowa be?[2]

In some ways, the state is a time warp. The state capital, Des Moines, the state's largest city, has just 214,000 residents.[3] Contained between the Mississippi and Missouri Rivers, 86 percent of the state's landmass is farm-land.[4] What rises from the soil and what perambulates atop it are what make landlocked Iowa hum.

The state is a place of extremes. By Labor Day, the sunbaked summer is over. The fall of dappled orange and red, everyone's favorite season, seemingly overnight yields to snow, sleet, and a curtain of steel gray that some years doesn't rise until spring.

Winter runs mid-October to mid-April—and that's a temperate year. Thirty to fifty degrees below zero with windchill is not uncommon. Teeth-chattering windstorms swirl and swell over the snowy meringue-white landscape. If you absolutely must make a road trip, blankets, flares, canned food (and can opener), and a fully charged cellphone are mandatory. If you ever get stranded in a snow drift on the side of a road, don't think of leaving your car unless you know exactly where you are headed and exactly how long it will take to get there. Even then, it's not a good idea. Best to stay with your vehicle and wait.

By the time Easter rolls around, a bluish-yellow winter pallor has washed over everyone's face. By June, be prepared for golf-ball-sized hail and pelting rain. Tornadoes and a wind phenomenon known as derechos are also apt to visit. Then, in two blinks of an eye, spring switches into humid, sticky summer when mosquitoes buzz next to your ears, sounding like miniature chain saws.

All of this topsy-turvy meteorology seems somehow to comingle to nurture the seed, nestled in the notched furrows of dark, alluvial soil, to produce magnificent corn.

All over again. Season after season after season.

. . .

In 1855, twenty-five-year-old Dennis Rice, on an exploratory trip from Chautauqua County, New York, imagined a steam-operated flour- and saw-mill along the rushing waters of the Wapsipinicon River in the northeast corner of the new state of Iowa. With his brothers Franklin and Gilbert, Rice platted the area and settled there, ensuring that the grid of a town growing up alongside the Wapsipinicon would forever be named Riceville.

Forty-seven years later, businessman F. A. Brown built above his Riceville hardgoods store on Main Street an eponymous opera house, which showcased a short film of the Wright Brothers' first flight at Kitty Hawk, and in 1915, D. W. Griffith's epic, *The Birth of a Nation*. Brown brought to Riceville's population of eight hundred traveling vaudeville, plays, circuses, and magic shows. The last performance at the opera house was in 1966, a variety show called "The Riceville Gaieties." Five hand-painted, thick, stage-wide curtains that once hung in Brown's Opera House now rest in storage in the Riceville Public Library, shown by appointment.

Chicago Great Western Railroad passenger trains used to pick up and discharge passengers in Riceville but in 1962, the town's stop was discontinued since hardly anyone made the 330-mile trip to Chicago any longer. Riceville's CGW depot closed in 1971 and eleven years later, the hot-rolled steel train tracks were extracted from the earth and hauled away. Instead of joining the rest of America, Riceville stayed put.

Today, the nearest traffic light is eighteen miles away. Riceville's only elevator raises and lowers corn and soybeans, not people. A 150,000-gallon water tank atop a tower delivers more than enough to serve the needs of everyone in town, with a little extra to extinguish any reasonable fire that needs quenching. As late as 1981, Riceville residents used telephone party lines, and today, all landlines start with 985. The city's telephone directory is six pages long. A tradition of the graduating class at Riceville High is silk-screened T-shirts with everyone's name printed on front.

The area's only growing population is Amish families. Several dozen live in nearby McIntire, and almost every year there are accidents and near-accidents of motor vehicles swerving to avoid horse-drawn buggies. Blond Amish children walk barefoot along the side of roads, the boys wearing suspenders, blue shirts, dark pants, straw-brim black-banded hats; the girls in long frocks and black-hooded bonnets. If a curious out-of-towner stops to inquire about directions, the children are instructed not to smile, and absolutely never to pose for photographs.

Riceville is an interlocking web of close-knit families, where everyone knows everyone else (as well as their cousins, first through fifth). There's no city gate to enter or exit, but there might as well be. Iowa farming towns are scattered fifteen, twenty miles apart, and each hamlet is a nation unto itself, wholly governed by generations of familial rules, customs, reputations, and property. Access is locked with few stray keys.

Locals can tell who's driving by the sound of a car or pickup. No one puts on turn signals because everyone knows where everyone else is going. As a greeting, farmers employ an index-finger wave from the top of their steering wheel. Unless it's a stranger. Then, the salutation might well be a cocked chin and an arched eyebrow. Locals pay attention to an interloper's license plates that if from Iowa, identify which of the state's ninety-nine counties the driver is from. Within hours, news of the sighting, the make of the vehicle, along with a drive-by description of the stranger make the local rounds. Phones ring. Neighbors peek out from behind curtains.

What ever brought you *here*?

The cliché about farmers being laconic, stolid, and stoic comes from somewhere. Whatever it is will get fixed, replaced, or returned to normal in due time. Patience may be a virtue, but it's the way to survive. Such behavior stems from the extreme weather, yes, but also from averse-to-change rural "values," which may be code for Christian, white, churchgoing, and not trusting anyone from anywhere else. If you don't like how things are around here, then you might think about moving. Say something bad about Iowa and prepare for an onslaught. Undying loyalty is required when it comes to the state and all that pertains to it. Sharp elbows belong somewhere else. With a degree of pride, residents like to boast they abide by something they call "Iowa nice." At least, that's what they say.

Prominent, long-standing Riceville families include the Asfahls, Bodenhams, Brunners, Christiansens, Congers, Dingers, Eastmans, Governs, Grupps, Lenths, Linkenmeyers, McGoverns, Mosers, Murphys, Setkas, Sprungs, and Swancutts. Five churches—Lutheran, Methodist, Catholic, Mennonite, and Baptist—aim to accommodate everyone's preference.

Chili, the go-to staple at church potluck dinners, crosses all denominations. Dinner and supper are two entirely different meals; dinner is served in the early afternoon, supper in the evening. At family gatherings, casseroles are expected, Red Waldorf cake is welcomed, and Jell-O salad served on a bed of wilted lettuce is pretty much hated by anyone under fifty. Every family seems to maintain a proprietary recipe for beer-cheese soup, as well as the location of a "secret" out-of-the-way glade in which to find wild morels, which, sauteed in butter, melt in your mouth. Fish served up for supper is never bought, but caught by either you or someone you know. The closest Riceville gets to a Starbucks is Andy's Mini-Mart, run by brothers Tom and Steve Anderlik, which opens at five a.m. so farmers can get their caffeine fix before sunrise. Locals leave their keys in the ignition, engine running, while dashing into the Casey's on Main Street to pick up a half gallon of milk while chitchatting with Karen Hartman, one of the five Blake sisters, behind the counter.

The closest "big" city is the Mitchell County seat, Osage (population 3,568), eighteen miles away, but Riceville residents don't often stray far. "I don't recall a single person from Riceville," said Monte Kloberdanz, seventy-eight, who was born in Osage, grew up there, and moved away for a spell, only to return several years ago. "Riceville's always been a peculiar little burg on the way to Cresco and Decorah. You never went there; you just passed through on the way to someplace else."[5]

Living in as self-contained a place as Riceville means that when Brenda Church's mother died this is what happened at Lindstrom Funeral Parlor on East Main: "I grabbed some clothes and the funeral director, Steve Quast, saw one dress, and said to me, 'Oh, let's put her in that one. She always wore that for visitations.'"[6]

If you're born in Riceville, chances are good that you'll die there—or within a radius of fifty miles. Residents at the Riceville Community Rest Home on Woodlawn Avenue are former farmers, agricultural salesmen, teachers, almost all long-ago graduates of Riceville High, right across the street.

About the only long-distance outing from Riceville might happen in late summer: the three-hour drive to Des Moines for the state fair to cheer on Miss

Riceville, take in the year's butter cow (six hundred pounds of butter sculpted in the shape of a bovine), and stroll the midway, Icee in one hand, cotton-candy beehive or corndog in the other. That'd be after standing in line for a grilled chop from the Iowa Pork Producers tent. A month or two later, after your crops are harvested, and depending on multigenerational family allegiances, football fans might convoy to Iowa City, Minneapolis, or Ames to cheer on gridiron warriors in black and gold, maroon and yellow, or burnt cardinal and gold. Once there, tailgating with brats and beer is a mandatory pastime.

When it comes to college as an *educational* institution, that's a different story. Higher education is wholly optional. Unless it's the University of Northern Iowa, seventy-five miles away, sending a child to college often means one less hand on the family farm or business.[7] College is expensive. Even with in-state tuition, plus room and board, four years at the University of Iowa these days costs in excess of a hundred thousand dollars. And really, is the course of university study germane to life back home? Many would laugh and shake their heads.

But the biggest risk: once in college, Riceville kids might choose to live somewhere else. They might also meet a future spouse who'll whisk them away.

Riceville kids are apt to marry a local girl or boy, have a brood of children, and work their grandparents' farm, then their parents', then their own. Intermarriage is when a Lutheran and Methodist get married, and more often than not it causes a rift with family members on both sides.

"No dating outside the faith," said Linda Ring Kinneman, who graduated from Riceville High in 1970. "That was the rule. There are cases of parents who didn't go to their children's weddings. Lutheran kids went out with Lutheran kids and married Lutheran kids. The same went for Catholics and Methodists."[8]

Jerry Koenigs, a farmer who has milked cows for more than seventy years, said, "Everyone is related and almost every family is intertwined. It's a good thing automobiles came along. It used to be just horses and buggies, and how far can you get on one of them? The next-door neighbor had a daughter who was around the same age as your boy, and the parents would get to talking, and next thing you know, the kids would get married. If it continued that way I think we'd have problems."[9] Koenigs was talking about genetics, too small a gene pool for the well-being of the next generation.

As in all small towns, gossip is everyone's business. Dishing about your neighbor surely beats another game of euchre. Relatives visiting from Winona? A new transmission on your pickup? A slammed door followed by the sound of squealing tires? Everyone's gonna know by sundown. Probably sooner.

Riceville City Councilman Dennis Leard, a relative newcomer to town who married a Riceville native, said, "When I moved here, I put up a six-hundred-square-foot shed behind our house. The lady across the street, she walked over one day and she says to me, 'Ya know, ever since you put up that shed, I can't see what you're doing in your kitchen.'"[10]

In addition to gossip and euchre, Riceville entertainment includes hunting, fishing, ice-skating, swimming and boating at Lake Hendricks, snowmobiling, horseback riding, pasture pool (golf), bowling, and scrapbooking. Riceville is the pheasant capital of Iowa. Every fall, woolly "buckskinner" reenactors armed with muzzle-loaded muskets, beer-filled Igloos, and packs of ornery dogs chase raccoons until they scurry up trees, causing a howling ruckus. Guns are as essential as Pyrex bowls and trickle battery starters. "Gun Control Means Using Both Hands" is a favorite local bumper sticker.

Just about every teenager has a summer job detasseling (snipping the tassel from the cornhusk so that stalks crossbreed) and walking beans (hoeing weeds from soybean fields). Summer Bible camp isn't required, but lots of Riceville parents think it ought to be. The first week in August every year is Wapsi Days (named after the Wapsipinicon River), during which there's a townwide sing, tractor pull, coin dig, duck float, pie bake-off, BBQ chicken dinner at the firehouse, parade down Woodland Avenue, and all the free watermelon anyone can possibly eat (more than a thousand pounds get trucked in). Other annual events: an Easter egg hunt at the rest home; milking contests between the mayors of Riceville and McIntire; frog, toad, and turtle races; a Little Miss Riceville pageant; Krazy Daze (sidewalk sales); and a polka worship service at the Lutheran church. On summer evenings after supper, when the mosquitoes finally stop buzzing and the mercury drops to a more civilized level, residents mow and edge their lawns with military precision, then sit on wooden swings on front porches with ceilings more often than not painted sky-blue.

Riceville has an underbelly, although hardly anyone talks about it, at least to outsiders they don't. Howard Wyatt, who ran a sawmill north of town and was appointed night marshal back in 1958, broke up his share of bar fights over real and imagined infidelities. During the 1970s and 1980s, couples used to throw house keys into a bowl at Murph's downtown to swap spouses. Word around town was that whenever a certain businessman cheated on his wife, her payback was a new car—and every year she'd get a new Ford LTD for his supposed indiscretion. Not that any of that was illegal. Or ever happened.

Almost everyone in Riceville knows of alcoholic teachers who stowed flasks in their desks and in snowdrifts outside school. Several teachers would go home for lunch and come back to classes snookered. There've been a number of not-so-discreet affairs of the heart between school administrators and their secretaries, between teachers, and between teachers and students. Perhaps Riceville has had more than its fair share of such "peccadilloes," but considering how shut off from the outside rural communities are, who really knows?[11]

If anyone wants to run for school board or city council, a vote tally of eighty will get a candidate elected. Until this year, the most conservative congressman in America, Steve King, represented Iowa's fourth congressional district, located just west of Riceville. One of King's declarations was that rape and incest through history made the United States the society it is today.[12] The few Democrats in town called King a white supremacist, a label he embraced; Republicans responded by saying King, like Donald Trump, spoke the truth even though the liberal media made him out to be a fringe lunatic.

Depending on the season, a profusion of hand-stenciled signs may advertise fresh-picked gladiolas (three for a dollar!), box traps, night crawlers, boar semen, or a demolition derby nearby ("First they were THRASHIN', now they're CRASHIN'!" reads a flyer taped to the window at the Riceville Pharmacy).

Popular expressions in this part of the upper Midwest include "Doncha know," "You betcha!," "Ope!," and "Uff-dah!," as well as the all-purpose declaration, "Could be worse," which serves as a handy response to pretty much anything—musings about the weather, the season's haul of Wyffels hybrids, the yield of starter sows and boars, your new brother-in-law, or how the Hawkeyes could lose Floyd of Rosedale yet again to the Gophers.[13] "Could be worse" is the quintessential answer to everything, cushioning the disappointment that happens after someone makes the mistake of expecting too much.

Ricevillians are resoundingly middle class. If you're poor or rich, you do your best to hide it. Five children in a family is considered on the low side of average. If kids outgrow their shoes, they likely go barefoot during the summer and into the fall ("The soles of your feet get tough," said Karen Schofield, one of nine children, who went to a one-room schoolhouse before enrolling in Riceville High and graduating in 1971).[14] Riceville homes are modest and compact without frills. If you ever take a vacation, you certainly don't brag about it.

As Jim Cross, who used to be editor of the *Riceville Recorder* and now is editor of the *Mitchell County Press News* in Osage, said, "I never can get a farmer to tell me how many acres or how many head of cattle he has. They won't talk about how much production they've had. We don't want to think we're better than anyone else. We don't want to make anyone feel bad. We don't stick out."

. . .

The experiment was one thing. If that had been it and Jane Elliott had quietly returned to Riceville from *The Tonight Show* and resumed her everyday life, everyone would have congratulated her, slapped her on the back, and that would have been that. Back to normal, to how it is. Elliott and Riceville might have gotten along just fine.

But Elliott wasn't about to squander her newfound celebrity. What stuck in the craws of nearly everybody in Riceville was what she did with the experiment, how far she took it, and how far it took her. That's what ticked people off, even after fifty years. Elliott used the experiment to make herself better than the rest.

It was more than that, of course. What came out of her mouth shocked residents. Locals couldn't believe their ears when they heard Elliott's accusations, made all the worse coming from one of Riceville's native daughters. The sentiment of almost everyone in town was that Elliott didn't care one whit about the experiment's impact on Riceville's children.

She wanted to make a name for herself. And if some money came her way, all the better.

Elliott seemed to thrive on casting shadows. She actually seemed to enjoy it.

At least, that's what people said. Ultimately, those shadows fell not just on Riceville, but on all of Iowa, and by extension on all of the Midwest and ultimately, on all of white America.

The nerve of that Jennison girl.

TWO

Dirty Little Bastards

JANE JENNISON WAS BORN at home on her parents' farm, four and a half miles northeast of Riceville, on November 30, 1933. The intern son of the town physician, Thomas Walker Jr., was home for Thanksgiving and delivered her. She was born Mabel Jane Jennison, the fourth in a family of six children, but almost immediately everyone forgot about Mabel and just called her Jane.

Her Baptist father, Lloyd Charles Jennison, had been the talk of Riceville when he, at age eighteen, married pregnant fifteen-year-old Catholic Margaret "Gie" (rhymes with He) Benson. It was a hurry-up wedding in nearby Cresco in 1927, officiated by the Reverend C. S. Carroll, a gospel minister. Both Lloyd and Gie were Riceville natives, as were their parents, and all were of Irish lineage.[1] "My father was one of the town's 'bad boys' and my mother, at fifteen, one of its innocent and naive girls," recalled Elliott, who said she believes her mother had been the victim of incest by an older brother. Gie's parents were so angry about their daughter's out-of-wedlock pregnancy and marriage to a Baptist that they were never to set foot on the Jennison family farm. Lloyd's family followed suit.[2]

The "intermarriage" between Gie and Lloyd made the young Jennison family outcasts. Jane's own cousins called the Jennison kids "dirty little bastards." It became young Jane and her gang of brothers and sisters against the world. At least, that's how she recalls it felt. "We were, in fact, discriminated against based on characteristics over which we had no control, and I hated it. In response, we circled the wagons. We self-segregated; we attempted to prove them wrong; and we pretended that we didn't care. . . . I learned about discrimination at an early age."[3]

Lloyd Jennison raised cows, sheep, pigs; he farmed corn, beans, beets, oats, and hay on a 150-acre farm with little topsoil, using a team of tired horses to till the hardly tillable, hard-rock land. During the fall of 1941, when Jane was eight, Lloyd had fifty-two hogs die from an outbreak of cholera.[4] "Goddammit, do your chores!" worked-to-the-bone Lloyd would yell to his gaggle of children, three boys (Charles, Sam, Steve) and three girls (Mary, Jean, and Jane).

Compact, jaunty Lloyd developed a reputation around Riceville as a contrarian, the farmer who always had an opinion and let everyone know it. "If you said to him, 'I wish this rain would stop already,' he'd come back with, 'Whaddaya talking about? We need the rain!'" remembered Patty Bodenham. "The Jennisons were people who wanted to do things their own way. All of them are strong-speaking people."[5]

Jane was ten before the Jennison farm got electricity or running water. She and her siblings slept on straw tick mattresses called shoddies, with sheets in the summer, scratchy wool blankets in the winter. Lights were kerosene-powered. Twice a week the iceman, Mr. Crabtree, delivered heavy oblong blocks in a horse-drawn wagon. On summer days, kids chased Mr. Crabtree's wagon as he tossed them ice slivers, as though feeding bread crumbs to a fluttering flock of trailing, chirping birds. On frigid winter weekends, Jane would awaken to the smell of flapjacks; in the autumn, it'd be green-apple pie. A treat for the Jennison kids was hot buttered popcorn dipped in fresh cow's milk. It'd sizzle and bubble like in a chemistry experiment. Ginger water was a treat. A patient white mare tolerated Jane and her brothers and sisters, all of whom would ride bareback while pulling a cutter sleigh in the winter and a surrey in the summer. When the Jennisons got a telephone, it was a party line. Each family along the line had a different ring; the Jennisons' was short-long-long-short. Everyone listened in on everyone else in what passed for entertainment, a diversion called "rubbering."[6]

One dreary winter day, Lloyd Jennison brought home a surprise—a dozen oranges, a delicacy in Iowa in those days. Against the ashen landscape, the oranges were bright, luminous balls. Jane and her brothers and sisters put quartered orange peels in their mouths and with iridescent grins chased one another in the dimming azure evening light. When they spit out the orange peels, they mimed smoking cigarettes, exhaling the frigid air into faux plumes of smoke.

During summers, the Jennison kids shocked oats, gathering bundles by hand, wrapping them in piles. Jane and her siblings didn't wear shoes, and the sharp, prickly stubble callused the bottoms of their feet, thickening their soles.

Six spirited kids nine years apart on a farm in the remote north-central plains of America during the Great Depression and the start of World War II. The Jennisons were the Ingalls family updated three generations. It made for impromptu games, wicked sibling competition, prodigious talent shows, daredevil acrobatics, and a parade of "watch-this!" pranks. A neighbor suggested to Lloyd that he needed to tame his feral clan, so with eight dollars borrowed from the Riceville State Bank, he brought home an Emerson radio that looked like a miniature church. The magical wooden box discharged a staticky torrent of words, music, and melodies that filled the remote prairie air. What an invention! Pulsating, aural entertainment from a case filled with glowing tubes and a tangle of wires. The whole family huddled around the talking machine and listened to *The Shadow, Mr. District Attorney, The Jack Benny Show, The Lone Ranger*, and *Oxydol's Own Ma Perkins*, Gie's personal favorite. Jane and her brothers and sisters used to sing off-key, at the top of their lungs, a popular radio jingle that went like this:

Me get a haircut
Shorter than a white man naked,
Drunk on a big
Case of beer

Racist and derogatory, absolutely. But during World War II in the middle of America, with NBC Radio's broadcasting coast to coast *The Adventures of Charlie Chan*, what was wrong with it?[7]

Lloyd Jennison's daily uniform was Red Wing work boots, blue denim overalls, a red handkerchief tucked in a back pocket, and a chambray shirt with sleeves rolled up past his elbows. He had a widow's peak, hazel eyes, and resembled actor Gene Kelly. Jane was her father's daughter. She was mesmerized by everything about him.

Lloyd was a natural storyteller, an armchair explorer, a man of dreams lost among the straight and narrow of Iowa's never-ending rows of corn. Jane's older sister, Mary Yager, described Lloyd as "gutty."[8] Along with the handkerchief, he always seemed to carry a dog-eared Louis L'Amour paperback tucked in one of his back pockets. Lloyd had an adage for everything, at least to Jane he did. He was a walking *Poor Richard's Almanack*. "You can make a dollar or a difference," he used to preach to anyone who'd bother to listen. "Git an education and git outta here!"[9] Gie, on the other hand, hammered to Jane, "Git married and stay put!"[10] It was that oppositional, push-pull dynamic that underscored much of Jane's early years.

Jane spent kindergarten through eighth grade attending Round Grove School, a one-room country schoolhouse in rural Mitchell County. Five-year-olds and fourteen-year-olds and everyone in between, all in the same room. A procession of barely paid but energetic teachers, all women under twenty-five, supposedly in charge, each a prestidigitator doing her best to pull rabbits out of multiple feed caps all day long. More disciplinarians and referees than teachers, they'd be exhausted by the end of the day, dispensing whatever instruction they could to an impossible range of children's talents, abilities, energy, and dispositions. *McGuffey Readers* were second only to the Bible in their utility. By default and necessity, older children were platooned to oversee younger kids, a practice Elliott would utilize in later years when she had her own classroom. Two Round Grove teachers would serve as inspirations for Elliott.[11]

At fifteen, Jane graduated and enrolled in Riceville High in town. Inside the city limits was where anyone who was anyone lived, and joining "sophisticated" "city" kids from the country required an adjustment for the Jennison tribe, especially Jane. The new pecking order put her on the lowest rung of respect and popularity: Jane was poor, undereducated, a pint-sized smart aleck with a family stigma in cliquey Riceville. For the first time, Jane faced competition to shine. She ultimately succeeded not only because she was smart, but because classmates assumed she wasn't. "We refused to live down to others' expectations of us," she'd recall.[12]

Her high school classmates included girls with the names Alma, Lavonne, Cleta, Vera, Velma, Velda, Delphine, and Zelda. Girls overwhelmingly outnumbered boys; there were twenty-seven girls and thirteen boys in Jane's class of 1952. Those odds made for packed home economics classes while the Corn Bowl Conference high school football teams scrambled for recruits. High school was a luxury that families with boys could hardly afford; young men routinely dropped out to work their family farms.[13] Education ran a distant third to feeding a family and providing an income.

Like her father, Jane fast developed a reputation as outspoken and opinionated. She had to run to keep up with her new classmates, and perhaps as compensation for her compact size, her mouth ran faster than her legs. She took to wagging her finger in the face of anyone foolish enough to stand up to her. Jane's classmates learned to steer clear of her. "We were dirt poor. We weren't supposed to amount to anything. We did, and we didn't do it quietly," Elliott would recall.[14] She and her siblings carried a well-deserved reputation as scrappy bruisers.

One of her classmates, Adolph Brunner, who still lives in Riceville, remembers Elliott as someone with a giant chip on her small-frame shoulders. With a name like Adolph during and after World War II, life wasn't easy for Brunner, who grew up speaking German and English at home. Even today at eighty-six, Brunner remembers students who taunted him mercilessly, and Jane and her brother Jim led the pack. "I got into a big fist-fight with him over it; it's something I've never forgotten."

Brunner's wife, Carol Lou, eighty-five, rejects any contention that Riceville locals treated the Jennison kids poorly because of their country upbringing, their "mixed" lineage, or their parents' shotgun marriage. "That Jane's parents were Baptist and Catholic had nothing to do with people's reaction to them," Carol Lou Brunner recalled, sitting at her kitchen break-fast table on an early-spring morning. "And that her parents had to get married, that happened all the time. Jane had an attitude and she's always had one. Even back in high school. You agree with her—or it's the highway. That's how it was then, and that's how it is now."[15]

Elliott readily concedes that she and her siblings were "sharp-eyed, quick-tongued, smart-mouthed hooligans who stuck together like white on rice, and we were ready to attack anyone who crossed any one of us." They were a tough bunch, the Bowery Boys transported a thousand miles west. "We were really aggressive and abrasive and obnoxious. . . . When all of us kids were in school together, it was like a circus of porcupines."[16]

Of the six, Jane was the most outspoken, and that's saying something. "Jane had a mouth," volunteered her sister Mary Yager, who also became a Riceville school teacher. "She was *very* honest. She didn't mind what people thought about her, and was clever enough to say what she believed in."[17]

Jane graduated ninth out of forty-one students at Riceville High.[18] In her class photo, she wore her brunette hair in a short curly bubble-cut bob; she had on cat's-eye glasses, a blazer, and a heart-shaped pendant around her neck. The Reverend B. H. Thorlakson, the local Baptist pastor, gave the class commencement address, titled "In a Democracy, They Teach to Live."[19] The senior class motto was "Tonight we launch, where shall we anchor?"[20]

High school diploma in hand, Elliott followed her sister Mary and enrolled in Iowa State Teachers College (ISTC) in Cedar Falls. During her freshman year, she lived with an aunt in Waterloo and rode the trolley eight miles to campus; in her sophomore year, she moved into the college dormitory. Elliott wasn't a particularly strong student. Her grades at ISTC were in the C range. Her best were Beginning Golf (A) and Beginning Folk Dance (A); her worst, Rural Sociology (D). In Child Development, Social and Economic History of the U.S., Children's Literature, and Language Arts, she received Bs. In American Government, Problems of Teachers, Teaching of Arithmetic, and Early Childhood Education, she got Cs. Elliott completed the two-year program in August 1954, which earned her a certificate to teach elementary school children in Iowa.[21]

Attending college seventy-five miles from home didn't allow Elliott to see much of the world, but it did give her a glimpse. When she was nineteen, she spotted a fellow student who opened her eyes. LeRoy Dunn was a standout tackle on the ISTC football team, who would be named an All-American. He also was the first Black person Elliott had ever seen up close.

In her life up till then, Elliott hadn't much thought of people as anything but white and Christian. Everyone looked like everyone else in Riceville. Whenever the infrequent topic of race came up at home, Lloyd and Gie Jennison referred to Black people not as Negroes, but as niggers, as did their neighbors and everyone else in Riceville. Like millions of white Americans at the time, Elliott's only connection with Black Americans had been through their portrayal in popular culture; for Elliott that meant mostly on radio and particularly on *Amos 'n' Andy*, a comedy show in which Black people were portrayed as swindlers or rubes.[22] It was that, Aunt Jemima, Uncle Ben, or *National Geographic* portrayals of half-dressed natives from faraway countries.

Elliott never talked to LeRoy Dunn, who was from Manly, a tiny town in Worth County. Just gazing at him had been enough. Did the black wash off? Why weren't his palms as dark as the rest of his body? Elliott was transfixed by Dunn's kinky hair, broad nose, and liver-colored lips. She would describe Dunn as a "big, black, beautiful man.... He had this great, beautiful grin and these wonderful white teeth."[23] Dunn's family had migrated to Manly for employment; the Rock Island Railroad had built a roundhouse there for servicing and storing locomotives in 1913.[24] Jobs, that's why any Black family would have moved to Iowa. Why else?

THREE

Pizzui

JANE ELLIOTT'S FIRST TEACHING JOB after leaving Iowa State Teachers College was third grade in Randall, Iowa, a town of fewer than three hundred, almost all Lutheran farmers and their families, in Hamilton County, fifty miles north of Des Moines. In 1954, she met Darald Dean Elliott, who would become her husband. Jane said she went out with husky, square-shouldered Darald because he resembled Marlon Brando (a fellow Midwesterner from Omaha). At the time, Brando was a huge movie star, fresh from his smoldering role as Stanley Kowalski in Elia Kazan's film adaptation of Tennessee Williams's *A Streetcar Named Desire*. Darald *did* look like Brando. Both had deep-set eyes, chiseled chins, thick eyebrows, and robust physiques. Darald was reflective and self-effacing, with a subtle and dry sense of humor. Perhaps he'd be the calming yin to Jane's intense yang.

Darald was an only child reared in Boone in central Iowa, where he had worked after school as a stock boy at the local National Tea Company grocery store. Despite Jane's parents' opposition to the union, the couple married on June 30, 1955.[1] Darald's mother, Bertha, threw a Sunday afternoon bridal shower for her new daughter-in-law. The wives of school superintendent William Devine and shop teacher Robert Hand organized a linen shower and luncheon for the new bride.[2]

Just as Elliott's own parents had done, the couple quickly started a family. They had four children in five years. Sarah was born in 1956, followed by Brian a year later, then Mary in 1959, and Mark two years later. Elliott quit her teaching job and the burgeoning family settled in Waterloo, where Darald got a job as manager of a brand-new National Tea supermarket at West Eleventh and Washington Streets.[3] The Elliotts lived in an apartment on Irving Street downtown, then in a small house on Littlefield Road, and finally in a Waterloo subdivision called Alabar Hills, where they bought a two-bedroom starter home at 1759 Corning Avenue. Six people in a one-bathroom, nine-hundred-square-foot home didn't afford much space, but with the kids doubled up, it suited all of them fine.[4]

In 1964, the Elliotts picked up once again and moved, this time to Riceville, where Jane was hired to teach third grade, along with two other new elementary school teachers, Ruth Setka and Dolores Steffen.[5] Jane and Darald moved into a house at 801 South Pine Street, close to downtown, for which they paid $905.[6] They also bought the dilapidated sixty-one-year-old Burke Hotel in Riceville from Jane's brother, Charles, who had renamed it the Jennison Inn. The coal-heated, ten-room brick hotel, across the street from the old opera house, had at one time been a popular lodging where traveling salesmen and pheasant hunters used to stay; now it was ramshackle and run down. Jane and Darald's idea was to fix it up and reopen the dining room and serve meals. Jane's parents, Lloyd and Gie, would handle the day-to-day operations. Aside from overnight lodgers, they hoped to rent rooms to "elderly people who want the friendly atmosphere of a 'home away from home,'" as a display ad Darald took out in the *Riceville Recorder* suggested at the time.[7]

Just before Jane and Darald packed up and moved to Riceville, they were thinking of renting, instead of selling, their Waterloo house, so they put an ad in the *Waterloo Courier*. When a prospective renter, who to Jane sounded Black, called and asked, "Do you rent to coloreds?" Jane staunchly replied, "This is an all-white neighborhood!" The caller promptly hung up.[8]

Elliott would later recall that her response had been automatic. Still, it made her feel "like a snake. I knew what I should have done—I should have said the neighborhood was white but that she could come and look at the house if she were interested. But, of course, I hadn't." Elliott had responded, she said, "out of fear of my neighbors' opinions. If we had rented to a Negro family and later wanted to move back, we would have had to face their anger."[9]

That circular, hypothetical reasoning was common for the era and the region. Waterloo, the only Iowa municipality with any appreciable numbers of Black residents (7 percent at the time), was strictly segregated, and middle-class Alabar Hills on the north side of town was an all-white enclave.[10] Redlining, neighborhood covenants, income disparities, and de facto segregation kept Black residents confined to low-income neighborhoods, almost all of them east of the Cedar River.[11] Black migration to rural Iowa was (and still is) practically nonexistent; the only exception was in and around a handful of cities when word circulated that packing plants, railroad companies, and farm-implement factories were hiring. Elliott's reply to the would-be renter had been spontaneous. "I didn't even think about it," she would later say. "That's just how things were."[12]

When Elliott started teaching in the fall of 1964, Riceville and Iowa were time capsules of rural America. The Vietnam War was still a "conflict" that had claimed the lives of 416 Americans, six of whom were from Iowa.[13] Democrat Lyndon Johnson was about to wallop Republican challenger Barry Goldwater in the November presidential election by 62 percent in Iowa, and by an even larger margin in Howard and Mitchell Counties, the counties Riceville straddles.[14] Riceville's population had slid to 898 residents, down 5 percent from the previous decennial census (the city's all-time high had been in the 1920s).[15] A glance at the *Riceville Recorder* from 1964 reveals a sampling of local events and exigencies at the time, small and large: Mosher Dry Goods offered a New Year's sale of half-price women's dresses, sizes twelve to twenty-four and a half; the Riceville Hatchery and Farm Store sought "old hens"; Mr. and Mrs. Roy Stark were "dinner guests in the home of Mr. and Mrs. Arthur Minnis Tuesday in observance of the birthday of the ladies"; a farm accident took the life of "young John Flugge, 13, the son of Mr. and Mrs. Albert Flugge. . . . [A]s the family was preparing to sit down for their evening meal, the body was found in the barn"; Immaculate Conception Church advertised a buffalo dinner with mashed potatoes, gravy, relish plates, and homemade bread; and by mid-May, pesky "horn, stable and face flies" were becoming a nuisance. Outside of a community-wide drawing for a free Holstein heifer, the year's biggest news (at least, the event that drew the most attention in the *Recorder*) was five Riceville girls (Miss Sheila Ellison, Miss Linda Fesenmeyer, Miss Pat Kubly, Miss Rita Sprung, and Miss Pat Winkels) vying for the title of Mitchell County Daily Princess. Miss Betty Ann Pitzen of nearby Stacyville won the crown; Miss Kubly was named Miss Congeniality. Judging was based on "healthy appearance, natural attractiveness, dairy background, public speaking and personality."[16]

Right from her first day at Riceville Elementary, Elliott, who was now thirty-one, carried a singular presence. She knew all about Riceville, what it offered and what it didn't, and set out to change as much as she could, one student at a time. Finally, she was the one in charge, at least of one classroom. From the start, she aimed to be different and was. She pushed boundaries, as well as buttons. Elliott was spirited and confident. She beamed "can do!" in a rural school that for years had made "can't do" the answer to almost any call for innovation. Elliott seemed to take pride in shocking not just the other teachers and administrators, but also her students and their parents. Enthusiastic and energetic, Elliott immediately made waves. To many, they were more like tsunamis.

To teach math and economics, Elliott promptly set up a store in the back of her classroom, Room No. 10, where her students swapped used items of clothing. It worked like this:

> The kids could go Christmas shopping for their brothers and sisters and parents in the Room Ten store, and in order to have money to buy things, you had to bring something from home to sell in the store. So, they'd bring in clothing that was in good shape. It was clean and had all its buttons and no tears. Then, we'd mark it up a third, so we had to figure out what a third of everything was. We'd put labels on the clothes and we'd rack 'em up and stack 'em up and set up a store. We made dressing rooms out of refrigerator boxes. The kids would try on the clothes and they'd come out and they'd say, "What do you think of this, Mrs. Elliott?" And I'd say, "I think that's just great, and it fits you and it really looks good." And one of them would say, "You look better in that than I did!" I was so delighted; here we were creating this family. It was just wonderful.[17]

Next to the store, she opened a class bank. When children deposited money, they'd get a handwritten deposit slip and handmade book of checks, each printed in the students' newly acquired, shaky cursive penmanship. One student, Brian Saltou, needed a white shirt to wear to an upcoming family wedding and spotted one on display in the class store. Brian took a liking to the shirt and decided he had to have it, but didn't have enough money to buy the shirt.

So Elliott decided she'd let him buy the shirt on credit, and every day, Brian would go to the blackboard to figure how much he had to pay back the bank for the shirt he'd bought on an installment plan. The resulting back-and-forth between Brian and Elliott seems spun from Abbott and Costello's "Who's on First?" routine.

"Where are you getting the money for the shirt, Brian?"

"I'm gonna borrow it."

"You can't just borrow money unless you intend to pay it back."

"Well, they've got lots of money. They might as well just give it to me."

"No, no, no! You can't do that! You have to sign an IOU and you'll have to pay that money back!"

"Well, how am I gonna pay it back?"

"You have to bring something from home and sell it to the store, because you can't just depend on the bank to furnish you the money for that shirt."

So, the next day, Brian showed up with a pair of pants and put them up for sale. Then, he showed up with a belt. Then a hat. Then two pairs of socks. Elliott had priced the white shirt at fifty cents, and each of the other items at a nickel and a dime apiece.

"What's fifty minus thirty-five minus fifteen, Mrs. Elliott?"

"Go to the board and figure it out."

When Brian realized he could finally buy the shirt, Elliott turned to him. "Aren't you gonna feel good when you wear that shirt at the wedding?"

"Yeah," Brian replied, "but I'm never gonna borrow another dime as long as I live!"[18]

Another student, Richard Linkenmeyer, wrote a check on his class bank account, but was notified by class bankers that it was being returned for "insufficient funds."

"Richard," Elliott said, "you just bounced a check and that's illegal. We're gonna have to start a jail, and you're gonna be our first inmate!"

At which point, Richard took three quarters he had in his lunch box, hurdled over three desks, and sprinted to the class bank to deposit the seventy-five cents in his zeroed-out account. "Boy, Mrs. Elliott, now I know what my dad means when he says he had to beat a check to the bank," out-of-breath Richard sputtered. "I'm never gonna do *that* again!"[19]

The class store and bank led to a perfect teaching moment when Elliott asked the students, "What do you want to do when you grow up?" and someone shouted, "Work in a factory like my dad!"

The response bothered Elliott, prompting her to come up with another class project.

Everyone made Christmas-present tags out of felt and paper in a class assembly line, and put the tags on sale in the school lobby. Some kids cut the felt material into shapes like Christmas trees, reindeer, Santa boots; other students composed haiku poems on the paper and pasted them onto the felt cutouts; another group created packages to showcase and sell the tags, twelve per container.

The piecemeal process took time and patience, and it wasn't long before students started complaining about how boring their jobs were.

"Welcome to life along an assembly line!" Elliott trumpeted. "Are you sure this is the way you want to spend the rest of your life—doing the same thing day after day after day? Maybe there's something else you'd rather be doing. Think about it."[20]

The class store, bank, and assembly line were three rings in a ten-ring circus Elliott managed every day in Classroom No. 10. Famed educator John Dewey, the father of experiential learning, would have approved.[21] So would Elliott's teachers at Round Grove, the one-room schoolhouse where she'd spent her first eight years in school. Now in her own classroom, Elliott was utilizing the talents and energy of students teaching students, just as her teachers had done two decades earlier.

In succession, Elliott made a home in Classroom No. 10 for a mouse, frog, a pair of gerbils (which turned out to be male and female, and promptly had a litter), a parakeet with periwinkle-blue feathers, and a slithering garter snake. The other teachers at Riceville Elementary had no choice but to roll up towels and stuff them in the cracks under their classroom doors to keep Elliott's peripatetic mascots from slinking in.

When students needed to feel fresh air, she introduced the insect unit. Elliott had her third graders bring in broomsticks, pillowcases, thumbtacks, and wire coat hangers to make butterfly catchers. She and her charges would fan out to chase the legions of monarch butterflies that floated onto the schoolyard from acres and acres of surrounding cornfields. For a biology unit, Elliott tromped over to Riceville Lockers to get a cow's eyeball, which she proceeded to display to the class. Half the kids loved it; the other half dove under their desks.

Elliott had her kids churn cream into sweet butter. She taught them how to hand-crank fresh ice cream. She encouraged her advanced students to make eight-millimeter movies, complete jigsaw puzzles during class time, and swing their partners during class square dancing lessons. Elliott and her kids would walk to the Riceville Rest Home across Woodlawn Avenue and bake cookies—for math lesson. The children would calculate how many chocolate chips they'd need if each of seven dozen cookies contained exactly thirteen chocolate chips. That surely beat drilling students on multiplication tables, as the other teachers did. More than making cookies for kids and seniors, Elliott had created in her students a brilliant Pavlovian response, forever connecting the lingering aroma of baking cookies with math.

She personalized the field trip by asking each student to adopt an honorary grandparent. To enhance the value of such cross-generational friendships, Elliott taught the children cribbage and had her students teach the residents how to play (even if they already knew). Competitive cribbage tournaments ensued. When a shortage of cribbage boards hampered play, Darald would punch out new boards in his woodshop, and the students would give them away as presents to their across-the-street buddies.

When a rest home resident died, Elliott would announce softly to the assembled children, "We've lost one of our people." What followed was a lesson in the taboo topic of death, seldom discussed among children. After a moment of silence, Elliott turned the somber news into a celebration of an appreciated, well-lived life.

Dean Weaver, who became superintendent during Elliott's tenure, recalled one afternoon when she waved him over to her classroom, so that her third graders could interview him press-conference style about what exactly it was that a school administrator did. When Weaver talked about balancing the school district's budget with the county's tax revenue, an idea sprang into Elliott's mind. That year, the budget had topped a million dollars, which spurred her to ask the students if they had any idea what a million of anything was.

The children looked down at their shoelaces. The best Elliott got was "a lot."

That prompted Elliott and her students to set out to count a million soybeans, but that year, soy prices were going through the roof. So, after the children got to ten thousand, Elliott switched to corn kernels, but it also happened to be a banner year for corn, which led her to swap corn for grains of rice. Every day, students would count rice grains one by one until the class had finally reached the million mark, just days before the school year was to end. It was a momentous event and Elliott held a class celebration to commemorate the calculating accomplishment.

When one girl asked, "Whaddaya gonna do with our million during the summer, Mrs. Elliott? We worked so hard counting them, you can't just throw them all away!"

Elliott replied, "I'll put 'em in my garage."

"Good! We'll wanna see 'em next year!"

Elliott took the soybeans, corn kernels, and rice grains home, stored them in one of the outbuildings at home, only to find that mice had eaten half a million, give or take ten thousand.[22]

Another time, Elliott got to talking to her class about the variety of trees in America, from palms in Florida to redwoods in California. She followed by assigning her students to write the governors of every state to ask for seedlings, and when they got them back from two dozen, the class planted saplings at the far end of the school yard and called it Liberty Line. (The trees are standing today.) On another occasion, students broadcast from a ham radio station based in her classroom, antenna wires strewn across the school roof.

Elliott was what many in Riceville might call a "kook," but that didn't bother her. She placed bets with her students that aliens would be found by the year 2000. She lectured them on the horticultural benefits of talking to houseplants. She railed against television. She tried (unsuccessfully) to convince the school administration to ban chocolate milk from the school cafeteria.

Of all her students, Elliott took particular interest in children who were slow readers, many of whom today might be diagnosed with dyslexia. In part, this was because Brian, her older son, had an impossible time learning to read. Elliott had taken a three-week course in Rochester, Minnesota, in Orton-Gillingham phonics, a multisensory approach to reading instruction, and started importing what she had learned to her students.[23] As a result, children who failed in other classes, who had been labeled "slow," got transferred to Elliott's Classroom No. 10.

One was Sandi Dohlman, who came to school with a host of learning disabilities. Dohlman recalled repeated sessions of frustration. "I had a teacher who slapped me. She told me I'd never amount to anything. I couldn't say my s's and my p-h's, and it frustrated her. But I was trying the hardest I could. Jane made us feel better about ourselves. She gave us confidence. She pushed us and she kept pushing us. She wanted to prove she could do great things with us. I tried harder because of her. We had been labeled 'the class that wouldn't succeed.' Teachers and pretty much the whole town said that, and we proved them all wrong."[24]

Todd Koenigs, also a slow reader, was another of Elliott's "problem" students. His mother, Sandy Koenigs, remembered,

I used to go to parent/teacher conferences and it always was, "Oh, that Todd is a horrible student. He's a terrible child. He irritates everyone. He's just awful." So, I wasn't looking forward to meeting his third-grade teacher. I told [husband] Jerry, "It's going to be the same story that I've heard before."

I come into her classroom for our conference and Jane starts out by saying, "Todd is a wonderful student! I love him! I wish the whole classroom was like Todd! He's so interested in things!"

Well, I thought she must be getting Todd confused with some other student. "Are we talking about the same child?" I asked.

Jane kept Todd interested and busy. None of the other teachers had done that. They just tossed Todd aside.

But when Todd had Elliott as a teacher, he soared.

To study the American Revolution, Elliott chose Todd to play Paul Revere and instructed him to go from classroom to classroom, flinging open doors, yelling, "The British are coming! The British are coming!" He'd slam each door and go to the next one, the next one, and the next. "He loved it. Who wouldn't learn in an environment like that?" Sandy Koenigs asked.[25]

It was classic Elliott. No wonder she got stares from the other teachers whose classrooms Todd had disrupted.

One of Elliott's most memorable inventions was Pizzui, a make-believe gremlin who used to creep around Classroom No. 10. Sometimes, Pizzui would fly. Other times, he'd hang from the ceiling. Occasionally, he'd hide in the closet or in someone's desk. He'd steal students' homework. He'd turn lights on and off. Pizzui could make windows slam shut. Elliott was so convincing about Pizzui's phenomenal powers that she made believers out of every student.

To aid Pizzui in his mischief, Elliott strung invisible fishing line to a poster hanging on the back wall, so suddenly, when the moment was just right, she'd make the poster crash to the floor. On occasion, Elliott would unaccountably speed up how fast she'd be writing on the chalkboard. When students would return from recess, they'd find painted footprints on the classroom floors and walls. Other times, everyone's rulers would go missing.

Must have been Pizzui!

"We were all freaked out! 'How could Pizzui do that?'" recalled Cathy Martin, who was in Elliott's third-grade class more than fifty years ago.

Pizzui's impromptu visits made a lifelong impact on Martin. "I was a shy, quiet kid. But after I got out, I changed. Pizzui was a part of what got me going. It might sound weird—I know it does—but Pizzui had a huge impact on who I became."[26] Pizzui opened Martin up to unforeseen possibilities that happen for good or for bad. Pizzui was kismet.

To Elliott, Pizzui was good-natured fun, telegraphing to her students that the best-laid plans of mice and children often go awry. Twists and turns were to be expected. Snow in May, hail in November—as any farmer can attest. Pizzui came and went wholly based on Elliott's whims. He was a manifestation of her quirky, powerful personality. Pizzui allowed Elliott to star as the wizard of Classroom No. 10, shocking, amazing, and awing impressionable eight- and nine-year-olds. It was a concept that would become a theme in Elliott's classroom and, in later years, her work as a diversity trainer. She was in control, rigging the game to her advantage.

Elliott was 100 percent all the time. She charged forward, always with a lesson in mind. "When she spoke, she spoke with certainty, in absolutes.

Always. 'This is fact.' 'This is the way it is.' She pointed a lot. But to me, all of it was refreshing," recalled Bill Blake, a former student, now an infectious-diseases physician in Atlanta. "To some kids, it could have been incredibly intimidating."[27]

When Elliott got fixated on certain topics of the day, all else receded. What Elliott wanted her students to do *now* was what they had to do *now*. She had rushes of creative ideas, torrents of synapse-firing vitality. Her demands could push students, and their parents, beyond their respective comfort zones.

From former student Cathy Martin: "She sent out a note to our parents prior to Christmas, saying the kids in third grade all should have Erector Sets for Christmas.[28] My parents had six kids, and no way was an Erector Set in the budget. My father didn't think she should have taunted our little minds to want one. You know how kids are—*I want it, I want it*! I didn't even know what an Erector Set was. A couple of kids got one, and I wanted to go home and cry my eyes out."

Another pet project was for Elliott's students to convince their parents to get rid of their TV sets. When that didn't work, if students got eight hours of sleep every night for a week, and their parents would attest to it, they'd get a prize of a pencil or sucker (Midwestern for lollipop).

"The forcefulness of her personality could cause problems. She was unapologetic about everything," recalled Blake.

The other teachers didn't quite know what to do about Elliott. They shook their heads and shrugged their shoulders. *Let Jane do what she does* was the prevailing attitude. What other option was there? Elliott wasn't the kind of colleague whom anyone, including older, more experienced teachers, could give a talking to. Nor could the school's principal. No one wanted to tangle with her.

Their reservations were as much about what they saw as Elliott's oversized personality and ego as they were about the innovations she was importing to school. She didn't seem to care much about getting along with the other teachers. If one of the teachers ever mispronounced a word, "she'd shoot you a stare that you'd never forget. Then *she'd* pronounce the word right, just to rub it in," recalled Ruth Setka, who had started with Elliott at Riceville Elementary in 1964.[29] As a teacher, Elliott was the same know-it-all who had picked fights with Adolph Brunner when they were trudging to school twenty-five years earlier as eighth graders.

From a school administrator's point of view, Elliott was as complicated as she was mercurial. "She got her kids thinking beyond boundaries, and other teachers got intimidated by her success," surmised Dean Weaver, the former superintendent. "She challenged her kids. She'd just go ahead and *do* things. They were the kinds of activities that gave administrators—and custodians—gray hair."[30]

Or as Elliott merrily put it, "I was constantly, constantly doing things that drove 'em nuts."[31]

She seemed to need to put herself on a collision course, turning fellow teachers into adversaries. Maybe it was a way to get back at those who used to whisper about the "poor Jennison kids" when Elliott was a child.

"She got away with things that none of the other teachers could ever do," Mary Lou Koschmeder, a Riceville teacher, remembered. "I didn't think it was proper at the time. Why she could do all these things I could never understand."[32]

Elliott's hands-on, anything-goes teaching style was as exhilarating as it was exhausting. After yet another day of nonstop activities, one of her students gushed, "This is so much fun, I don't wanna go home!"

"Well, I do!" Elliott replied, trying to catch her breath.[33]

As though she didn't have enough happening in her classroom, Elliott squeezed into her lesson plan a unit she called Hero of the Month. In January 1968, she chose Babe Ruth; in February, she picked a trifecta of American heroes—George Washington, Abraham Lincoln, and Martin Luther King Jr. In March, it was Davy Crockett. To commemorate the frontier trapper, Elliott sewed a coonskin hat with a long furry tail, which everyone in class took turns wearing, including herself. She stopped off at Riceville Lockers and got the men behind the counter to fill a burlap sack with deer bones—hunters didn't want the bones; all they cared about were the heads, antlers, rump (for jerky), and marbled loins (for steaks). She took the bones home and split them lengthwise, scooping out the gooey, black marrow. Elliott's students the next day would munch on cracked-wheat crackers topped with marrow to taste what Winnebago Indian children used to snack on before Lorna Doones and Oreos were invented.

No matter how many balls Elliott kept suspended in midair, she always left time for Magic Circle. This was when Elliott and her students would pull their little chairs close together, lowering their voices and their guard. The children made a promise: nothing in Magic Circle would ever leave Magic Circle. Whatever anyone said in Magic Circle would stay in Magic Circle. It'd be their secret. Magic Circle would be time for reflection and honesty—before the next day's roller-coaster ride.

FOUR

Elysian Fields

ELLIOTT GAVE ALL OF HERSELF to Classroom No. 10. She was a blur in constant motion. In addition to being nonstop teacher, she was wife and mother to four children, daughter to two aging parents, sister to five siblings, and aunt to flatbeds overflowing with visiting nephews and nieces. Jane and Darald maintained their family's packed workaday routine like young, prospering families everywhere. Darald commuted daily to his job at the National Tea Company market in Waterloo. He was a member of the Iowa National Guard and, later, the Masonic Lodge in Osage. On top of her teaching, Jane was elected first vice president of the Riceville PTA. She played bridge with other wives in town and joined a league at Riceville Bowl. The Elliotts had a succession of dogs, including Spooner, a black schipperke with no tail, and a border collie the family named Catastrophe.

By the time 1968 rolled around, Jane and Darald's oldest child, Sarah, was twelve, an age when life and its vicissitudes can be either vexing or carefree, and for Sarah it was wholly the latter. For Sarah and her eleven-year-old brother Brian, her closest in age and partner in crime, Riceville was an enchanted forest with preternatural paths, mysterious meadows, and seraphic bluffs. Elliott encouraged her kids to have imagination and they delivered in spades. Riceville's Lake Hendricks could very well have been the Indian Ocean, Highway 9, the line demarcating the Sahara Desert from the equatorial savanna.

Sarah and Brian were natural risk-takers. They egged each other on, daring, double-daring, and triple-daring each other. No boy was ever going to best Sarah, particularly if he was a year younger. Each day was an adventure, a safari that took Sarah and Brian on peril-filled, white-knuckle expeditions to and from school. Danger lurked everywhere to a wide-eyed tomboy with her daredevil brother in tow. Benevolent souls protected the dynamic duo, but as in all perilous journeys, sinister forces could materialize at any moment.

Reva Clark, who sold Avon beauty products and kept a collection of hundreds of salt and pepper shakers in her kitchen, living room, and dining room, had nine toes. She lived in a tiny cottage with her mother and baked the best sugar cookies this side of Mason City. Bill Fuoss was a sharp-eyed sentry who kept track of everyone who made their way past his house at 704 Pine. Winnie Robinson, a devout Christian who darned Darald's socks and made him sweet-grape jelly, mowed her lawn every Saturday with a push mower whose blades went *chut-chut-chut-chut*. Stanley and Marsha Grupp (Tom Brokaw, a South Dakotan, is Marsha's nephew; he worked construction for Stanley in the summer of 1957) lived at 205 Pine, and every winter Stanley plowed mountainous drifts of snow onto his yard and made forts for his son, Conley, who in the summer raced a go-kart in circles around the neighborhood followed by the Grupp's ferocious Doberman. Mary Rosensweig's brother, Fred Wieland, always had a wad of chewing tobacco in his puckered cheek. Marian Schmidt, who taught sixth grade, and her niece lived around the corner. Ruth and Stan Setka, Mary and Keith Yager, and Russell Ring and his family lived down the block. Donald Johnston, the school superintendent, lived in the yellow house at the far end of the street. Ada Crum, First Baptist Church's oldest congregant at ninety-five, was on constant patrol from her porch at Third and Walnut every afternoon, inspecting those who walked by. Miss Crum's father, a blacksmith who lost his left leg in the Civil War, used to run the Riceville stagecoach service.[1]

Sarah and Brian rode a series of ponies, first Brownie, then Fred, followed by Thorn. The pair rode everywhere, except downtown. Downtown was no place for ponies, particularly ponies with children atop them. In the fall, flocks of mallards with shiny green heads, along with gaggles of Canada geese, squawked overhead, *yeeb-yeeb-yeeb-yeeb*, flapping their wings, crisscrossing the gray Iowa sky. The commute was strictly north-south, and those commuting seldom parked in Riceville. Where'd their endless journeys end?

Rest was never in question when it came to the rafters of wild turkeys in and around Riceville. Full-feathered, strutting in military formation right next to Sarah and Brian, jousting for ownership of the pair's lookouts and trails. They certainly weren't like chickens, who'd raise a ruckus whenever a chipmunk skittered by. Gazes of raccoons and an occasional prickle of porcupines completed the neighborhood brigade.

A flock of what-me-worry sheep grazed in a pasture close by. Sarah and Brian would corner a lonely ewe, grab hold of her, and burrow their hands into the thick coat of matted, oily wool, and then drop to their knees as the bewildered animal tried to shake them off. That led to a wild ride, dragging the buckeroos to the far end of the pasture in a fantail of flying, gloppy mud. When they'd get home, Sarah and Brian would be covered in sludge, reeking of musky lanolin. "In the bathtub!" Jane would bellow, allowing just the tiniest trace of a smile that only Darald would detect.

To get to school in the deep, heavy snow, they'd walk in the same footprints they'd made the day before. They'd scoop out a track of snow to fashion a makeshift luge and careen down snowbanks slick with overnight ice. In the fall, they'd pick low-hanging apples and pears, taking bites from each, then launch the "mortars" at enemy targets. As they made their way home, whack-a-gopher was the game. That and drown-a-gopher. On weekends, they'd thread nightcrawlers onto yellow and red hooks and drop lines to tempt walleyes and crappies in the Wapsipinicon River to nibble. Back home, Jane would scale, bread, and fry up the catch for supper.

Before the Opera House on Main had closed, it'd been the place for community variety shows, one of which had Jane lying supine in a black-and-silver magician's box with her head sticking out of one end and her stockinged feet dangling out the other, all the while crooning Frank Sinatra's "The Curse of an Aching Heart."

"You made me what I am today, I hope you're satisfied," Jane belted out as she awaited being sawed in half and magically reattached.

As a finale, Sarah and her friend Linda Murphy sashayed onstage in bath towels and go-go boots, trilling Nancy Sinatra's "These Boots Are Made for Walking."

It was a self-contained world. If anyone needed anything, Mosher's Dry Goods or Bill's Barn on Main Street had it. For footwear when hand-me-downs no longer fit, Art's Shoes over in Osage was the place. Entertainment was taking turns sticking your feet into the Art's X-Ray Pedoscope to see the bones inside.

Another treat was heading over to Riceville Bowl or the Rack 'N' Roll, which had card and pool tables and a racy reputation.[2] For a special outing, there was Watts Theatre, a Technicolor palace with 580 seats in Osage, the county seat known as the City of Maples. For hormone-charged teenagers or large households ("The whole family is welcomed, no matter how noisy the children are!"), the Starlite Drive-In on Highway 218 outside Waterloo, Iowa's first, was a crowd-pleaser, even though the projector broke down with maddening regularity.[3]

It was an Elysian life. In many ways, it was perfect.

FIVE

From Memphis to Riceville

ON THE EVENING OF APRIL 4, 1968, Elliott was sitting on the living room rug in the house on South Eighth and Pine Streets, preparing her next day's lesson plan, the "Indian unit." The dinner dishes were washed and dried, as were the children, who had simmered down and, teeth brushed, were in bed, save for Sarah, who was finishing her homework at the kitchen table. Darald was working on a shop project, something for the supermarket, and Spooner, the family dog, was minding his own business, for a change, sitting quietly at Elliott's side. Every once in a while, he'd open his mouth wide, yawn, and then snap it shut. That's what Spooner did.

At the moment, Elliott was facing a monumental task: wrestling bed-sheets she had spread out over the living room floor, which when stitched together would become Classroom No. 10's Indian teepee. The makeshift teepee had been an epic hit ever since she'd started at Riceville Elementary four years earlier, and her third-grade kids this year wouldn't stand for anything less than Mrs. Elliott's full-on annual Indian Teepee Show. Their older brothers and sisters and friends had raved about the Indian unit, and Elliott couldn't very well disappoint. The other teachers might sniff at all of her for-gracious-sake class projects, but Elliott didn't pay much heed to static in the hallways or teachers' lounge. Sitting in a teepee, with just a flashlight for illumination, while Elliott incanted wide-eyed stories about Indian survival on the northern plains of what would become the state of Iowa—what kid wouldn't love Mrs. Elliott's class that day?

History shouldn't come from a textbook, she knew. It needs to wow students, wake them up like ice water splashed on their faces. Learning ought to be thrills and chills. Were the other teachers *trying* to make their lessons dull?

Maybe Pizzui would make a guest appearance tomorrow. Pizzui as an Indian? A cowboy? Even Elliott wasn't sure when or in what incarnation Pizzui would show up in Classroom No. 10.

She needed to finish painting the "Winnebago" stencils on the teepee sheets. Tomorrow, she'd figure out how to get the lopsided cone to stand up straight with wooden sticks inside as support beams.

Elliott's gift for teaching came from her father. She knew that. Lloyd Jennison had been her hero even before she knew what heroes were and what they did. Along with Darald, Lloyd Jennison was as honest a man as she'd ever known. He was a poor man's philosopher. Words never failed him. Lloyd could summon forth another, and another, and another maxim for every occasion. Jane couldn't help but smile when she flashed on one of his favorites, an adage he delivered with regularity as though he were a sage Indian chief dispensing wisdom for the ages. It was a Lloyd Jennison special, the "Sioux" prayer that went: "Oh, Great Spirit, keep me from ever judging a man until I have walked a mile in his moccasins."

Spooner yawned, got up, and ambled over to Brian's room, where he plopped down with a thud on the foot of the bed and curled up like a donut.

Lloyd Jennison's well-worn maxim would fit perfectly with the unveiling of the teepee tomorrow. As a kind of christening of the makeshift teepee, Elliott would impart the lore to her third graders. It'd be a natural, especially the part about the moccasins. She might even try to convince Art Olson, who owned Art's Shoes, to lend her a pair of real moccasins. After slipping in and out of the teepee, the kids could take turns careening down Riceville Elementary's waxed hallways, maybe not for a mile, but enough to feel what it'd be like to be an Indian. Well, sort of. Elliott would join in the fun, putting on the soft-leather moccasins, skidding down the corridors, too.

Did Elliott ever consider the commotion she caused? Or the example she set?

The truth was she relished her role as the black sheep at Riceville Elementary. She delighted in being different. It was who she *tried* to be, even as a country kid growing up outside Riceville city limits. Now as a teacher with her own classroom buoyed by energy and enthusiasm, Elliott reveled in tweaking the other teachers. If they couldn't handle her passion for teaching, that was their problem. Elliott was as much about doing what would educate her students as she was about getting even.

Case closed. Back to the teepee.

She got up from the floor and turned on the black-and-white, nineteen-inch Zenith television. The pickings were slim—a toss-up between *Ironside* with gravel-voiced Raymond Burr and *Bewitched*, starring nose-twitching Elizabeth Montgomery. Elliott didn't like TV, but she liked sewing less. She kept the volume low; she didn't want to disturb the children. That's all she needed. She flipped the dial.

But all she got were news bulletins—grainy, flickering pictures of a motel terrace with black metal latticework. The same thing on every channel. Serious men with big microphones. Special reports.

She heard a name, King.

A group of Black men stood milling around. There seemed to be great confusion. Elliott held her breath. Her heart seemed to skip a beat.

Someone had killed Martin Luther King Jr.

Reports came on from New York, Atlanta, Detroit, Los Angeles, then back to Memphis.

"Darald! There's something on the television you need to see!"

She was practically in tears.

Elliott didn't know much about Black people, but why should she? There had never been a Black family in Riceville. Black Americans lived in other places, in big congested cities, in crowded, dirty ghettos, as far as she knew. She flashed on LeRoy Dunn, the football player she had gawked at that one afternoon at Iowa State Teachers College. She recalled the time when that woman in Waterloo had called and asked if she rented to colored people.

Blacks were more an abstract concept than anything else. Everyone was white in Elliott's particular world. She couldn't begin to imagine what it'd be like to live in a city like Chicago or St. Louis, where tens of thousands of Negroes lived. She had read about marches for equality and sit-ins in places like Selma and Birmingham. But those places were so far away they might as well have been the moon.

"Someone shot King!" Jane shouted to Darald.

"Martin Luther King?" he yelled back.

"Yes!"

"Is he dead?"

"I think so. But I dunno. *Shush*!"

"Where was he?"

"Somewhere in the South. Memphis or Nashville. One of those places. I'm not sure."

"*Shh*!"

News bulletins—"We interrupt our regularly scheduled programming to bring you this special news report"—always gave Jane shivers, and tonight, the goose bumps on her arms had spread to her back and shoulders, the same sensation she had when she stepped into the meat freezer at Darald's market. "The Reverend Martin Luther King Jr., thirty-nine years old and a Nobel Peace Prize winner and the leader of the nonviolent Civil Rights movement, was assassinated in Memphis tonight. A sniper's bullet cut down Dr. King as he stood on a hotel balcony in Memphis. Within an hour, Dr. King was dead. That happened at seven p.m. Eastern time. The nation was shocked. President Johnson expressed horror."[1]

News reports from Memphis followed, about rock throwing, rioting, looting, shootings, a curfew, and National Guardsmen deployed to quell growing civil unrest. ABC went to newsman Tom Jarriel: "This is where the shooting occurred tonight, where Dr. King was killed. The Lorraine Motel was a favorite place for Negro leaders to stay while in Memphis. It's a very nice, new, modern motel. He was on the second-floor balcony, standing where these two officers are, talking to some of his aides at the time of the shooting. The shot apparently came from an apartment building directly across the street."[2]

Darald switched to CBS, to Walter Cronkite: "Good evening. Dr. Martin Luther King Jr., the apostle of nonviolence and the Civil Rights movement, has been shot to death in Memphis, Tennessee. Police have issued an all-points bulletin for a well-dressed, young white man seen running from the scene. Officers also reportedly chased and fired on a radio-equipped car containing two white men. Dr. King was standing on the balcony of his second-floor hotel room tonight when, according to a companion, a shot was fired from across the street. In the friend's words, the bullet exploded in his face."[3]

The camera switched to a reporter holding a microphone at the mouth of a distraught Black man, tears streaming down his cheeks, as the reporter asked, "When our leader was killed several years ago, his widow held us together. Who's going to control your people?"

"*Your* people?" Jane asked Darald. "What's he mean by *your* people?"

Darald shook his head, either to agree with Jane or to shush her.

Jane felt a jumble of emotions colliding in her head, the least of which was that she'd have to postpone hoisting the precarious Indian-unit teepee tomorrow. All these sheets on the living room floor. The Indian emblems she was going to stencil on them. An hour earlier, she'd been so enthusiastic. Now with tonight's bulletin, what was the point? An experiment in relativity and context. One moment, a seemingly essential activity seizes all of our attention. The next, the earth moves. What was once urgent becomes inconsequential.

Of course.

She'd ditch tomorrow's teepee and talk to the children about Dr. King's assassination. How could she not? Making like nothing had happened would be a crime. Even for third graders. Especially for third graders. Her kids needed to know. They had studied Dr. King in their Hero of the Month unit in February. They'd want to know.

She already knew what the other teachers would do tomorrow. Nothing. They'd ignore the news. If it didn't fit into their lesson plans, forget it. What relevance did Dr. King have for these kids, anyway? The other teachers would sweep the murder—*that's what it was, wasn't it?*—under the rug.

But how could Elliott offer any kind of explanation for *why* Dr. King had been killed? How could she explain to eight- and nine-year-old children the savagery of murdering a man, any man, but especially this man, because of the color of his skin and his ambition to unite others into a nonviolent political movement? That's why King had been killed. Was there any other way around it? Even for third graders?

How could her kids, who had never encountered a Black face, even begin to comprehend the horror of such an act?

Elliott's first instinct was that she'd personalize the death. She'd ask the children how they'd feel if their own fathers had gone off to work one day and never came home. But that wouldn't get at what had happened in Memphis, she realized.

And, then, in a nanosecond, in her living room on Eighth and South Pine, as the numbing TV reports continued, as Elliott would later recall, she had an epiphany, a revelation that would change everything.

At the time, Elliott had no idea of its significance, how a single thought would alter everything that henceforth was to happen, how her life would forever be different, as would the lives of tens of thousands of others.

That evening, with Darald sitting beside her, Elliott envisioned what she would do the following day. She'd combine the Indian unit and February's Hero of the Month unit into one. She'd compress two disparate items into a single, multipurpose lesson, and top it off with the maxim her father had taught her, the "Sioux" adage about walking a mile in someone else's moccasins.

Now in rapid succession, all kinds of thoughts converged. In an instant, she recalled a book she'd read, Leon Uris's World War II novel *Mila 18*, about the German invasion of Poland, and how the Nazis had used eye color to determine who would live and who would die, that the Nazis had looked at blue-eyed people as good and pure, and those with brown eyes as genetically inferior, scourges to be eradicated.[4] That's the way she thought she remembered it, at least.

And so it was in that moment, on this early-April evening as dusky twilight folded into night, that Elliott recalls she came up with her experiment to demonstrate to third graders what it was like to be Black in America. The idea was sketchy at first, but the more she thought about it, the sharper the focus would become.

Elliott would import a variation of the Nazi experiment into Classroom No. 10.

Tomorrow in class, she'd separate her students by the color of their eyes. The brown-eyed kids would get all the privileges they could ever want. They'd get extra time at recess. Elliott would make a point of praising the brown-eyed children as smart, hardworking, thoughtful, dependable, responsible, and honest. She'd clap them on their backs; she'd offer them praise and encouragement.

But she'd go further.

She'd instruct the brown-eyed children that they shouldn't associate with the blue-eyed students, even if they were friends, especially if they were friends. Blue-eyed people, she'd say, were shifty and no-good. They were trouble. It'd be best to ignore them, to shut them out of their lives like they'd never existed. If the blue-eyed kids got pushy—and that's what blue-eyed people were like—Elliott would tell the brown-eyed students that it'd be all right to push them right back. She'd give them permission to put the blue-eyed kids back in their place, where they belonged. It'd be okay to shove them if they kept trying to hang out with the brown-eyed kids. The brown-eyed children should do whatever it took to keep the two groups separate. It was the brown-eyed kids' right and duty to do so. This was America.

People make sense out of tragedy in different ways, and as Jane and Darald continued watching the numbing news reports that night, gobsmacked, she kept refining the activities she'd try out the next day. Ideas came storming into her head. She sifted through dozens, rejecting some as impractical and outlandish, assessing others as plausible and possible, ready to import into Classroom No. 10.

Elliott did whatever it took to get through to her students, to teach them what they needed to know. In her mind this April evening, separating her students according to eye color sounded simple, even elementary. *But that's what the kids are*—elementary school children. Elliott's job was to make them *think*. That's what this experiment would do.

But could she justify something so harsh without first explaining to the kids that it would all be make-believe?

Elliott pondered this. If she came clean before she even started, then the experiment would fail. Abstractions might work in college, but in third grade, she knew better. She realized that she'd have to be dead serious about the experiment for it to work. There'd be no explaining that what she was about to unveil would be made up. It would have to be real. Elliott would have to make it real. She'd have to sell it to her kids as real.

This way she could truly teach them about Martin Luther King Jr., maybe even why King had so outraged a white person that he had used a gun to shoot the civil rights leader dead.

Would the experiment be going too far?

With Darald sitting in his easy chair and the newsmen talking, Jane wrestled with defending what she already knew she'd spring on her kids tomorrow.

Pizzui had been her invention and Pizzui was made up. What was the difference? Elliott had come up with the concept of Pizzui to create an environment of spontaneity and surprise. Maybe Pizzui had spooked some students. That could have happened. But that was all right because so many other kids, like Cathy Martin, had responded so well to him. Pizzui and his antics had been for the greater good of the students. No one could argue that Pizzui hadn't served the purpose of fostering student excitement to learn.

If Pizzui had worked, then why not this—that brown-eyed people are better than blue-eyed people, *if* it taught her kids a lesson that was real, significant, and urgent?

And it *would* work, Elliott figured, for the same reason that Pizzui had worked. Children are at their most impressionable in third grade. They trusted Elliott. They hung on her every word. It wouldn't even dawn on the kids that she could be lying.

Elliott also knew she couldn't get permission from the students' parents. Besides there not being enough time, that'd be letting the cat out of the bag, giving away the trick's reveal. Nor could she let Mr. Brandmill, the school principal, know about it. Dinsmore Brandmill was a nice man, but did she really need to go through him to do her job? If she just went ahead with the experiment, then no one could tell her no. The chestnut "Better to ask forgiveness than permission" crossed her mind, but Elliott wasn't the kind of teacher who'd ever ask to be forgiven anyway.

By God, I'm going to do it!

By now, the teepee was yesterday's news. She had put it out of her mind. To make tomorrow's eye-color experiment believable, she knew she'd have to come up with a plausible reason for splitting the class into the two opposing groups. To these kids of the rocket age, she knew she'd have to say the experiment's rationale had something to do with science. Whenever in doubt, science to the rescue.

Elliott would explain that the pigment in students' eyes, which made for blue or brown irises, indicated whether the students were smart or stupid. She'd say the kids with blue eyes didn't have brains of the same size as the kids with brown eyes. She'd tell them that blue-eyed children were inferior. *But* that it wasn't their fault. They couldn't help it. That's just how blue-eyed kids were made. Don't blame them. Pity them.

She'd go further. She'd ridicule the blue-eyed children and would poke fun at them. She'd encourage the brown-eyed students to do the same. Those with blue eyes shouldn't even think about doing their homework. But, once again, they shouldn't feel bad about it. Because no matter how hard they'd try, no matter how hard Elliott sought to teach blue-eyed kids, they just wouldn't be able to understand. *And it wasn't their fault.* That's just how blue-eyed people are.

In the event that two or three blue-eyed kids did finish their homework? Elliott would doctor the assignment so they'd get the answers wrong.

Of course, that would be only *if* they handed in their homework. Blue-eyed people are lazy. They're dishonest. They can't be trusted. They cheat. Everyone knows that. At least, every adult knows it. That's just how they are.

To be fair to the blue-eyed students, Elliott would reverse the experiment the next class day, which would be Monday, after the weekend, after all that had happened had sunk in. On Monday, she'd have the brown-eyed kids take the place of their blue-eyed counterparts. The brown-eyed students this go-around would be the kids the blue-eyed children would pick on. They'd be the inferior kids. They'd get to know what it had been like for the blue-eyed kids on Friday. That'd tie up the experiment nicely. That's when she'd intone her father's saying about the moccasins: "Oh, Great Spirit, keep me from ever judging a man until I have walked a mile in his moccasins."

A possible hiccup: Did any of the kids have green eyes?

She did a quick inventory. Julie Kleckner and Ricky Sletten did, and Kim Reynolds had either hazel or green eyes, Elliott wasn't sure which. She'd lump the three of them into the blue-eyed group. Elliott had blue eyes, so she, too, would be part of the blue-eyed bunch. That'd be good. She'd assign herself to be in the genetically inferior half tomorrow.

In the unlikely event that any of the students questioned her or the experiment, Elliott would tell the children that it was about time they learned the truth, that now that they were in third grade they were old enough to understand.

"Are you sure you know what you're gettin' yourself into, Jane?"

"Don't you see? That's exactly why I'm doing it! Because they *are* just kids. Now's the time to undo the damage they already have. Don't you see why I've got to do this?" A tone of exasperation crept into her voice.

Darald knew better than to talk his wife out of much. When she got an itch, she'd scratch it till it bled. "Remember," she told Darald in a voice he knew all too well, "teachers are supposed to teach. That's what they pay me to do. And that's what I'm gonna do!"

Darald, the businessman-grocer, seemed to recognize the risk. "You realize you could lose your job over this," he said, not mincing his words. Whether that was true, Darald didn't really know, but it might catch his wife's attention. "You could get into a heap of trouble introducing something like this, you know that."

"And if I get fired, then I'll come and work for you!" Jane's humor in full bloom.

Darald never let much bother him. Sleep came easy to him. Jane, on the other hand, mulled over everything, from stop-and-chats at the post office to conversations she and her father had had two decades earlier. In bed now, she was way past Darald's reticence about tomorrow. Backing off wasn't an option.

A series of questions flooded her:

What effect would the experiment have on the kids?

Could it get out of control?

How would I feel if a teacher tried the same experiment on my own children?

What if I can't make it work?

What if I do more damage than good?

What if the children learn how good it feels to be on top and are too satisfied to give up the perks that go with being superior?

What if I make a child cry?

Jane sat up, wide awake, careful not to stir Darald, practical, likable, non-confrontational Darald. The children need to see the world as it is. Why not go for broke?

She knew the stakes, or at least, she thought she knew them. Perhaps because of that, she found herself doing something she seldom did. With Darald sleeping fitfully at her side, Jane found herself whispering one of the few prayers she'd ever learned by heart. "Lord, make me an instrument of thy peace. Lord, make me an instrument of thy peace. Lord, make me an instrument..."

Counting sheep or reciting devotions never worked for Jane. After a half an hour of tossing under the covers, she got up, put her slippers on, padded to the kitchen, and pulled out some lined paper and started a letter to a friend from teachers college, Mickey Alcorn. Why not try out the experiment on Mickey? Mickey had always been Jane's sounding board.

April 4, 1968

11:30 p.m.

Dear Mickey,

My God! It's happened again! "The land of the free and the home of the brave..." has witnessed (permitted? promoted?) the assassination of another thinking (and therefore dangerous) man. I'm angry and anxious and ashamed—and inadequately prepared to answer the questions my third graders will ask tomorrow.

But I'm not alone in my inadequacy, Mickey. I've been watching these white politicians and news analysts all evening and so far no one had been able to empathize with the Black. They can sympathize and analyze and dramatize and criticize and categorize but not one can truly empathize. They all keep bringing up J. F. K.—to prove, I suppose, that they've suffered as the Black man is suffering—and they also keep bringing up words like "riot" and "bloodbath" and "violent" and "anger." It's as though they are saying when we whites lost a leader we mourned in a decent and respectable manner, but who can tell what you people will do?

Now, if we "educated" adults can't understand what has happened, how can I expect my nine-year-old children to? How can I explain to these white children in this white community the hazards of being black—or brown—or yellow—in this "sweet land of liberty"? And if I should find a way to explain this do I dare use it rite [sic] away or must I wait until the experts have had several more conferences and have done a dozen more studies and have definitely proven the necessity of using this kind of experience as to the third grade level? I mean, where does this fit into the state course of study?

Mickey, do you remember how frustrated I used to be when I'd come back to T.C. [Teachers College] after spending a weekend at home arguing about race with my dad? Do you remember how we decided that if blue eyes ever went out of style we'd all be in big trouble? Well, what do you suppose would happen if I introduce a color bar into my classroom tomorrow morning? What if blue eyes did, in fact, go out of style for one day in Room 10? Could this help my people to learn a little bit about how it feels to be black?

What would the experts say about that kind of thing? I know what the administration would say, "How will it improve their results on the Iowa Tests of Basic Skills?" Well, frankly Mickey, I think educators should spend more time teaching people to relate to one another and less time teaching them to relate facts! My dad says the world is full of educated fools and I think I'm beginning to see why he's rite [sic]—too much emphasis on Reading, Writing, and Arithmetic and too little emphasis on Reason, Rights, and Responsibilities.

I also think empathy is more effective than empty sympathy, and I want my children to empathize. Just last week when we began our Indian unit we learned the Sioux prayer that goes, "Oh, Great Spirit, keep me from ever judging a man until I have walked a mile in his moccasins."

Could a day of discrimination at the third grade level help my people to walk in a Black child's moccasin?

I'm going to try it, Mickey, and I hope the Great Spirit will be on my side tomorrow!

Regards,

Jane E.[5]

By 1:30 in the morning, Jane started rubbing her eyes. She gathered up the bedsheets on the living room floor, folded then, and put them away. The Indian unit would have to wait. Tomorrow would be a busy day. She could hardly wait.

SIX

The Experiment

STEVEN ARMSTRONG WAS THE FIRST to show up in Classroom No. 10 on the morning of Friday, April 5, 1968.

"Hey, Mrs. Elliott," Steven said as he slung his books on his desk. "They shot that King last night! Why'd they shoot that King?"[1]

Steven was an alert, savvy kid. The son of a Mitchell County road-maintenance worker, he looked like he'd stepped right out of *The Little Rascals*. Mischievous, self-assured Steven ought to be commended for bringing up last night's terrible news, but this wasn't the time. Not yet, at least. "We'll talk about that a little later," Elliott told him.

More students filed into the classroom. Debbie Anderson, Alan Moss, Jeanette Goodale, Billy Thompson, Danny Lewis, Byron Bucknell. And just as the bell rang, Lowell Sprung, Ted Perzynski, Cindy Meyer, and Nancy Schumann raced to their desks. By 8:35, all twenty-eight children had found their places.[2]

The children seemed particularly eager that day. Spring's warmth was palpable. The school year would be over in six weeks. And then summer. Glorious summer.

But third graders are always eager and enthusiastic, always raring to go. Third grade was the last grade before kids, even rural kids, started getting moody and cliquish. Once children were in fifth and sixth grades, they really weren't children any longer. Third grade was a magical, in-between moment for kids, but also for their teacher.

That didn't mean that Elliott would let her students walk all over her. She was strict, a stickler of a teacher. Her most repeated classroom refrain was, "Good listeners have quiet hands and feet." If you were in her class, you had to listen and behave, or face Mrs. Elliott's wrath—the wagging finger, furrowed forehead, darting eyes, then drop-dead stare. She didn't take back talk. What she said went. Mrs. Elliott was the one in charge. It was the price to pay. But activities in Classroom No. 10 were usually so much fun, it was worth it.

After the commotion of books, notebooks, pens, pencils, and rulers falling into the right or wrong places, the squeal of sneakers skidding and Mary Janes sliding, cotton dresses and chino pants against varnished wooden desks, kid-sized chairs getting dragged back and forth on the linoleum floor, Elliott announced that she had cooked up something special for the day. And it wouldn't involve spelling, arithmetic, or penmanship!

A spontaneous cheer arose from the children.

YAAAAAAAAY!

This was going to be one of Mrs. Elliott's great days off. Maybe we'll plant herbs in the schoolyard for botany unit. Or maybe Mrs. Elliott will take us to Cliff Pearce's farm and we'll scream at the top of our lungs in his silo to study the science of echoes. Maybe Clarence Prange at the Riceville Livestock Pavilion will let us pretend-bid for the week's calves, cows, and bulls. Might Pizzui make a surprise appearance? With Pizzui on the loose, you had to hang on to everything.

The kids' cheery disposition comforted Elliott, but at the same time, stabbed at her. She still had time to change the lesson plan. Maybe it would be going too far. Were these children ready to be exposed to such a horrific dose of make-believe? If she were going to call off the experiment, this would be the time. No one would be any wiser.

In the hours between writing the letter to Mickey and now, Jane had realized that Darald had been right. At least, some of what he had said made sense. Elliott never liked to admit when such an occasion happened. But she could be wrong, and today could very well be one of those times. If she did go ahead, she knew there'd be consequences. The experiment wouldn't be just another activity in the long line of Mrs. Elliott's class projects. Those were *exercises*, nothing compared to the deceptive experiment Elliott was about to unleash. Today, Elliott would *lie* to her kids to provoke them. She would encourage students to act on their impulses, however cruel they might turn out to be.

The way she saw herself through this conundrum was that the experiment would be for the students' good. But lying, knowingly misleading children, encouraging bullying? An adult—a trusted teacher—lying to hammer home what she believed was a fundamental truth vital to her students' cultural well-being?

Could Elliott justify this?

She knew she was complicating matters by not running the experiment past Principal Brandmill or alerting the kids' parents. But if Elliott had clued them in every time she'd come up with a "teaching moment," she'd never have accomplished half the things she'd introduced in Classroom No. 10. The assassination of Martin Luther King Jr. was fresh in her students' minds—at least, it should have been. If there ever were a time, this was it.

Besides, Elliott knew sooner or later she was bound to get into trouble. It was just a matter of time before she'd get called into the principal's office for *something*. Since she had started at Riceville Elementary, Elliott had gotten accustomed to scowls from the other teachers. But that was their problem, not Elliott's. She reported to the students, not the other teachers. And parents? Could Elliott, in good conscience, ever give control over what she could and could not teach to her students' parents? Elliott was in it to stimulate, to provoke. Wasn't that what a good teacher does? Yes, some parents had asked Brandmill to reassign their daughters and sons to other teachers' classrooms, and that was fine with Elliott. If parents thought their children weren't able to learn from her, then they ought to have the right to transfer them somewhere else.

Thus far, Brandmill had supported her. Maybe that's because as a child he had had polio, resulting in a deformed arm, and was dyslexic himself.[3] It was the principal's job to listen and be agreeable. If parents or teachers had problems with Elliott, let them discuss them with Brandmill. That was *his* job; Elliott's was to teach.

What was the worst that could happen?

Why not?

She took the class roll. Then, as she did every morning, she stood, faced the flag, placed her right hand over her chest, and led the children in the Pledge of Allegiance.

As they did every morning, the students remained standing and sang "God Bless America." Per their usual, it was an off-key rendition, a medley of tentative sopranos and wobbly altos.

Now was the time to return to Steven Armstrong's prescient question.

Elliott started out gingerly. She asked what the children knew about Negroes—that was the word, at least the polite word, that people in Riceville used. After a collective pause, without any prompting, came an onslaught: Negroes are dumb, they don't bathe, they have a hard time keeping jobs. One boy said Negroes like to riot in cities, stealing anything they can get their hands on. "They just go in and take whatever they want. Televisions, stereos, cameras. I seen it on TV."

The students said all this without malice, as though sharing that they had eaten Cheerios or Quaker oatmeal for breakfast. That's just the way Negroes are. Everyone agreed, nodding their heads in unison.

"And how do you know all this?" Elliott asked, doing her best to keep her voice neutral.

"My dad said so."

"On TV you see 'em killing people."

"Their houses are all broken up and dirty."

"My dad says they'd better not try to move in by us!"

"If you're gonna get kidnapped, it'd be a Black person who'd do it."

"If a Negro man ever found you in a bathroom, he'd kill you."

There was a collective pause, as though the students were thinking, "Why are we wasting our time talking about Negroes? Who cares about Negroes? What does any of this have to do with *us*? Can't we just get on with the class project Mrs. Elliott promised?"

Elliott walked over to the blackboard and picked up a stick of chalk, which snapped in two the moment she started writing, creating a plume of white dust that floated to the floor.

She picked up another stick and wrote three words in perfectly looped cursive: DISCRIMINATION, PREJUDICE, RACISM.

They were a mouthful for third graders, and Elliott pronounced each slowly and with purpose. She repeated them.

Elliott said that because of the color of their skin, Negroes had a terrible time—from the instant they awoke in the morning to the moment they drifted off to sleep at night, from when they were born to when they died. And it was all because of these three words—*discrimination*, *prejudice*, and *racism*.

The students reacted the way Elliott knew they'd react. One girl with short hair, clipped bangs, and cat's-eye glasses like Elliott's said she thought that was terrible. A boy in the second row wearing a plaid shirt volunteered that he once saw a Negro man in Rochester, Minnesota, and "he looked like he'd been dipped in chocolate." Another boy in the back with dungarees and a striped shirt said that when he was at the state fair in Des Moines, he saw a Negro and asked his mother why the man was "so dirty." Several students laughed in a good-natured way. If there was any malice, Elliott didn't notice it.

The children's remarks were a nice setup. But to move forward, Elliott knew she needed to involve the students in a more visceral way.

That's when she started.

"How do you think it would feel to be a Negro boy or girl? It would be hard to know, wouldn't it, unless we actually experienced DISCRIMINATION ourselves. Would you like to find out?"

This time there wasn't a chorus of *YAAAAAAAAY*. The reaction was a curious, quizzical silence. Julie Kleckner cocked her head. Ted Perzynski raised his eyebrows. Best friends Ricky Sletten and Lowell Sprung shot each other what-the-heck looks.

Elliott stood in front of her twenty-eight students, each displaying a combination of uneasy wonder and anticipation. No sense of alarm had crept into any of the kids' faces, at least none Elliott could discern.

"It might be interesting to judge people by the color of their eyes," Elliott teased. "Would you like to try?"

What had Mrs. Elliott cooked up this time?

There were some preliminaries to take care of. First, Elliott asked the children to identify one another by eye color. The children paired off, staring into each other's eyes. Kids with glasses had to take them off.

"He's got blue eyes!"

"Mrs. Elliott, Debbie's got brown eyes!"

"Blue!"

"Open your eyes wider!"

"Her eyes aren't brown *or* blue!"

Elliott had been right. Julie Kleckner and Ricky Sletten did have green eyes. Kim Reynolds had hazel eyes.

Elliott told the children to stand with the others who had the same eye color. Jostling and shuffling, the brown-eyed and blue-eyed students quickly formed two groups. But Julie, Ricky, and Kim didn't know where to go.

"What are *we* supposed to do, Mrs. Elliott?" Julie asked, afraid she'd be left out.

"Which group are we supposed to join?" Kim asked.

Elliott lumped Julie, Ricky, and Kim with the blue-eyed kids. This being Iowa, fifteen students had blue eyes, and ten had brown eyes. With Julie, Ricky, and Kim, that meant that there were eighteen children in the blue-eyed group and ten in the brown-eyed group.

Elliott issued more directives. "All you brown-eyed children, push your desks to the front of the room."

The children looked puzzled. "You heard me. Push them to the front. You're the smarter kids. That's where you belong!"

The comment didn't seem to register with the children, so Elliott repeated it.

"Go ahead," she told the brown-eyed group. "You ought to be sitting up front. Blue-eyed children, push your desks to the back. As far away as you can!"

There was no recognition among the children of what Elliott was suggesting. Had the kids heard her right?

The order meant that all the children in Classroom No. 10 had to move their desks to make room for a new configuration of furniture. *If Mrs. Elliott says it, I guess that's what we have to do.* Students jockeyed their desks next to their best friends of the same eye color in the front and in the back. It caused a momentary uproar. The sound of furniture being moved on the linoleum floor made for a racket up and down the hallway.

"Do it quickly," Elliott said, her voice turning shrill. "We don't have all day! Come on, children! Hurry up, hurry up!"

Something was about to happen. Some of the kids seemed excited, others seemed unsure and wary.

By now, the hubbub had died down. The kids were waiting for Mrs. Elliott to spring on them whatever it was she had in mind.

With the furniture rearranged, Elliott pronounced that this is where everyone deserved to be.

There was a marked change in her tone. Mrs. Elliott sounded testy and annoyed. She tapped her foot impatiently.

"*You* are the superior children," Elliott said, pointing to the brown-eyed kids up front. "And *you*," she said, arching her eyebrows toward the blue-eyed children, "are inferior! You know what 'inferior' means, don't you?"

Without waiting for an answer, Elliott said peevishly, "Well, that figures." The kids didn't seem to follow.

"See, the blue-eyed children aren't as clean as the brown-eyed people up front. They can't even keep their desks clean! It's true! Just look at their desks! Take a look for yourself!"

In fact, the desks of the brown-eyed children were tidier. Maybe that was because there weren't as many of them; maybe it was because the brown-eyed children had had more time to put their stuff in order. But Mrs. Elliott was right. The desks up front looked neater and more organized. Everyone could see that.

The brown-eyed students responded by cheering, while those in the blue-eyed group sat motionless and glum.

"The brown-eyed people are the better people in this room," Elliott said. "They are cleaner. They are smarter."

Elliott went around the room slowly, making eye contact with each child until she got a nod back.

"They are not," one blue-eyed boy said under his breath from the group in the back.

"Oh, yes, they are!" Elliott said, her eyes open wide. She wagged her index finger at the blue-eyed boy with the audacity to question her.

"Brown-eyed people are more intelligent than blue-eyed people. It's about time you knew the truth. You're old enough to know this."

She slowed her cadence. This was the students' cue to pay attention. Quiet hands and feet.

"Do. You. All. Understand?"

"Yes, Mrs. Elliott," the class answered dutifully as one.

"Brown-eyed people," she continued, "are better than those with blue eyes. Blue-eyed people don't take good care of things. You give them something nice and they just wreck it.

"Think about this with the people you know. Think about your own brothers and sisters who have blue eyes. They're always messy, right? They are!"

Elliott could see the students taking all this in, considering the eye color of their siblings and friends, maybe of their own parents. If Mrs. Elliott said it, it must be true. There was no arguing with her. Several brown-eyed children had impish smiles creeping up on their faces.

By now, Elliott realized an unmistakable change had transformed all the children. A chasm had begun to divide the kids. The desks up front already said that. The brown-eyed children looked smug while their blue-eyed counterparts in the back fidgeted, looking down at the floor or their desks.

This was what Elliott had been waiting for, and for the briefest of moments, she shivered.

"Do blue-eyed people remember what they've been taught?" Elliott asked.

Without a moment's hesitation, the brown-eyed kids responded with a resounding "NO!"

"Can we trust blue-eyed people? Do they *ever* do what they're told?"

"NO!" the brown-eyed children shouted back.

Elliott could see that the blue-eyed kids didn't like this, but they said nothing. It was as though they had become mutes.

Elliott rattled off a list of requirements for the day, which included a decree that the blue-eyed group must use paper cups if any of them wanted to drink from the water fountains in the hallway.

"*Why?*" a blue-eyed girl asked haltingly, on the verge of tears.

"'Cause we might catch something from you," a brown-eyed boy shot back.

All the students looked toward Mrs. Elliott, who pleasanty nodded. "That's right," she said.

If eyes, no matter their color, are windows to the soul, then Elliott had given herself the almighty ability to peer into twenty-eight souls that morning. She had become instigator and witness to a nightmare about to unfold.

The empowered brown-eyed kids proceeded to berate the blue-eyed children mercilessly, and Elliott did nothing to stop them.

Instead, she egged them on.

When a blue-eyed boy mumbled an answer, Elliott raised her voice and ordered, "Speak up, James!"

James was tongue-tied. He slumped in his chair, drooped his shoulders, and said nothing.

"Well, whaddja expect, Mrs. Elliott?" one of the brown-eyed boys up front volunteered. "He's got blue eyes!"

"That's just how those blue-eyed people are!" Elliott crowed. "Isn't that true?"

"Yes, Mrs. Elliott" came the reply, this time from all the children.

All year long, Elliott had organized her classroom on the basis of row leaders, with one child per row in the first seat taking charge of everyone behind. Row leaders were chosen because they were smart, mature, and responsible, Mrs. Elliott's lieutenants. But today all that changed. Any blue-eyed student who had been a row leader was now in the inferior group and, by default, was an underling.

Watching the drama unfold, blue-eyed Elliott knew it was only a matter of time before the children would make *her*.

That moment came sooner than expected.

About an hour into the experiment, a brown-eyed girl asked, "Hey, Mrs. Elliott, how come you're the teacher if you got blue eyes?"

It was an impertinent question, and just before Elliott could answer, brown-eyed Steven Knode jumped in. "If she didn't have 'em blue eyes, she'd be the principal!"

Elliott couldn't help but grin, at least to herself, not just for Steven's insight, but because Mr. Brandmill, the principal, did, in fact, have brown eyes.

To the class, Elliott responded with a forlorn shrug, as though to concede how fortunate she was that the brown-eyed men in charge had allowed her to be a teacher despite her blue eyes.

Next, she informed the children that no one from the blue-eyed group would be allowed on the playground equipment, because, she said, "They're careless. Everyone knows that. They might break something."

Elliott went further, instructing the brown-eyed children not to allow any of the blue-eyed kids to play with them—even if they were friends. "Brown-eyed children need to play only with brown-eyed children. Blue-eyed children, you play among yourselves. There will be no exceptions. Does everyone understand?"

"Yes, Mrs. Elliott."

Elliott issued more rules. The blue-eyed children would have to wait for the brown-eyed students to finish before being allowed to eat lunch. For recess, the brown-eyed children would get five more minutes.

"Do you understand, children? Have I made myself clear?"

"Yes, Mrs. Elliott."

On her way to school that day, Elliott had thought about adding geography to the experiment, and it came to her to show a world map to her students. She wanted the children to see where Africa is and how large it is in comparison with the United States. Just as Elliott pulled down the metal clasp to the map, the clasp slipped out of her fingers. The map retracted, spinning round and round on its roller, making the flapping sound that everyone who attended school prior to PowerPoint remembers.

"Well, I've done it again," Elliott muttered as much to herself as to the children.

"You got blue eyes, haven't ya?" brown-eyed Debbie Hughes declared to everyone.[4]

Debbie's mouthy rebuke was a stunner. The students laughed uneasily. Tossing a wisecrack at a teacher, especially someone as fierce as Mrs. Elliott, showed a lot of gall for a third grader, and for an instant, as Elliott was later to recall, her first reaction was to backhand Debbie, a temptation she fortunately resisted.[5]

"Oh, Debbie, you know she's never done that right," said a blue-eyed girl in the back row. Elliott couldn't help but grin, as did three or four of the children in the front of the room.

For the rest of the morning, Elliott was unrelenting. While on the playground, brown-eyed Bruce Fox would later recall, "Mrs. Elliott told a boy who was getting bullied that the next time that happens, 'You smack 'em in the nose.' She put her fingers together in a fist to show how it ought to be done."[6]

If blue-eyed students were playing jump rope or kickball, Fox remembered, Elliott urged the brown-eyed kids, "You take it away from them! That's your right! *Do it*!"

A brown-eyed student, Debra Anderson, recalled, "One of my friends had blue eyes, and I couldn't play with her. I kinda hung out by myself and played on the swings and the monkey bars. I felt sick."[7]

Green-eyed Julie Kleckner, who'd been folded in with the blue-eyed kids, tried to play with two brown-eyed girls but they pushed her away. That was bad enough, but back in the classroom, Elliott humiliated Julie by ordering her to kneel in front of everyone and apologize to the entire class.[8]

Ricky Sletten, the other student with green eyes, also was made to pay for his eye color. He and Lowell Sprung were standing in line next to each other before going off to lunch. Forgetting for a moment Mrs. Elliott's rules, Ricky and Lowell started talking, and as soon as Elliott noticed the transgression, she yanked Ricky out of line, lined him against the wall, and told him to "Shut up!"[9]

Ricky reacted by flinching, brushing against Mrs. Elliott. That earned him a trip to Mr. Brandmill's office.

For all the terror Elliott had unleashed that morning, she noted assorted instances of good. Several of the slower students with brown eyes, given a boost of superiority, had transformed themselves into confident class leaders. They whizzed through reading, reciting sentences and paragraphs without hesitation. All this was at the expense of the blue-eyed students, now so unsure of themselves that several stuttered when called on. Some mumbled, which prompted Elliott to scold them. "Speak up!" she bellowed.

When music period began and the children moved to another classroom, Elliott headed to the teachers' lounge. At that moment, five teachers were in the lounge, eating their lunches and chatting. Two were playing cards.

By then, Elliott felt a heady sense of accomplishment. The classroom experiment had worked. Elliott didn't know how she felt or should feel— either ecstatic or heartbroken. But she was bursting to tell the other teachers what she had done.

Elliott started by asking what the other women were doing to bring last night's news about the King assassination into their own classrooms. These were veteran teachers; several had taught at Riceville Elementary for as long as twenty-five years.

Something happened last night? seemed to be the collective response.

Elliott couldn't help herself. She spilled to the room what she had cooked up that morning. She wanted the other teachers to know.

Elliott wasn't sure what she was expecting. Certainly not a clap on the back. Maybe just a nod of approval.

But all Elliott got were giggles. The teachers in the teachers' lounge couldn't stop laughing.

"I don't know how you have time for all that extra stuff," one teacher, Angela May, said, Elliott recalled. "It's all I can do to teach reading, writing, and arithmetic."

The others seemed to agree, then looked toward the most experienced teacher in the group.

"I don't know why you're doing that," she said, as though settling the matter, Elliott recalled. "I thought it was about time someone shot that son of a bitch."[10]

———

SEVEN

"Did She Really?"

ELLIOTT RECALLED THAT SHE FELT as though she'd just been punched in the stomach. For a moment, she couldn't breathe. "Nobody looked shocked, and nobody gasped. Every one of those teachers either smiled or laughed and nodded because she [the senior teacher in the group] had expressed their feelings perfectly."[1]

Elliott slumped back to Classroom No. 10 as best she could, wounded and deflated, fully realizing, if she hadn't before, what she was against. How could Elliott countenance such bigotry? Surely, the teachers' views would get to the students in ways large and small, blatantly and subtly.

As best she could, Elliott tried to regain her composure. By the time she found herself once again in front of her class of twenty-eight familiar faces, she resumed what she had started that morning with even more purpose and determination.

A smart, tall, blue-eyed girl by the name of Carol Anderson, who never had problems with arithmetic, started making all kinds of mistakes when Elliott called on her. When Carol walked across the room, her shoulders slumped and she dragged her feet. Carol had always had ramrod-straight posture, but since the morning, she had turned into a different person. Anyone could see that all the confidence that had once defined her had disappeared.

During recess in the schoolyard, Carol, flushed and red in the face, came running to Elliott, sobbing. Three brown-eyed girls had ganged up on her, and one of them had hit her, warning, "You better apologize to us for getting in our way because we're better than you are! Mrs. Elliott said so!"

Elliott looked at Carol and said with a degree of resignation that that's just the way brown-eyed girls are, and that Carol ought to stick up for herself. She better defend herself, or the next time she'd really get hurt.

By now, each of the ten brown-eyed students had turned into an acknowledged leader, both in the classroom and on the playground. They lorded over their blue-eyed counterparts. The brown-eyed children barked out orders and the blue-eyed students followed them submissively. Some in the blue-eyed group glanced toward Elliott for guidance and support, but all she did was nod and smile, thereby granting more power to the brown-eyed children. By three that afternoon, the blue-eyed children were groveling before their brown-eyed overlords. Blue-eyed Theodore Perzynski and hazel-eyed Kim Reynolds looked pasty pale, as though all the blood had drained from their faces.

The experiment had worked beyond Elliott's wildest expectations. She shuddered to think what would have happened if she had tried the experiment out for several days or even weeks. Once again, to justify what she had put the children through, she went back to why. These white children had tasted for one day what Negroes experience their entire lives, even though Elliott really had no idea what Blacks went through. Their lives were as foreign to her as they were to her students.

Elliott couldn't come clean to the students about the experiment just yet. The blue-eyed children would get their turn dominating the brown-eyed kids Monday. That's when the brown-eyed children would get their comeuppance. Elliott was relieved that part 1 of the experiment had happened on a Friday. It'd give the children the weekend to mull over what had transpired, to let the experiment sink in. Let them gloat or stew, depending on which group they'd been in.

But before she let them go that Friday, Elliott convened Magic Circle, as was the custom in Classroom No. 10. She listened to what the children had to say, but most were too shell-shocked to say much. Alan Moss likely spoke for the blue-eyed group when he announced, "I wanna go home and dye my eyes brown."

That evening, Jane described to Darald what had happened. He still wasn't sold on what she had done, but Jane being Jane, there wasn't much he could say to change her mind. As much to process all that she'd seen and experienced, Elliott wrote again to Mickey Alcorn, her college friend. Elliott and Alcorn had taken classes and studied together, visited each other's homes. They had talked about everything, from boys to what their futures as teachers and women would be like.

"I tried the eye-color thing today and I've never spent such a miserable day in a classroom. Thank Heaven today is Friday and how I dread Monday! What you are about to read may sound like science fiction but this is how it was."

Elliott gave Alcorn a point-by-point description of the day, and then wrote, "This all sounds pretty horrid, doesn't it? Well, it was.

"This morning segregation turned my happy, secure, loving, appreciated and appreciating third graders into two races, one of haughty, arrogant, insolent, presumptuous, exultant, jubilant, swaggering bullies and the other of confused, ashamed, crushed, crest-fallen, actually servile underlings! I know it sounds impossible, but I watched it happen and I'll never forget it. . . . I've learned more today than I did in all those classes at ISTC [Iowa State Teachers College]."

Elliott wrote that she was hesitant to repeat the experiment on Monday, but had no choice. She had to give the same rights to the blue-eyed children that she had given the brown-eyed kids. Anything less would be patently unfair. "I can't just call the whole thing off on Mon. a.m. because I can't leave these blue-eyes down—and those brown-eyes up!"

Elliott ended her letter by quoting Shakespeare. "I feel like Macbeth, 'steeped in blood so far that to go forward is no more painful than to go back.'[2] If I were a drinking person, I'd get thoroughly snookered tonite [sic] and so I'd forget this sick situation. Let's face it. I'm a coward, due to my blue-eyes, no doubt."

. . .

"So, you mean it was all just for fun?" Julie Kleckner asked Monday morning when Elliott said she was going to reverse the experiment and today make the blue-eyed children the superior group. Elliott hardly thought that Friday had been fun, but she smiled just the same.

As she had done previously, Elliott ordered the students not to dally. "Hurry up, hurry up, children. We don't have all day!" She informed everyone that today the brown-eyed students would be the shifty, dumb, lazy children. "Don't ever think you can trust them!" Elliott said, pointing at the brown-eyed children. "'Cause if you do, they'll rob you blind! Brown-eyed people are liars, that's what they are! They steal, they rob, they make us blue-eyed people miserable. That's just who they are, and there's nothing we can do about it."

As the children had done Friday, they listened attentively and followed Mrs. Elliott's instructions. This time around, it was the brown-eyed children who moved their desks to the back of the room while the blue-eyed children sat up front.

Sitting with his brown-eyed counterparts, Dale Brunner knew what was to follow. He'd seen it played out on Friday. Dale closed his eyes for a moment. He hated what had happened. Perhaps when Dale opened his eyes, everything would be back to normal and Monday would be just another day at school.

Some of what had transpired Friday happened again, but with a twist this time. Instead of the blue-eyed kids retaliating against the brown-eyed children for their behavior Friday, Elliott noticed that everyone seemed kinder today. The blue-eyed children had seen the cost of their brown-eyed aggressors' conduct and chose not to duplicate it, even when they had the opportunity. Nor did the blue-eyed kids revel in their newly granted superiority. They didn't seek to exact revenge. Some of that had to do with the fact that the experiment's raison d'être had pretty much already been revealed, but Elliott speculated that it was more—a newfound sense of compassion and empathy.

The experiment had worked. The children had walked a mile in someone else's moccasins.

At three in the afternoon, Elliott ended it. In Magic Circle, almost immediately, the children hugged each other. Some cried. Everyone had gone through a trauma together and all had seemingly survived. The children in Classroom No. 10 bonded as never before. That's what shared adversity can do, Elliott reflected. They talked about what they had experienced as a class. As a kind of shorthand, Elliott said that henceforth they'd call the experiment Discrimination Day.

"Boy, President Johnson should go through what we did," Billy Thompson said. "Then he'd do something different."[3] Elliott wasn't sure exactly what Billy was referring to, if anything in particular, but it comforted her, nonetheless.

When she reminded the children that the impetus for both days had been Martin Luther King Jr.'s assassination, someone asked if Dr. King had any children, and when Elliott said four, she sensed that the students were reflecting about how they might feel if their fathers had died, and in such a violent way. However a person dies results in the same finality, but Dr. King hadn't died while working an auger during harvest season, a fatality not unheard of in farming communities. Elliott made it clear to the children that someone had killed Dr. King because of the color of his skin. There was no sugarcoating the facts, at least not in this class and not after Discrimination Day.

Elliott suggested that the children might share their sympathy in a letter they'd all write together to Coretta Scott King, Dr. King's wife. With the children's input, Elliott composed a condolence note and the students signed it. Elliott stuck the letter in an envelope addressed to "Mrs. King, Atlanta, Georgia," and on her way home that evening, she dropped it off at the post office on East Main Street.

Back in school the next day, Elliott wasn't yet finished with Discrimination Day. She asked the children if they wouldn't mind another assignment: writing short compositions about their reactions to the experiment.

"Let's do it together and we'll share everyone's theme in Magic Circle," Elliott suggested. "That'll make it easier." It was hard to disagree with Mrs. Elliott, so the children got out their pencils and tried their best to express their thoughts about what had transpired. The kids finished their compositions within thirty minutes.

Elliott was proud of the children's essays and shared them with her mother, Gie, over lunch at the Jennison Hotel the next day. At that same hour, M. E. Messersmith, the editor of the *Riceville Recorder*, also happened to be eating in the hotel dining room. Everyone knew Messersmith as chain-smoking Smitty, and when he, Jane, and Gie got to talking, Elliott showed him the compositions. Messersmith read them over lunch and was bowled over. The twenty-eight papers were snapshots from a generation of heartland Americans not even adolescents. The themes spoke volumes about how youngsters process complex issues such as discrimination, prejudice, racism, as well as death. While the essays demonstrated how children internalize traumatic events, they also showcased the experiment Elliott had tried out. The compositions displayed Elliott's teaching techniques as much as what the students could learn from them.

Messersmith asked Elliott if he might publish the compositions, and she readily agreed. If the teachers in the teachers' lounge didn't appreciate Elliott, perhaps the rest of Riceville would.

To his very core, Messersmith was the consummate community newspaper editor. Smitty knew so much about what was going in town that everyone called him "Mr. Riceville." Nothing got by him. That didn't mean Messersmith printed everything he found out; hardly. That would be the kiss of death for a local newspaper. Neighbors carrying on affairs or teenagers joyriding at midnight on Highway 9—everyone already knew those stories in minute detail by the time the paper came out. Readers didn't want to see that in their newspaper, anyway. But publishing the children's stories made sense. It's what small-town newspapers do. Printing the kids' names under their literary masterpieces would appeal to parents, grandparents, neighbors, everyone. In addition, Messersmith figured that running the essays would be a fitting way to cover the King assassination by publishing "the local angle." Not least, the children's compositions would provide Messersmith with copy, filling up editorial space with copy between the *Recorder*'s display advertisements, including two that ran side by side every week, one for a funeral parlor and the other for a furniture store—Chisholm's—which were one and the same.

Messersmith picked out the best of the essays, made corrections, and published twelve of them on page 4 in the April 18 issue under the headline, "How Discrimination Feels."[4]

On Friday I felt happy because the people with brown eyes got to do everything first and we got five extra minutes of recess. I felt sad for the people with blue eyes because they got to do everything last. On Monday, I felt mad and I wanted to tie the people with blue eyes up and quit school because they got to do everything first. I felt dirty. And I did not feel as smart as I did on Friday. —Debbie Anderson

Our room heard about when Martin Luther King died and we wanted to see what it felt like to be a negro child, with black skin. The brown eyed children were the whites and the blue eyed children were the negroes. This was Friday. I have brown eyes. I was happy. The brown eyed children were hot shots. I felt good inside. On Monday I felt mad because I was being discriminated against. The blue eyed people got to be first in line and the teacher just explained to the blue eyes their mistakes and bawled us brown eyes out. I was sick. —Sindee Hockens

On Friday I felt good because I had brown eyes and we got to be row leaders and we got to sit any place in lunch. The blue eyed people had to be the unlucky ones and they were mad. On Monday I could have locked them in jail because I was mad. The blue eyes got to be first in lunch line, and got to be first in lunch. And I got five minutes extra of recess. I didn't want to work. I didn't feel like I was very big. —Dale Brunner

On Friday we practiced discrimination. The brown eyed boys and girls got to do what they wanted to do. I am brown eyed and the blue eyed boys and girls had to do what we wanted. I felt good inside. On Monday we had the blue-eyed people do what they wanted to do. I felt like I was going to tie all the blue eyed people in the corner. I am brown eyed so I felt like crying. —Billy Thompson

Last Friday the people in Mrs. Elliott's room who had brown eyes got to discriminate against the people who had blue eyes. I have brown eyes. I felt like hitting them if I wanted to. I got to have five minutes extra of recess. And when we went to reading class we could sit wherever we wanted to. On Monday, April 8 the blue eyes got to discriminate against the people who had brown eyes. And I have brown eyes. I felt like quitting school. The blue eyed people got to do everything that we got to do on Friday. But they got to have a recess on Monday and we didn't. I felt mad. Thats what it feels like to be discriminated against. I wont ever discriminate against people again. —Debbie Hughes

On Friday we practiced discrimination. The brown eyed people got to do things first. I have blue eyes. I felt like slapping a brown eyed person. It made me mad. Then I felt like kicking a brown eyed person. I felt like quitting school. The brown eyed people got five extra minutes of recess. On Monday, I was happy. I felt big and smart. Then we got 5 extra minutes of recess. We got to do everything first. And we got to take out the play ground equipment. I do not like discrimination. It makes me sad. I would not like to be angry all my life. —Theodore Perzynski

On Friday, April 5, we had Discrimination Day. The people with brown eyes could do almost anything. The people with blue eyes could not do half the things the people with brown eyes did. I felt left out because I have blue eyes. I felt like giving them all black eyes. On Monday, April 8, we had Discrimination Day again only the people with blue eyes got to be the [big] wheels. Boy, was that fun! We got to do all the things first. That was living it up. I felt like I was smarter, bigger, better, and stronger. —Dennis Runde

On Friday we had the brown eyed people get to be the smarter ones and the blue eyed people were the negroes. I had blue eyes. The brown eyed people got to be first, got to drink out of the water fountain, got to bring out the toys, got to do the fun things, and to have more recess. I felt mad because I felt like I was left out. Martin Luther King was killed because he was trying to help the negroes. He died trying to help stop discrimination. He was a preacher. —Julie Kleckner

On Friday I felt real sad and left out. The brown eyed people in room 10 got to play with the toys and the blue eyed people didn't. I have green eyes. I could have cried because the brown eyed people got to play with the phones and we didn't and we didn't get to drink out of the fountain, and didn't get to work on the teepee. I felt like crying and being a drop out, and tieing the brown eyed people up. On Monday I was happy because we discriminated against the brown eyed people and I felt smarter and gooder, and cleaner than the brown eyed people. —Kim Reynolds

On Friday, the people with brown eyes did everything first. The rest did everything last. They got to take out things to play with and the rest didn't. And I was a blue eyed person. And did I get mad. Why, I felt like never coming back to school! But on Monday, April 8, the blue eyed people did everything first. We did things we couldn't do on Friday. Then I didn't feel sad. I felt very happy then. Martin Luther King wanted negroes to have what they wanted just as white people do. And he was killed for doing this. He was killed by discrimination. —Carol Anderson

Friday we practiced discrimination. Friday the brown eyed people got to do what they wanted to do and Monday blue eyed people got to do what they wanted to do. I have blue eyes. Friday I wanted to hit the brown eyed people. I felt mad Friday. But Monday, I didn't mind that. We got to have five more minutes of recess. And you even got to go outside even if we didn't have our work done. Boy, was that fun. —Alan Moss

On Friday the people with brown eyes got to have a recess and art and I have brown eyes. I was happy. We did the same things on Monday except the people with blue eyes got to have long recess and p.e. and I felt like blowing the teacher sky high. —Bruce Fox

Messersmith's feature immediately got people talking, even though by the time the kids' essays had been published everyone in town had already heard about what Elliott had done in her classroom. The consensus was almost wholly negative. Who had given Elliott the right to bring up King's assassination—and to third graders? And separating children, pitting them against each other based on the color of their eyes, saying that genetics made some kids better than others because they had blue or brown eyes—what in the world had gotten into her?

To residents who went back a ways—and that was pretty much everyone— Elliott was still Jane Jennison, Lloyd and Gie's headstrong daughter, the girl who had grown up on the outskirts of town, was educated at one-room Round Grove School in the country, and never fit in with the girls and boys from inside the city limits. Elliott was as much an outsider as anyone could possibly be who had grown up in Howard or Mitchell County. This experiment of hers proved it. If she enjoyed shocking the locals, then she'd certainly achieved her goal.

Word circulating around Riceville was that Elliott didn't care one whit about the third-grade children she had used as her subjects. She had tried the experiment out to to shock everyone. And to draw attention to herself.

That was only the beginning. With a mounting degree of certainty, residents began whispering that Elliott had stolen the classroom experiment she had tried out—not that it had served any purpose to begin with. Soon rumors were flying all over Riceville. There were different versions of where Elliott had gotten the experiment from, but almost everyone seemed certain that she had stolen it. The experiment wasn't hers. No way had Elliott come up with the idea. Just about everyone in town was sure of it.

EIGHT

"Here's Johnny!"

ON THURSDAY, MAY 30, 1968, Jane and Darald got up before dawn and drove the twelve miles to the Minnesota state line, passing the Dairy Queen in Spring Valley, then got themselves to the Minneapolis–St. Paul International Airport, where they boarded a Northwest Airlines DC-8 to New York, the first time either of them had ever been on an airplane.

They were alternately terrified and mesmerized. Two Iowans thirty thousand feet high in crystalline-blue skies, winging their way to New York City. They took turns pointing an Instamatic camera at every river they thought might be the Mississippi.

The previous week had been surreal. This fantastical airborne journey had started in the early afternoon of May 23 when Elliott had been summoned to the principal's office on Riceville Elementary's intercom. Something about a long-distance phone call.

"Who in the dickens could be calling me?" Elliott wondered aloud to her students. "Long distance?"[1]

Elliott ruled out an emergency, Darald, her kids, her parents, her brothers and sisters; they were all fine and certainly they weren't "long distance." She could count on one hand the people she knew outside Iowa.

"Maybe it's Mrs. King!" Julie Kleckner volunteered. "Maybe she's thanking us for the note we sent her!"

The kids immediately warmed to Julie's idea. They agreed it had to be Coretta Scott King calling Mrs. Elliott long distance.

As soon as Elliott rounded the corner to Mr. Brandmill's office, she could see the principal's secretary motioning Elliott to hurry. The secretary looked as though she were directing traffic, moving her right hand back and forth hurriedly.

"Quick, Jane! It's from New York! New York's calling!"

Elliott had no idea who it could possibly be.

New York? New York City?

She straightened her shoulders and stepped to the desk in the main office. "This is Mrs. Elliott," she said into the phone.

No one could have prepared her for who was on the other end of the line. It was Johnny Carson.

Not an assistant, a producer, or a long-distance operator. It was Carson himself.

Before Elliott could catch her breath, Carson announced, "We'd like you to come on the show and talk about the experiment you did on the kids in your class, the one separating the blue-eyed kids from the brown-eyed kids."

Her first thought was that this *has* to be a joke. Darald must be trying to put one over on her. Or maybe it was Sam, her brother.

But the call was legit. It was indeed Carson, the king of late-night TV.

Elliott listened amazed, actually speechless, and before she knew it, Carson had handed off the phone to a producer, a man by the name of Carsey, who talked to her about logistics. Everything would be paid for, he said, which meant the plane fare, two nights at a "fine" New York hotel, taxis, meals, entertainment, the works.

Elliott regained her composure, and asked Carsey whether he'd pay for Darald to accompany her. "I consented to go if they'd pay expenses for Darald and me," she would recall. "I neglected to mention that I'd go even if they wouldn't!"[2]

"Yes, absolutely, bring your husband," Carsey replied, who said that Elliott would be scheduled to appear May 31, a Friday night. That was in eight days.

Elliott hung up as though all of this had been a dream. For a moment, she didn't quite know what to say, an unusual sensation for her.

Meanwhile, Brandmill's secretary couldn't stop talking. Johnny Carson on the school phone. An all-expenses-paid trip to New York. By plane. An appearance on *The Tonight Show*!

Elliott couldn't wait to tell Darald to pack his bags. But first, she needed to tell her students.

She flipped the office switch to the class intercom.

"Was it Mrs. King on the phone?" one of the kids asked.

When Elliott said no, a collective groan arose from the class.

She paused for a second, and with all the fanfare she could muster, announced:

"BUT IT WAS JOHNNY CARSON!"

No one said a word.

"Johnny *who*?" Theodore Perzynski asked.

"Who's he, Mrs. Elliott?" someone else shouted.[3]

Carson surely wasn't Paul Harvey. Nor was he Billy Graham, Richard Nixon, or Elvis Presley.

But still.

In fact, Carson wasn't much of a household name in Riceville in 1968. Locals, of course, knew who he was and were familiar with *The Tonight Show*, but few stayed up late enough to watch it. If you had to be in the fields before sunup the next morning, late-night TV wasn't for you. The local ten o'clock news was about it, and that was on too late.

That evening, in another letter to Mickey Alcorn, Elliott would write, "I'm not terribly flattered by the invitation."[4] She was turning modest, at least on paper, overplaying her self-effacing Iowa roots, minimizing what by all accounts was an extraordinary turn of events. In reality, Elliott was agog with anticipation.

If she was going to pull off this trip of a lifetime, she had an awful lot to do and just a couple of days to do it all. Jane's parents and sister Mary would babysit the children and Spooner. Darald surely could take two days off from the grocery store. Mr. Brandmill would give her the time off from school. That was for starters.

Elliott had a pretty, sleeveless black dress with a lace pattern along the neckline. That would work fine. The hemline was a little short, but Elliott was trim and slender, didn't have anything to hide, and the last thing she wanted to do on national TV was project the image of a prim-and-proper Iowa schoolmarm. Elliott was a pixie with a ready smile. She was smart and articulate. And she had great legs.

But how'd Carson and his staff, ensconced in a television studio in a hermetically sealed high-rise in New York, ever get wind of Elliott and the experiment she'd tried out eleven hundred miles away on twenty-eight Iowa third graders?

Two days after Messersmith ran the student essays in the *Riceville Recorder*, Elliott's loyal friend Charlotte Button tore the page 4 article out of the *Recorder* and sent it directly to Carson, along with a letter. Within days, Button's package somehow had gotten into the right hands.

Messersmith described what happened in a front-page story in the *Recorder* under the banner headline:

Through news sources and a letter written to the Tonight Show by Mrs. Don Button, the [third grader third-grade students' compositions] were brought to the attention of Johnny Carson of the nationwide network show.

On Tuesday, May 21, a call was placed from New York City to the Riceville Recorder concerning the example. Questions were asked about Mrs. Elliott, about Riceville, the school system, and whether or not Mrs. Elliott might consider appearing on the Tonight show.[5]

There was talk that newswire services had picked up the story of the classroom experiment and the student essays from the *Recorder* and that was how the Carson people had found out about Elliott and the experiment. But the wires didn't run any story about her until after she had appeared on the show.[6] Messersmith's daughter, Gail Messersmith Morris, who worked part-time at the newspaper, remembered, "Dad put it in the newspaper and from there it kinda ran on its own."[7]

Word of Elliott's upcoming appearance on national television spread instantly, and in next week's *Recorder* the Riceville Community Club took out a quarter-page boxed ad on page 2, with a photograph of Elliott, that read:[8]

> "Hello"
> Johnny Carson
> And the
> Tonight Show
> Thanks for inviting
> Mrs. Jane Elliott
> To appear on your show
> Best Wishes
> ARE EXTENDED FROM A SMALL TOWN
> TO A BIG CITY!

That Carson's personnel had vetted Elliott through Messersmith played nicely to Smitty's role as Mr. Riceville. Messersmith had unwittingly served as impresario for Elliott. Behind the scenes, he had become a queenmaker. At least that's the impression Smitty spread around town.

Jane Elliott on *The Tonight Show* might very well have been the biggest local news since Dennis Rice arrived along the banks of the Wapsipinicon River 113 years earlier. For a small-town newspaper publisher, such an appearance of a local resident on national TV was too great an opportunity to squander. All Messersmith asked of Elliott was that she plug the *Recorder* when she appeared on *The Tonight Show*. As a kind of kickback for printing the students' essays, as well as endorsing Elliott to the Carson producer who had called him, Messersmith had published a special front page of the *Recorder*, gave it to Elliott, and instructed her in no uncertain terms to hold it up during her appearance with Carson. Elliott owed him as much. She wasn't so sure, but agreed to take the fake newspaper with her to New York.[9]

If Elliott had ever dreamed of exposure beyond Riceville, this would be her break. But only if she could seize it. Elliott might use her national TV appearance to convince other teachers to try out the experiment in their own classrooms. She might be able to export the experiment to other school districts in other states. Perhaps she'd get invited to teachers' conferences to talk about what she'd done back home. Who knew how far Elliott could take this opportunity. That is, if she wanted to make something of it.

In a stab at local humor, Don Button, Charlotte's husband, circulated a flyer around town.[10]

RED ALERT—RED ALERT—RED ALERT

Greetings to All:

The eyes of the world will be focused on Riceville, Friday, May 31, as one of the third grade teachers of our nationally recognized school system will be interviewed on the Johnny Carson Show.

She will be discussing the recent race riots which broke out when a Black Angus Cow tried to move into the same pen with a White Shorthorn steer at the local stockyards.

Stay tuned to NBC for further details.

THE ABOVE MESSAGE IS SENT ON BEHALF OF THE RICEVILLE COMMITTEE FOR EASING RACIAL TENSIONS IN THE GREATER RICEVILLE METROPOLITAN AREA

Love, Don

P.S. Seriously—Johnny Carson really does intend to interview her on Friday. Her name is Jane Elliott and she teaches third grade in Riceville. She ran an experiment in discrimination in her classroom shortly after Martin Luther King was assassinated and had the children write letters telling how they felt about discrimination. These letters were printed in our local paper and Char sent them to Johnny Carson. Johnny Carson called Mrs. Elliott and asked her to come on the show.

Fantastic but true!

Button's citywide alert, of course, wasn't necessary. By Thursday evening, everyone in town knew about Elliott's big invitation.

The Tonight Show producers had reserved a room for Jane and Darald at the Warwick Hotel, within walking distance of venerable 30 Rockefeller Center, where the show's taping was scheduled for Friday evening. After landing at JFK, Jane and Darald got in a taxi and told the driver to take them directly to the NBC studios. They were giddy, taking in all there was— skyscrapers, gridlock, wall-to-wall people.

Jane and Darald walked into the NBC Building's art deco lobby, their heads swiveling. No one wasn't bowled over by seventy-story Rockefeller Center, a temple to power, capitalism, and wealth.

John Carsey, the Carson producer who had talked to Elliott over the phone a week earlier, was in a meeting, but an assistant told the receptionist to tell the couple to head directly to the Warwick, check in, and show up tomorrow afternoon at the studio for makeup. In the meantime, the NBC receptionist advised them, "Enjoy New York!"

The Warwick was where all out-of-town *Tonight Show* guests were put up. Built in 1926 by newspaper magnate William Randolph Hearst for his paramour, Marion Davies, the hotel featured a gilt-covered grill portico heralded by twin Greek sirens, Peisinoe and Aglaope. Whenever Cary Grant was in New York, he stayed in the wraparound terrace suite atop the hotel, the apartment where Davies had lived.[11]

As soon as Jane and Darald arrived at the hotel, they checked in, then promptly left. New York awaited them. They walked, gawking, up and down Broadway and Times Square, then over to Fifth Avenue. Darald was particularly taken by the identical yellow cabs that were seemingly everywhere. They got back to the hotel elated and exhausted.

Early the next morning, they went to Battery Park and took the ferry to the Statue of Liberty. On their way back to the Warwick, Darald bought shoe polish, deodorant, shaving cream, a razor, and cigars for a post-show celebration; Jane purchased curlers, bobby pins, and a can of Helene Curtis hair spray. They bought two New York souvenir books, along with presents for Jane's parents and the four children.[12]

Jane and Darald wanted to give themselves plenty of time to get to NBC's Studio 6B, where the show would be taped. Darald dressed in a dark suit and silk tie, Jane in the sleeveless black dress with lace. They took the hotel's mahogany-paneled elevator down to the lobby. To anyone who saw them, the couple looked like two urbane sophisticates, perhaps spun from a John O'Hara story, out for a stroll, an early dinner, and an evening of theater.

They walked through the Warwick's ornate lobby and passed two silvery-haired women sipping martinis in the first-floor bar. The women glanced over at the couple, especially Brando-look-alike Darald, and raised their eyebrows. Just as Jane and Darald approached the hotel's revolving door, the porter crossed the red-carpeted lobby and approached Darald, discreetly tapping him on the shoulder.

"Sir, your fly," the porter whispered. "It's unzipped."[13]

Darald quickly remedied the exposure. Embarrassed at first, then struck with the mirth of the circumstances, Jane and Darald broke into nonstop laughter.

They walked with purpose arm in arm the five blocks to Fiftieth Street and Sixth Avenue, where the couple was greeted by an NBC receptionist in a maroon-and-gold uniform, who sent them to the sixth floor.

Jane's first reaction was to notice the young women. "Carson's office is a maze of amazing maidens," she later wrote Mickey Alcorn. "No one looks over eighteen and Darald didn't overlook them for a minute. Their skirts were as short as possible and their hair as long as possible and Darald kept watching. . . . His eyeballs may never get back to normal."[14]

Through the bevy of pulchritude, producer John Carsey emerged. He greeted the couple in a busy, I've-got-*thousands*-of-things-to-do kind of way, and led Jane and Darald to a room lined with mirrors.

Carson's invitation to Elliott to appear on the show had been an experiment itself. The NBC publicity team certainly hadn't shied away from announcing why she would be a guest on the show. In its publicity packet to newspaper TV editors across the nation, she was identified as "school teacher Jane Elliott (who teaches race relations in an unusual manner)."[15]

A year earlier, Carson had told author Alex Haley for a *Playboy* interview that he sympathized with Black protesters. In a restrained, all-holds-barred interview, he allowed, "It all comes down to just one basic word: *justice*—the same justice for *everyone*—in housing, in education, in employment and, most difficult of all—in human relations. And we're not going to accomplish that until all of us, black and white, begin to temper our passion with compassion."[16] Carson's attorney Henry Bushkin mildly suggested that the entertainer was "strong on integration and civil rights, skeptical of the military and war, big on personal responsibility."[17]

Three months before Elliott was to appear, Carson had invited singer Harry Belafonte to substitute for him for a week, during which fifteen of Belafonte's twenty-five guests had been African Americans, including Martin Luther King Jr., singers Lena Horne and Dionne Warwick, actor Sidney Poitier, comedians Nipsey Russell and Bill Cosby, and NBA star Wilt Chamberlain, along with Senator Robert F. Kennedy and Native American activist Buffy Sainte-Marie. This had been the second time Carson had asked Belafonte to sub for him. Carson and his producers had given the Black entertainer the power to give America's top-rated late-night program the social consciousness that Carson himself wouldn't provide the nation.[18]

With her off-beat experiment, Elliott might prove to be tonic for the show. "Johnny prefers to look for non-celebrities who'll make human-interest stories," reflected Fred de Cordova, *The Tonight Show*'s longtime producer, who would take over from Rudy Tellez in 1970. "We subscribe to fifty-seven newspapers from small towns and cities all over the country, and that's where we find some of our best material."[19]

As a plucky Iowa schoolteacher, Elliott might impart some wisdom from deep within the corpus Americus. Dorothy Gale slipping in through the nation's back door to teach us a lesson. Featuring Elliott on the show might turn into a disarming way to proclaim that tucked away in a rural recess of America, a teacher was doing something innovative and imaginative to narrow the awful Black-white divide undermining the nation.

As Elliott's face was being plastered with pancake, Carson's head writer, Walter Kempley Jr., a veteran of *The Jack Parr Show* and *The Jackie Gleason Show*, dropped in to introduce himself. Kempley, also an Iowan, from Fort Dodge, who would become a legend in comedy writing, gave Elliott a pep talk. When she asked about producer Carsey's earlier admonition to "punch it up," Kempley advised, "Tell them what you did in your classroom, and you'll be great. Break a leg!"[20]

At exactly six o'clock, Carson sidekick Ed McMahon came out on-stage to loosen up the mostly out-of-town studio audience. Big Ed tossed out a few groaners, careful not to step on anything topical Carson might use that evening.

After Carson's monologue of one-liners, his trademark seven-iron golf swing, and a glut of commercials, it was time. "I want you to welcome Jane Elliott from Riceville, Ohio," Carson announced, as she walked from behind the curtain to greet America.[21]

Almost all of *The Tonight Show* tapes prior to 1970 are lost today. In a cost-cutting move, NBC erased all the show's tapes so they could be reused, and because of that, there's no way of knowing exactly, word-for-word, what transpired more than a half century ago. But those who saw *The Tonight Show* that last Friday in May likely forgot about James Garner and the Box Tops, although not about Elliott.

Elliott's message on *Tonight Show* No. 1442 came across blunt and unfiltered. Blacks in America were treated as second-class citizens and whites didn't have a clue about it. And even if they did, the last thing whites were about to do was reshuffle the stacked deck Blacks had been dealt. Elliott's solution was to teach children, kids as young as eight years old, the damage that whites imparted every day to Blacks. And the best approach was to follow Lloyd Jennison's "Indian" maxim: to walk a mile in someone else's moccasins.

Elliott couldn't get all that out, sitting between McMahon and Carson, in the same chair where Martin Luther King Jr. had held forth four months earlier. But her appearance was a beginning. Carson didn't anoint Elliott, but her national debut gave her a kind of benediction from America's most popular secular priest. She'd been launched, just as Carson had launched other innovators, albeit most of them entertainers, into the stratosphere.

Midwesterner to Midwesterner, by purpose or default, from henceforth on, Elliott would now have the bona fides to tell her story. As she volunteered to Mickey Alcorn the following week, "I stepped thru the curtains and into history."[22]

Producer Carsey had given Jane and Darald passes to the Latin Quarter, a Manhattan nightclub, where Bobby Vinton was performing that evening. Jane and Darald took a taxi to Broadway and Forty-Seventh Street, at the north end of Times Square, and heard Vinton sing his trademarks "Blue on Blue" and "Roses Are Red (My Love)." All the while, Darald made sure to keep an eye on the time. They left just as Vinton's first set was over to get back to the Warwick by eleven.

Jane and Darald quickly changed into their pajamas and jumped into bed. Jane couldn't bear to watch herself on the television and pulled the covers over her head while Darald thoroughly enjoyed his wife's introduction to America.

In retrospect, Elliott was fortunate not to have been scheduled to appear on *The Tonight Show* the following week. On Tuesday, Carson's show was preempted for news coverage of the California presidential primary, and when New York Senator Robert F. Kennedy was gunned down on the floor of the Ambassador Hotel in Los Angeles on June 5, 1968, nonstop TV coverage took over for two days. Comedian-pianist Victor Borge and starlet Joey Heatherton had been scheduled as Carson's guests the next night, but that show also was canceled, as was the show the following night.

As for how Elliott played back home, that's a whole other story. The Minnesota Twins were battling the Chicago White Sox in Comiskey Park that Friday evening. The two teams were a popular matchup, as fierce a Major League Baseball rivalry as northeastern Iowa had. After nine innings, the Twins and the White Sox were tied, 1–1. The game would go fourteen innings and wouldn't end until Luis Aparicio bunted in Dick Kenworthy in a suicide squeeze play at 12:20 a.m. for a 2–1 White Sox win.[23] The Waterloo, Iowa, NBC affiliate KWWL stayed with the deadlocked game till its early-morning conclusion, preempting *The Tonight Show*. After the local news aired, following the game, as a courtesy to viewers, Channel Seven aired Elliott's portion of the Carson show, but by then it was after one a.m. and almost everyone in Riceville was asleep.

As for holding up Smitty Messersmith's special edition of the *Riceville Recorder*, the one he had given Elliott, that was something either she forgot, never found the appropriate moment for, or just refused to do on principle.[24] Messersmith was so angry at Elliott's lapse that, other than a tip of his hat and a cursory greeting, he never talked to her again.

———

NINE

Back Home

ELLIOTT RETURNED TO RICEVILLE INVIGORATED. Publicly, she minimized her fleeting minutes of fame. "OK, so I was on the Johnny Carson show. Local girl makes good. Goes to New York City and . . . whoopee!"[1] To her college friend, Alcorn, Elliott wrote, "Well, I've 'seen the elephant.' Oh, my!"[2]

Despite such outward indifference, Elliott's experience in New York had introduced her to a new world, and she was buoyed by the responses she had gotten, both from her own circle of friends, as well as from strangers wanting to know more about the classroom experiment she had evangelized, however briefly, on national TV. Judging from the mountains of letters she received, the experiment suggested a remarkably simple solution that might chip away at the runaway racism and bigotry that had culminated in the King assassination. A schoolteacher from Iowa had captured the attention of hundreds of thousands of late-night TV viewers with a visionary cure to America's racial divide. It seemed too good to be true.

Elliott returned to Iowa with the zeal of a missionary. If Elliott intended to capitalize on the national exposure that had dropped into her lap, she would have to move fast.

In most rural communities, a local teacher who'd been invited to sit between Johnny and Ed would have been accorded returning war-hero status. Folks would have gathered at the nearest airport, cheering as her prop plane taxied to what passed for a terminal. There would have been banners and placards welcoming her home. The entire town would have clapped her on the back. Everyone would have swelled with a profusion hometown pride. A hayrack ride, the equivalent of a ticker-tape parade, would have been organized and Elliott would have sat high on the top bale, waving to the crowd, as the high school marching band high-stepped behind her.

But that didn't happen in Riceville. Smitty Messersmith, who felt Elliott had snubbed him, ran nothing about her triumphant return, and almost all news of Elliott was subsequently banished from the pages of the *Riceville Recorder*.[3] Messersmith's job wasn't to educate Riceville readers, it was to deliver what they wanted, and the last thing they wanted was to open up the local paper and read anything about Jane Elliott.

Outside of the experiment, what was it that had so rubbed the locals the wrong way?

For starters, there was Elliott's grandstanding performance on the Carson show. Riceville residents maintained a running ledger of unspoken rules, mostly negatives ("Don't do this, don't do that, *never* do that!") and Elliott had breached pretty near all of them. Such rural praxis started with modesty. *Blend in. Be inconspicuous. Don't make waves. Calling attention to yourself in any and all forms is poor manners.*

But way before the experiment and her debut on Carson, Elliott had rankled parents, neighbors, and residents in Riceville. Not only was she perceived by many as a know-it-all motormouth, she was a woman and she had gone to college. That made her different, and not in a good way, at least to many in town. Yes, she was a teacher, the default profession for women, but she also was ambitious and outspoken. To many in a small, conservative farming community it seemed like anyone, particularly a woman, who attended college usually came back with a license to express an opinion at any and all occasions. In 1968 in rural Iowa, women were supposed to get married and have a family, and if their husbands were farmers, work the land.

So here comes Jane Elliott, née Jennison, hired to teach farmers' children multiplication tables, penmanship, and assorted other skills, and what does she do? She makes a spectacle of herself on national TV, touting some experiment about *what*?

What did discrimination have to do with anything that third graders in Riceville needed to know?

The implicit message Elliott had telegraphed to the nation was that the good people of Riceville were a bunch of racists. Whether she actually said that wasn't the issue. Why else would our eight- and nine-year-old children need to go through such a classroom experiment if we weren't? Our kids must have picked up those attitudes from somewhere.

To many in Riceville, what Elliott had done had been a disgrace. She'd been an embarrassment. Her bragging had been one thing, but her waxing about Blacks and racism and why our children needed a lesson to eradicate bigotry smeared not just Riceville, but the whole state of Iowa. *What do we know about prejudice? We don't discriminate against Negroes. How could we? We've never talked to a Negro in our entire lives! What the hell was the Jennison girl talking about?*

That Elliott had tried this experiment out on kids without first asking parents' permission, that also stuck in the locals' craws. *As though our children were piglets in some ag experiment at Iowa State!*

Some of the attacks went deeper, bubbling up from a well of paranoia in and around Riceville. The media at the time portrayed Blacks rioting, burning down city blocks, and looting stores, not in Des Moines, but in cities like Chicago, Minneapolis, and Detroit. Not next door, but not far away, either. These were terrifying images to an all-white community. Word started circulating that Elliott's supposed proselytizing sermon on TV might even trigger an influx of Negroes into tiny Riceville. However nonsensical this scenario seems, the reasoning went something like this:

If Negroes somehow got the notion that local children were being indoctrinated to welcome them, then wasn't Elliott's TV pitch just an invitation for Negroes to pick up and move to Riceville? Elliott's experiment and her gloating about it coast to coast showed the rest of America that Riceville would welcome Negroes with open arms. Elliott was sending a signal to Negroes to relocate to this ecumenical gem hidden in the thicket of America's vast corn belt. And everyone knew what would happen next.

Our schools, churches, neighborhoods, and businesses would be overrun with them. Negroes would be our neighbors, they'd be working side by side us on our farms, they'd marry our children. That Jennison girl is promoting the end of white civilization as we know it.

This, of course, was the most preposterous of all the responses to Elliott's national exposure and message. It was a tired canard that reflected a host of racist attitudes, culminating in white hysteria. Such thinking presumed that Blacks would move to an all-white farming community in Iowa with no promise of employment or housing, based on what they might, or might not, have heard on a single late-night television show. At its worst, the speculation confirmed what some white Americans in cities large and small thought at the time: that Blacks were members of an itinerant tribe ready, willing, and capable of infecting white families and their "values." And once they moved, they would spread crime, filth—and, worse, miscegenation to white communities across the land.

"People were frightened," remembered a former Riceville native, now in her mid-sixties. "There was rioting going on in cities. It was on TV every night. People in Riceville were scared out of their wits, and Jane was throwing gasoline on all their fears."[4]

The reality was that few locals knew exactly what Elliott had said on the Carson show because almost no one had stayed up late enough to watch. Since the extra innings of the White Sox–Twins game had preempted *The Tonight Show*, driving even the most curious to bed before her appearance was aired locally, Riceville residents relied on gossip to determine what she actually said (or didn't say).

The reaction to Elliott was a permutation of how many of the locals had long felt about Jane and the rest of the Jennison family. That came in part from Elliott's "And-Why-Can't-I?" attitude. It was difficult for anyone to feel neutral when it came to her.

"Iowa is a whole different place, even for the Midwest," reflected eightyish JoAnne Machin, who grew up in nearby Osage. "How Jane presented herself, she was always combative. That's off-putting to people around here. It's as though she's laughing at anyone who doesn't agree with her. She enjoyed being the bad guy. People here, they don't want to rock the boat. We do what we're told. We're polite. And Jane, she never cared about that. She *wanted* to rock the boat. She's like a little banty rooster."[5]

Jerry Koenigs, who for years has considered himself a supporter of Elliott, winced and conceded when asked about her, decades after her debut on the Carson show: "She can be awfully tough on people." Added his wife, Sandy: "Jane is very abrasive. I like her myself. But you have to know where you stand with her. You have to go along with her line of thinking to get along."[6]

All of it made for a kind of civic combustion when Elliott returned home from New York City in late spring of 1968.

On the morning after Jane and Darald got back, one of her oldest friends, a woman Elliott had known since their days attending Round Grove School together, walked right past her at the post office with nary a hello. The woman looked through Elliott as though she didn't exist. Their families knew each other; their kids played with each other; their husbands made time to visit with each other. At first, Elliott figured the woman must not have seen her. That had to be it. Or that she was in a hurry. Or that she was feeling under the weather.

Then, as Elliott recalled, the next Sunday, she, Darald, and their kids had plans to go with another couple and their children to Lake Hendricks for a June picnic, only to be informed at the last minute that the outing had been canceled.

The husband was the local insurance agent, and the last thing he needed was for locals to start gossiping about *him*. Insurance was a business based on local trust. Without it, insurance was nothing. If the insurance man and his family went to Lake Hendricks with the Elliotts, it'd be like consorting with the enemy in full view. It'd be all around town by sundown.

"I'm coming down with something," the insurance man's wife explained to Jane, sniffling into the phone. "I'm sure you understand."

Jane shrugged, piled the kids into the flatbed of Darald's pickup, and they all went to the lake anyway—where they saw the insurance man and his family sitting around a checkerboard tablecloth as everyone munched on fried chicken and potato salad while merrily chatting away with *another* family.

"But Mom, what are they doing at the lake?" twelve-year-old Sarah asked. "I thought Mrs. _____ said she was sick."

Neither Jane nor Darald could come up with an answer.

More followed. Elliott played in a weekly bridge club with Jackie Lawrence, Marian Krall, and Hazel Dinger. The four women alternated homes every week, serving coffee and sweets—until Elliott returned home from New York and Marian Krall informed her that the weekly bridge club wouldn't be convening any longer. At least, that's the way Elliott remembered it.

The same thing happened with a couples' bowling league at Riceville Bowl. Jane and Darald weren't invited anymore to participate. At least, this is how Elliott recalled the events.[7] "I became the invisible woman when I came back from the Carson show," Elliott said.[8] No one point-blank told Elliott she wasn't welcome. She'd get the message. The idea was to punish and isolate. That same message would filter down to the four Elliott children.

"Friends like them we don't need," was Elliott's rejoinder to Darald and the kids. "How good could they have been if they're treating us like this?"[9]

The community-wide ostracism worked, just not in the way it was intended to. It made Elliott more certain of herself, what she had done in Classroom No. 10, on the Carson show, and what she hoped she would do in the months—maybe even years—to come.

Ricevillians may have put her on a spit, but many outside Mitchell and Howard Counties celebrated what they had heard. Teachers across the nation contacted Elliott as word circulated about the eye-color experiment.[10] Elliott heard from educators as far away as California and Florida, who showered her with praise and were eager to try out versions of the experiment in their own classrooms.

How many schoolteachers anywhere could boast of such sudden reach, influence, and recognition? It gave Elliott confidence to carry on.

At thirty-four, Elliott had also turned into a role model for women coming of age professionally in Iowa and elsewhere. While there weren't many professional women in Riceville, her presence inspired others pushing against what years later would be known as "the glass ceiling."

"I didn't have a TV, but I heard Jane was going to be on *The Tonight Show*, and I was desperate to see it," recalled Mary Noble, who grew up in Riceville and in 1968 was a twenty-three-year-old library-science student at the University of Iowa. "We weren't allowed to have radios or TVs on after ten at night because the landlord was living downstairs. But my girlfriends and I were crazy to see the show, so we knocked on the door of a nice young woman across the hall who had a TV. '*Please*, can we watch *The Tonight Show*? *Please*!' And we did, even though it was way past midnight.

"Jane was rather, I would say, saucy in her appearance and set Johnny Carson back on his heels a little bit. I don't recall what she said, but I remember it was a little bit suggestive. All of us were whooping and hollering loudly. We were just so proud of her."[11]

Some sent letters of congratulation. "You were terrific!!" Hazel Farus wrote Elliott. "Felt very proud and elated to sit here in my room and watch someone I know so well on one of my favorite programs. . . . Bet you are having a ball tonight—truly hope so."[12]

Another friend wrote, "Wow! Were we proud of you! Headlines, TV appearances, dinner at the Latin Quarter! Have you landed yet?"[13]

A teacher from Worchester, Massachusetts, sent Elliott a letter asking whether the experiment would work on her fifth graders. "Be prepared to be shocked, appalled, and frightened," Elliott wrote back immediately. "Also be prepared to learn things about your students and yourself that you have not been aware of or chose to ignore. Such was my experience and how thankful I am for it."

Elliott suggested that the teacher ask her white students to list stereotypes they'd heard about "people who are different from ourselves." Then have the students read "[news]papers, the ads, magazines, even their school and library books to find writing that attempts to perpetuate these myths. TV commercials are particularly rich sources for this kind of research."[14]

The letters Elliott received weren't just fan mail. Elliott got racist screeds, some addressed to her, others sent directly to Riceville Elementary principal Brandmill, and others forwarded from *The Tonight Show*.

"Have you ever lived in the deep south among negroes?" asked Ruby Thompkins, from Montgomery, Alabama. "The southern negro is lazy, shiftless, indolent, will lie and steal, and living together as man and wife without being married—all of this is part of their way of life."[15]

Another came from Baltimore. "When you have a gang of blacks under your window at all hours, when you come home from work to find your apt. robbed and ruined, when you have a pack of them living over you, and under you, when you pay for everything and work like hell while the blacks get it for free, when you can't open your door at night any longer, when you take your life in your hands just riding in a public bus, then you will have a FEW problems that you know nothing about."[16]

On the Sunday after Elliott had returned home, Iowa's largest newspaper, the *Des Moines Register*, published a page 1 story in the lower right-hand corner, headlined "Brown-Eyed Prejudice for Those with Blue." The nineteen-paragraph, unbylined article was a rewrite from Smitty Messersmith's *Riceville Recorder* story with one update, the news peg, buried in the last paragraph: "Mrs. Elliott appeared on the NBC 'Tonight Show' in New York Friday to describe the experiment and the children's reaction to it."[17]

At the time, the *Register* was well regarded and well read, considered among the top ten newspapers in the United States. Iowa's largest newspaper and the state's paper of record, the *Register* circulated in each of the state's ninety-nine counties.[18] The *Register* article, prominently displayed on the heaviest read of all publication days, didn't much advance Elliott's story, but it conferred on her more legitimacy. Within Iowa, the coverage carried more weight than her national exposure with Carson had.

The *Register* story also did something else: it forced the Associated Press's hand. On July 12, the AP moved a seventeen-paragraph story on its national wire with a Riceville dateline, under the byline of a Des Moines–based AP reporter, Celiene Nold. The story didn't have much that the *Register*'s piece (or Messersmith's story) hadn't featured, except several quotes from Elliott, including, "I think these children walked in a colored child's moccasins for a day" and a last-paragraph tagline: "Up until the lessons, she said, the children's only impression of 'colored people' had been 'burn baby burn and what they saw on television.'"

The AP story ran in scores of newspapers in cities including Philadelphia, Oakland, Baltimore, and Tucson. Many ran photographs the AP had sent with the story, including one that showed smiling kids playing on swings while another group of students stood shooed off to the side. The evocative shot made for prominent display in the newspapers, giving Elliott more of a national platform.[19]

First the Carson show, then the *Register* front page, followed by a national wire story. News of Elliott and the experiment was circulating throughout America.

TEN

What Some of the Kids Said

THE OPINIONS OF THOSE WHO HAD READ about Elliott, seen her on television, or gossiped about her ought not be the only litmus test of what Elliott did in her classroom. Perhaps the strongest test of the experiment's impact ought to be determined by the children used as unwitting subjects.

Elliott had surely pushed the limits, particularly in a public school third-grade class in rural America in 1968, and some students, along with their parents, said so. The experiment might have sounded like a miracle cure to some on the outside looking for a remedy to centuries of systemic racism, but for many in Riceville it came with side effects.

For certain students, the impact was substantial; for others, it was minimal. While the experiment lasted only two days, some students would remember it in minute detail for the rest of their lives as though it had been etched in the amygdala of their brains. Others would forget all traces of it, as though it never happened. Some students ultimately felt betrayed by Elliott and what she tried out in her classroom. That Elliott continued some form of the experiment for years to come brought additional accusations.

As the Classroom No. 10 children in that first year grew older, some expressed the belief that Elliott had abused her power by intentionally deceiving them. At what point does teaching turn into bullying, even if the classroom activity is for what the teacher might perceive as the class's "greater good"? In her apparent rush to make sense of the King assassination, Elliott may have failed to fully consider the myriad implications and consequences of her actions.

One of the students of that day, Kim Reynolds Huemann, would later recall, "I always felt isolated anyway, and she being an adult and a teacher, I just felt that all my feelings of abandonment and the dysfunction of my home life were being justified in some way. After that experience, I did not apply myself and I didn't care if I lived long enough to see if anyone would notice. I was a troubled child with a lot of problems within my own self. And then this 'lesson' on top of my feelings of being left out! Yeah, you could say I felt pretty darn right awful. I became very reserved and just didn't learn after that. After that experiment, I didn't know who I could trust as a friend."[1]

Bruce Fox, today a nurse, remembered: "Jane always was domineering. You were afraid of her. This was out of the blue and got sprung on us. It was a break from the 'See Jane, see Dick run' kinda stuff. But no one was going to challenge Mrs. Elliott on it. That was her teaching style. She didn't have a lot of sympathy if it interrupted her teaching methods."[2]

Sharon Cummings Zobeck, who came from a family of twelve brothers and sisters, recalled, "I can't stand the woman to this day. When I was in her class, she was a loud, overbearing bitch (excuse my language!) who thought she was right and only she was right. I think Jane Elliott is a fake and should never have been able to be around kids, let alone teach them."[3]

Vickie Bill Roethler, who has seven sisters and five brothers, remembered the day of the experiment this way: "I hated that class. We were treated like third-class citizens. She was the worst teacher I ever had."[4]

For Kay Worple, who was in a subsequent 1970–71 class, the experiment has lasted a lifetime. "None of us have forgotten the exercise, even though it was fifty years ago. What sticks out in my mind were the hurtful things she said. She wanted to bring tears to your eyes. I understand what she was trying to do. I get what she was trying to do. But it wasn't a racial thing; it was a bullying thing.

"When she brought it up—'How would you guys like to try this?'—kids that age, we're up for anything. I guess there's no way I could imagine what she was going to do. We're eight going on nine. We were too young."

When Elliott started berating Worple and others in the blue-eyed group, "I remember sitting at my desk, being told that my house was so junky. It was humiliating for a kid to sit there and listen to all that. I was a shy little girl. I never would have said anything negative against another person.

"'I lied to you!' she told us. A teacher is the person you feel you need to go to if you need something. That day, she became a person I feared. She got personal, and that was just wrong. A teacher is not who you expect something like this to come from. It'd be like having your mother doing it to you. It's abusive. Like children abused by their parents. I've thought about this my whole life. What would make her want to do this? What in God's green earth was she thinking when she did this?"[5]

Others were more neutral. "I knew it was an exercise, so I just played along. I don't think it was a bad thing," recalled Pat Johnson, whose mother was a school bus driver in town. "I wasn't affected one way or another. It made me think that people who are colored might not have it as good as the white folks because they're in the minority. I'm just not sure third grade was the right age."[6]

"I remember those two days like they were yesterday," Alan Moss recalled. "I never knew what prejudice was and today many of my best friends are Blacks. I think that's because of Jane Elliott." Moss, though, also carries another memory. He said that Elliott "humiliated me in school. She wrote on my papers, 'Messy Moss,' and soon the kids would pick up on that and my nickname became Messy Moss. That didn't feel so good."[7]

Complicating matters is that some of Elliott's most enthusiastic former students have chosen in recent years not to talk about their experiences in her class. They give various reasons for their silence, including local opposition in Riceville to Elliott, as well as a desire to assure that some degree of sympathetic understanding of the issues Elliott raised will be included in any media representation of her. Others said they are so tired of inquiries about Elliott that they refuse to discuss her further.

The other teachers at Riceville Elementary—and not just those who were in the teachers' lounge on April 5—don't hold back when assessing Elliott. The experiment crystalized resentment that had been building ever since Elliott joined the faculty. Elliott didn't play by the same rules as the others, they said. Some local teachers stayed angry decades after the experiment.

"Third grade was too young for an experiment like that," reflected Dorothy Wallace, who taught first grade and had been at Riceville Elementary since 1955. "She was very rude to the other teachers. She certainly didn't make the other teachers very comfortable. I think she wanted to make a name for herself. People felt she was domineering. If you could see the expression in her eyes when she pointed her finger at you, it was like she'd like to mop up the floor with you."[8]

LaVonne Moses, who taught first grade at Riceville Elementary for thirty years, recalled: "Little third graders were very upset and couldn't sleep at night.... She had some complaints from the principal for that." Elliott, Moses said, was the kind of person who "liked to talk, but she didn't like to listen. A lot of people are afraid of her. She has a vicious mouth and she'll come back and stab you."[9]

Mary Lou Koschmeder, who taught seventh and eighth grades in Riceville for twenty-five years, remembered, "She always seemed to have the children stirred up. She seemed to enjoy humiliating the kids. I know some of the children were hurt really deeply and still are today. She intimidated everyone."[10]

Ruth Setka, who started at the Riceville public schools the same year as Elliott, taught fourth and fifth grades at the time of the experiment, and continued teaching for thirty more years, said, "I think third grade was too young for what she did. Junior high, maybe. Little children don't like an uproar in the classroom. And what she did caused an uproar.

"Jane was always angry. Always. Maybe she developed that as a kind of defense. I wouldn't say I hate Jane, but I'm tired of hearing about her and her experiment. With Jane, you're always afraid she'll take something that you said and chew on it, and something will come out entirely different."[11]

Parents, too, had problems with Elliott. "I think the experiment really did a number on these students," said Mary Myers, whose son Rusty was in Elliott's class. "I think it was horrible. It was disgusting. Kids are the most susceptible when they're that age. It wasn't right to do."[12]

Carol Lou Brunner and her husband, Adolph, were two years behind Elliott as students in Riceville High, and their son Dale was in the 1968 class when Elliott unveiled the experiment. Both said it caused Dale, a naturally shy boy, all kinds of problems.

"A lot of the parents were really upset with her, and still are," Carol Lou said. "They felt like she was making it so those kids didn't trust anybody, whether they were Black or white. Dale was the kind of person who liked anybody. But after that, he kinda wondered about people. To me, she created hatred. She taught kids to hate. I talked about it with Dale when he came home that day. When it came time for parent-teacher conferences, I let her know I didn't think much of that experiment. She just kinda laughed. She never gave me an answer that made me think she was sorry."

Added Adolph: "You wonder what she was doing and what she hoped this would do for her. She just went ahead and done it. What kinda griped me was she didn't even ask permission of the superintendent to do it. It bothered Dale, I can tell you that."[13]

ELEVEN

Rotarians

THE SPATE OF STORIES ABOUT ELLIOTT, as well as the hoopla swirling around her after the Carson show, spurred the Rotary Club in nearby Osage to invite Elliott to appear as a speaker at its monthly luncheon. Wes Birdsall, the treasurer of a local agricultural services company, was the designated chair of the Tuesday, August 20, 1968, men's lunch club, and the way he envisioned the event, Elliott would give a breezy, impressionistic talk about Darald's and her trip to the Big Apple, as well as her time with Johnny Carson on *The Tonight Show*.[1] Birdsall and the other Rotarians weren't much interested in hearing about the classroom experiment and any impact it might have had on the students. They wanted to hear about Elliott's high-flying trip to New York City.[2]

Elliott had other ideas. If she was going to serve as noon-hour entertainment for a men's club, she wasn't about to give them a sunny travelogue.

"I thought, 'Oh, ho, ho, ho, ho, this is not what *I* want to do,' so I said to the man who called me, I said, 'Would you like to put them through the exercise?' He said, 'Yeah, let's do that.' I said, 'Can you be fired?' He said, 'No, I'm the boss where I work.' I said, 'Good, then let's put 'em through the exercise.'"[3]

This time, Elliott would spring the experiment on adults, not children. That'd be a first.

If the Rotarians thought they were going to hear an entertaining account about a pair of hapless Iowans lost in New York, they were in for a surprise. This was just the opportunity Elliott had been waiting for.

At noon on the day of the luncheon, Elliott instructed the Rotarians to stand in a line while she inspected each man to determine his eye color. She leaned in close to the men, her nose almost touching theirs. Once she determined eye color, Elliott invited the brown-eyed men to help themselves to the buffet. There were a few "What the heck is this lady doing?" glances, but "Iowa nice" meant "Iowa nice," particularly when it involved a young schoolteacher from an adjacent town down the road, so the men followed Elliott's instructions. Rotary luncheons were fun—guys joking, eating and drinking together. A break from whatever it was they did sunup to sundown. No one quite knew what to make of Elliott and what it was she was doing. As at all their lunch meetings, the men anticipated having a swell time.

As the brown-eyed men began loading their plates with slices of baked ham and pork tenderloin, mashed potatoes, and mushy green beans, Elliott directed the blue-eyed Rotarians to stand against the back wall and wait their turn. Only when every brown-eyed man had finished serving himself would the blue-eyed men be allowed to start. Elliott was insistent. There would be no exceptions.

Whatever this schoolteacher was doing, well, the blue-eyed men hoped it didn't involve waiting any longer. Rotary was a friendly service club. The men were hungry and had work to get back to. Finally, when the last brown-eyed man had finished, Elliott gave the blue-eyed Rotarians the go-ahead to start in the food line.

But just then, a latecomer rushed into the meeting.

"You! You, come here," Elliott instructed the man. "Let me see you up close. Let me see what color your eyes are.

"Yep, a brownie. You go to the head of the blue-eye line. You get to eat before they do." She handed a plate to the brown-eyed man, who may have been a plant Elliott had arranged beforehand.[4]

This did not sit well with the blue-eyed men, who were getting hungrier, grumpier, and angrier by the second.

"Whaddaya think you're doing?" the first blue-eyed man in line asked Elliott.

"Don't blame me for the color of your eyes," she replied. "Let this man eat. He deserves to eat before you!"

"What the hell does this lady think she's doin'?" another blue-eyed man asked.

Elliott said nothing.

The blue-eyed men had no choice but to wait, follow the brown-eyed latecomer, and then fill their plates with what was left on the buffet table. A chill descended on the usually upbeat Rotary luncheon.

When all the Rotarians finished eating, Elliott instructed the waiters to clear the brown-eyed men's plates, but informed the blue-eyed men that they'd have to bus their own dishes.

By now, the blue-eyed men had gotten Elliott's drift. Never before had anyone been so rude to the Osage Rotarians.

Three blue-eyed men found a black Magic Marker and in large block letters wrote on the paper tablecloth, "ELLIOT GO HOME!" and held it up in protest. The subversive act was half in anger, half a joke.

Elliott had pushed the men far enough. It was only a matter of time before they'd pull something like that, she knew, but this mild insurrection was even better than Elliott had expected.

The men had spelled her name wrong.

"You have to expect mistakes when you're dealing with blue-eyed people," she announced. This infuriated the men even more.

Instead of taking their dishes to the kitchen, half the blue-eyed Rotarians stormed out of the restaurant. As they filed through the doors, Elliott mused loudly at their backs: "Blue-eyed boys are all right, I suppose. But you wouldn't want your daughter to marry one, would you?"[5]

As far as anyone seems to remember, that was the extent to which Elliott connected eye color to race in this first-run adult version of the experiment. Perhaps she wasn't as ready to explicitly reveal the experiment's point to a roomful of grown men as she had been to third graders. Maybe that was as far as she was prepared to go that day. Maybe she had run out of time. Perhaps she had gotten cold feet, although considering Elliott, that scenario seems unlikely.

A week after the luncheon, Elliott received a rather stiff thank-you note from Rotary luncheon chairman Birdsall, which read in part, "You are to be commended for your imaginative teaching methods and the clarity with which you present your ideas."[6] Manners were manners.

Elliott was obstinate, everyone knew that, but with September and the beginning of the school year around the corner, few in Riceville expected her to continue with this experiment on another class of third graders.

Hadn't she gotten the message? What did it take to get through to her?

TWELVE

"Eye of the Storm"

SEVERAL DAYS BEFORE ELLIOTT appeared before the Rotarians, she had received a call from a Washington, DC–based reporter by the name of Stephen Banker, who had heard about Elliott through the AP wire story, and wanted to film her classroom experiment and insert a segment about it into a Canadian Broadcasting Corporation documentary about pervasive racism faced by Canadian Inuits. At the time, "Eskimos" were the targets of racist epithets in Canada's western provinces; "niggers in parkas" was just one of the slurs being hurled at them. The CBC documentary was to be aired by Canada's premier news magazine, *The Way It Is*, similar in format to *60 Minutes*. Banker hoped to explore the issue of racial prejudice and offer up an innovative method that might reduce it.

Elliott invited Banker to Riceville, and he and a two-person crew packed their bags and headed for Iowa. This time, Elliott alerted the principal, Dinsmore Brandmill, and the superintendent, Donald Johnston, who decided it would be prudent to inform the school board of the trio of visitors before they commenced filming. This time, Elliott sent notices to parents that their children would be filmed and recorded, and she asked them to sign waivers.[1] This time, Brandmill and Johnston insisted that Banker and his crew agree that they wouldn't disclose the names of students or where the experiment took place, other than a small farming community somewhere in Iowa.[2]

Once again, Elliott reprised her role as a reluctant media star. "I was far from eager to go through the experience again," she would write. "It forces a teacher to do deliberately what she normally tries hardest to avoid: to deceive her students, to tell them something she knows is not true. It's a complete reversal of ordinary good teaching. And besides that, you work and work to build up a good rapport with your students, and then for two days you delib-

96

erately destroy it, knowing you will somehow have to build it up again when the lesson is over. It's a sickening experience to cause children with whom you've identified closely that much pain, even if you're convinced that the lesson is important."[3]

Elliott would later say she felt "like a monster picking on a child I would normally help. . . . I kept wanting to say to the class, 'What's wrong with you? Why don't you stand up and refuse to put up with this? Why don't you defend each other from me?'"[4]

Elliott might have expressed overt qualms about subjecting a new crop of students to the experiment, but she was carried away by the potential payoff of appearing on television once again. Any ostensible reservations were masked by full-throttle enthusiasm, this time with journalists recording the experiment. Any concern she might have had was mitigated by the greater good she banked would come from another round of splitting her third graders into two opposing groups. That potential good would be magnified by the prospect that coverage of the classroom experiment would be broadcast coast-to-coast on Canadian television.

Elliott made several modifications this second time. The most significant was the introduction of armbands that she would have the children place on each other's arms to denote the day's inferior eye-color group. These armbands would simulate Jewish stars on cloth swatches that Jews were forced to wear by Nazis, a reference to what Elliott said were the antecedents of the experiment. Elliott's armbands would show at a quick glance which children could be picked on and ridiculed and which children were that day's leaders. Students no longer had to peer into one another's eyes to determine who would be the day's second-class citizens. The armbands were badges of inferiority, invitations for the other eye-color group to bully. They also were a striking visual cue, tailor-made for TV.

As Elliott had done in the spring, the blue-eyed children would be the first victims, followed the next day by the brown-eyed children. This year's third-grade class had twenty-four students.[5] While parents had been informed of Banker and his crew, and had signed releases, neither they nor their children had much of an idea of what would transpire. Students from last year's class could have told them, but apparently few did, at least not in detail.

With half the students wearing armbands, much of the same torment that beset Classroom No. 10 the preceding April took place again. This time around, though, there were a few classroom heroes. Paul Bodensteiner steadfastly refused to go along with Elliott and her instructions. When she informed students that eye color determined personality, character, and intelligence, Paul heatedly responded, "It's not true! That's not fair!"

Undeterred, Elliott tried to appeal to Paul's self-interest. "You should be happy! You have the right color eyes!"

Paul, one of eight siblings and the son of a dairy farmer, didn't buy the mollifications. "But it's not true and it's not fair no matter what you say!" Elliott nodded neutrally and went on with the experiment.[6]

On the second day, with the eye-color groups switched, brown-eyed Sandra Stark burst into tears as she looked on while blue-eyed Malinda Sunnes and Donna Jo Linkenmeyer played on the swings in the playground. As Sunnes remembered it, Sandra could join the pair, but only "if we asked her."

Back in the classroom, if a brown-eyed child knew the answer to whatever Elliott was seeking, she'd ignore the student. "That day, she wouldn't call on you, even if you were blue in the face. We didn't know what was going on," recalled Sunnes.[7]

Another student, Dale McCarthy, recalled that when Elliott set out the premise of genetic superiority based on eye color, "You didn't know whether to believe her or not. But at that age if someone tells you something, especially the teacher, you believe it."

McCarthy remembered Joe Marr and Paul Bodensteiner, the same boy who had stood up to Elliott, getting into a fight on the playground, and when the other boys ran to Elliott for help in detangling the pair, "she didn't say anything. She made it sound like it was the brown-eyed kid's fault, that brown-eyed kids always get into fights. That that's just the way they are. We stood there and felt like crap. She really humiliated the kids. You had a worthless feeling."[8]

To Malinda Sunnes, her memory of the two-day experiment was that it lasted much longer; the experiment remained so vivid in her mind that she recalled it lasted "at least a week, maybe more; it seemed more like three weeks. At least."[9] Such a striking impression underscored how deeply the experiment had cauterized at least one former student's memory.

For Banker and his documentary film crew, Elliott was a dynamo. She came across as telegenic, focused, and certain, a natural for television. She was a one-woman force selling an experiment to challenge children's preexisting conceits about race and racism. Banker got such strong footage that he didn't have to tuck his report about Elliott into the larger CBC story about racism and the Canadian Inuit.[10] Banker had more than enough to stand alone as one of four segments in the hour-long newsmagazine broadcast on Canadian television on the evening of October 6, 1968.

Just as in the aftermath of the Carson show, reaction to Elliott and the experiment was swift and sure. Many viewers were appalled at what the CBC had broadcast. The protest was so spontaneous and so great that, in addition to registering complaints with the CBC, enraged viewers called random Canadian newspapers and radio stations to vent their anger at what they had seen.

"An unusual number of viewers phoned in to *The Citizen* to protest even the showing of the film, which depicted a class of young children taking part in a chilling demonstration of how bigotry is born," wrote Frank Penn, the television critic of the *Ottawa Citizen*, the next day.

Penn wrote that the experiment "was clearly close to traumatic for the youngsters. By the second day all of them were uneasy and tense, and some were upset by the experiment. For an adult viewer it was a powerful illustration of the ease with which prejudice flourishes. It may even have been a wonderful object lesson for the children. But I confess, I'd be mightily reluctant to have any children of mine subjected to it."[11]

So many viewers called in to complain to newspapers, radio stations, and the CBC that the show's producers hurriedly invited Elliott to Toronto to appear before a studio audience to explain more fully her intention with the experiment.

Elliott found herself in the middle of a made-for-TV maelstrom. "Their switchboard had nearly blown a fuse as viewers from across the country had called in demanding to know what in Hell was going on with those poor little kids in Riceville, Iowa," she would later recall (although Riceville had never been identified in the segment). "Immediately two hundred angry Canadiennes raised their hands and commenced to interrogate me as to what I thought I was doing with those poor little white children and that eye-color thing."

One was a white woman who asked Elliott, sitting on a stage upfront, "Don't you think you could do great psychological damage to a child by doing that exercise with them for a day?"

Fielding such a question would become Elliott's stock in trade. Elliott responded that she was much more concerned with the damage done to Black children every day of their lives, not make-believe hostility faced by a white child for one day.

"That's different," the woman replied sharply. "They're used to it. They can take it."

Point, game, match for Elliott.

Just as the exchange was getting more heated, Elliott and her interlocutor were interrupted by another woman who stood up to great fanfare.

"Mrs. Elliott," the older woman started, "I came here to tell you how much I hate you. I am Jewish. I was born and raised in Germany. We went to a Jewish school. Every morning when our headmaster came in, we would bow and say, 'Good morning, Herr Headmaster.' One morning he came in with two SS troopers and one of the troopers said to us, 'In the future, you decadent Jews will no longer bow and say, "Good morning, Herr Headmaster." You will salute and say, "Heil Hitler."' The atmosphere that you created for the blue-eyed children in your classroom that day reminded me of the atmosphere that the Nazis created for the Jews in Germany."[12]

All Elliott could do was agree as the crowd clapped wildly, providing an electrifying out for Elliott and CBC executives. It was unclear whether the audience members were signifying their disapproval of Elliott or their support of the Holocaust survivor. When Elliott left Toronto, she hadn't changed many people's minds, but she once again had a sense of how explosive experimenting on elementary school children was when it came to the topic of race.

Back in Riceville, if the locals were still looking for a reason to make Elliott into an outcast, they surely found one now that the experiment had been brought into the homes of tens of thousands of Canadians courtesy of the CBC. If the other teachers at Riceville Elementary hadn't turned their backs on Elliott before, they did now. Elliott took to calling herself "the invisible man" and "Typhoid Mary."[13]

The next fall Elliott was one of seventeen statewide teachers nominated to be Iowa Teacher of the Year. Another third-grade teacher, from Des Moines, ultimately won the honor, but Elliott's name being placed in contention rankled her fellow teachers enough.[14] Teachers as a professional group are as catty and cutthroat as any other, and when they saw Elliott hurdle to the front of the pack throughout the state that was bound to smart.

To be sure, the reaction around town wasn't just because of what Elliott had done in her classroom and how she had capitalized on the experiment. Her personality continued to prickle the locals. The wife of the school custodian complained that Elliott routinely snubbed everyone at school. "She wouldn't even speak to school maintenance personnel when she met them face-to-face in the hall."[15]

That reaction spilled over to some of the elementary school children. "Kids in Riceville were fearful of her," recalled Brenda Church, today an attorney who grew up in Riceville, moved to Arizona for three decades, and relocated back to her hometown. "We were all happy *not* to be in her class. That's completely aside from that experiment. She'd punished kids. Lots of time-outs. She had this way about her that was intimidating. None of us wanted to be in Mrs. Elliott's class. Pushing the envelope was something she liked to do."[16]

Elliott marched on in her role as the demanding teacher and odd woman out. Occasionally, she was rewarded with some redemption—of a sort.

When Elliott's students took the bus to and from school, high schoolers would occasionally let the third graders know what they thought of Elliott. "You're the kids who have that nigger lover for a teacher," was a common refrain. "You must all be nigger lovers in that class."

"Boy, Mrs. Elliott," a wide-eyed eight-year-old reported to her one day. "Did I learn something on the bus this morning! We already know more than those high school kids do. We know it's wrong to use the word 'nigger' and we know there's nothing wrong with being one either!"[17]

While Elliott's popularity continue to plummet locally, her stock beyond Riceville kept soaring. Admirers flooded Elliott's mailbox with letters and phone calls, heralding her ingenuity. That, in turn, prompted Elliott to do whatever she could to advance her growing national reputation. She wrote an essay about the experiment and submitted it to *Reader's Digest* during the summer of 1968.[18] She submitted the same essay to an educator's journal called *Scholastic Teacher*, which published her two-page article in April and named it a runner-up prize winner in the category "Promising New Practices." Loretta Marion, the journal's editor, wrote to Elliott that the experiment "merits national attention as an innovational practice in education."[19]

"Living in an all-white Iowa farm community, my students have no direct experience with race problems," Elliott wrote in the essay. "Their knowledge of the black man is limited to what they see on television. Some have never seen a Negro. This is unfortunate and needs to be remedied."[20]

Trying to drum up more national interest, Elliott pitched herself and the experiment to a wider circle of powerful media influencers, including the education editor at *Time*; Art Linkletter, the host of the popular daytime variety show, *The Linkletter Show*; Joey Bishop, the host of a late-night show that competed with *The Tonight Show*; George B. Leonard, a senior editor at *Look*; and James Case, the education editor at the prominent literary magazine *Saturday Review*.[21]

None of the magazines or television shows responded positively to Elliott's entreaties, but that did nothing to dampen her enthusiasm. If anything, it accelerated her campaign to advocate for the merits of the eye-color experiment. She spoke before the Iowa State Education Association in Des Moines in April, followed by another gathering of Rotarians, this time in Keokuk, a Mississippi River city 250 miles southeast of Riceville.[22] Elliott started off by asking those with brown eyes to stand. Seventy-five people got up, not knowing exactly why or what was in store for them. Elliott told those standing that they were inferior to anyone with blue, green, or hazel eyes, and then explained her premise. But that was as far as she took the experiment that evening.[23]

One event at a time, Elliott was creating a national platform for herself. The Carson show, *Register* piece, AP story, CBC segment, the teachers' magazine article, along with assorted speaking engagements, had given her a forum, as well as a growing legitimacy. Elliott's grit was beginning to pay off.

That the classroom experiment came from a dot of a town in rural Iowa made her all the more curious as an authority on race. That the experiment had Nazi undertones, was promulgated by a photogenic and articulate white school teacher, and appeared progressive in the context of a sharply divided nation also seemed to tilt in Elliott's favor. That she was media friendly and savvy didn't hurt, either.

The payoff for all of her promotional efforts came soon. In the summer of 1969, a producer from ABC News in New York, William Peters, called Elliott and asked whether she would consent to having a documentary film crew travel to Riceville and film the experiment for a half-hour program that would be part of the network's weighty *Now* documentary series.

Elliott expressed the same reservations she had shared with Mickey Alcorn in the aftermath of *The Tonight Show* and with Stephen Banker, the CBC producer. "My first thought was, 'Oh God, here we go again!' My second thought was, 'Are these people crazy? Isn't there more exciting news out there?'"[24]

She told Peters to look at Banker's *This Is Now* CBC segment, "to give him a chance to change his mind. That didn't work. I sent him to my principal and superintendent, thinking they could get me off the hook. That didn't work" either.[25] To those who knew Elliott, all this was orchestrated modesty.

William Peters, forty-eight at the time, was a good choice to produce a documentary on Elliott and the classroom race experiment. Born in San Francisco and educated at Northwestern University, he was a blue-eyed, bow tie–wearing intellectual patrician. Peters had cut his teeth in television, books, and magazines, an unusual trifecta then as now for a journalist. He had produced two award-winning TV documentaries, *Storm over the*

Supreme Court in 1963 and *Africa* in 1967. Peters had also written two books, *The Southern Temper* in 1958 and *For Us, the Living* in 1967, coauthored with Myrlie Evers, about slain civil rights leader Medgar Evers, Myrlie's husband. In 1956, Peters had written one of the first national magazine articles about a Black twenty-seven-year-old Baptist minister, Martin Luther King Jr., for *Redbook*, titled "Our Weapon Is Love."[26]

Once again, Elliott received permission from Dinsmore Brandmill and Donald Johnston, as well as from parents of the children enrolled in her third-grade class for Peters and his crew to film the students. At least one student's parents did not consent and chose not to have their child participate. This time, there would be no stipulation that either the names of the students or the identity of Riceville would be kept confidential. Everything would be on the record. No one in Riceville would have vetting power to control what Peters and his crew would film or broadcast.[27]

By now, more than a few parents had complained to Brandmill and talked to him about having their children transferred to Helen Weaver's third-grade class, an accommodation that Brandmill automatically accorded parents. This was due not only to fallout from two years of the experiment, but also to Elliott's reputation as a hard-knocks, no-nonsense teacher.

"Usually the father would tell the principal not to 'put my kid in that nigger lover's classroom,'" Elliott recounted, "and the principal never had to ask, 'Which nigger lover do you mean?' We all knew there was only one. One father said, 'I don't want my kid in that nigger lover's classroom, but I want him to learn to read, so put him in there, anyway.'"[28]

Elliott seldom conceded her reputation as a difficult, overbearing teacher, opting instead to label the parents' alleged racism as the reason for their dislike of her. Many parents volubly disparaged Elliott's version of their motives. They insisted they'd pulled their kids out of Elliott's class because they believed that Elliott would not serve their children well as a teacher. One former student recalled that another teacher had advised her parents to "'do whatever you can to get your son out of that class.' She actually called Mom and told her that Jane wouldn't be good for my brother. She told Mom she needed to get up to the school and do something. Jane could be like a pit bull."[29]

Elliott did have experience teaching children with reading disabilities, so Brandmill made it a point to place poor readers and low-aptitude students in her class. Some in town suggested that the parents of such children had all but given up hope for any academic success for their children and that Elliott was their last resort. Other parents were not the kind to second-guess the school administration. Still others simply were too busy with their jobs and their families to seek to intervene.[30]

With sixteen students in Elliott's class, Peters and his crew had committed to start filming in Riceville during the last week in February, so Elliott had all fall to prepare her students for the in-class documentary, scheduled to last four days. Elliott and Peters agreed that there would be no mention of the upcoming televised experiment to the students and no coaching of them. They would simply be told that a news crew would be arriving and would be spending time in their classroom to film them. When the children asked why ABC had chosen their class, Elliott told them, "Because they're looking for the greatest group of third graders they can find and where would they go except to my room?"[31]

When Peters's eleven-man news crew arrived, they brought with them heavy, bulky equipment, which they placed up and down a five-foot-wide swath on one side of Classroom No. 10, along with a serpentine maze of wires, tape, and cables. The crew covered the windows with heavy black-out drapes and set up bright lights inside the classroom. Peters encouraged students to mingle with the visitors the day prior to filming. Before Elliott launched the experiment, the crew filmed a day of normal classroom activities. The idea was to acclimate students, so they'd be comfortable with the cameras, sound-boom microphones, and operators recording their every move. This was imperative once the experiment began. Like an early reality TV program, the students were unpaid, real-life actors playing their natural roles as third graders. Elliott instructed the children to ignore the hubbub on the sidelines and not look at the cameras. As a reward for their efforts, Peters gave kids assorted snippets of audiotape and film to take home as souvenirs.[32]

With high-wattage lights on, cameras rolling, and microphones picking up the lowest-decibel student asides and whispers, Elliott started off the experiment by having the students recite the Pledge of Allegiance and sing "God Bless America," as was customary. She then asked the children to make an eye-color inventory, recording the names and eye colors of each student. This time, Elliott discarded the idea of armbands in favor of simple cloth collars attached with a straight pin. The armbands had been too literal, too much of a reminder of the gruesome history they came from. The collars, simple swatches of dark cotton cloth, served the same purpose, but worked better.

This year, the two days of the experiment happened to fall on National Brotherhood Week, which gave Elliott cause to start the first day off by asking students what the word "brotherhood" meant to them. A lively exchange followed that nicely set the scene. Two members of Peters's television crew were Black, but none of the students seemed to notice.

"It might be interesting now to judge people today by the color of their eyes," Elliott asked, easing into the experiment. "Would you like that? It sounds like fun, doesn't it?"

As the students had responded during the two previous years, this year's crop replied with a resounding *Yeah*!

Elliott chose to reverse the two groups this time. The blue-eyed children would be classified as the superior group the first day, and the brown-eyed kids would be superior the second day. This year's split between blue-eyed and brown-eyed children was even, eight to eight; no one had hazel or green eyes.

When Elliott instructed the blue-eyed children to use the straight pins to fasten the cloth collars around the necks of the "inferior" brown-eyed students, the humiliation that they would feel became personal. Draped on the shoulders of the brown-eyed children, the collars were yokes, symbolically weighing the wearers down. To further make her point, Elliott announced, "We aren't always close enough to see your eyes, and we want to be able to tell even when your back is turned. We wouldn't want to make a mistake."

As in the previous two Classroom No. 10 experiments, Elliott noticed that cliques among students formed immediately. The blue-eyed children started strutting around the classroom as the brown-eyed students slumped. At midmorning, on the playground, brown-eyed John Benttine hauled back and slugged blue-eyed Russell Ring after Russell called him "Brown Eyes!"

Elliott was on the playground, saw what John had done, and didn't bat an eye. Nor did she come to Russell's aid.

The next day, Elliott had the blue-eyed kids wear the cloth collars, with the same instructions. Much of what had transpired the previous day happened again. As was Elliott's practice, when the day ended, she had all the children gather in Magic Circle. When asked how the inferior group wearing the collars felt, blue-eyed Greg Johanns replied, "Like a dog on a leash." Raymond Hansen replied, "Like you're chained in prison and someone threw the key away." For brown-eyed Sandi Dohlman, the experiment "proved that people do treat people differently because of their color."[33]

The results at the end of two days were just as dramatic as they had been during the previous two years. When Elliott told the blue-eyed kids they could take off their collars and throw them away, Raymond Hansen stomped on his and ripped it into two. Blue-eyed Brian Saltou did his best to destroy his collar, first stepping on it and then picking it up and biting it to tear the cloth into pieces.[34]

There was some unintended drama the cameras didn't capture. Russell Ring, who had left his glasses at home the second day, had somehow swallowed one of the straight pins that Elliott had used for fastening the collars, and was rushed to the hospital, eighteen miles away in Osage. Sheila Schaefer ran into the steel post of one of the swing sets on the playground and got a whopper of a blue-and-purple bruise on her forehead. Elliott didn't know whether these accidents happened because of the students' excitement at the cameras or because her own performance distracted her from more fully supervising the children. Or whether they would have happened anyway.

Elliott had asked her friend, photographer Charlotte Button, to take photographs of the children, with and without the collars. Button's black-and-white photographs showed the agony of each student singled out as unworthy, and later, freed and happy once the collars were removed. The photographs were testament to the power of two days of discrimination, not based on skin color but on eye color. At the conclusion of each day, Elliott had students draw self-portraits.

Wearing an eight-button jumper in her first picture, brown-eyed Susan Ginder depicted herself as crestfallen and dejected; in the second drawing, she was smiling ear-to-ear. Frowning blue-eyed Brian Saltou looked far away and alienated in one sketch, wildly enthusiastic and energetic in the other.

"It was dynamic and very exciting and a frightening thing to watch," recalled Peters, stunned by what he and his crew had caught on film.[35]

ABC was proud of the work and did its best to drum up viewership for the show, which was titled "Eye of the Storm." *TV Guide* ran a promo of the program (with a photo of frowning blue-eyed Russell Ring wearing a collar), as did the *New York Times* (with a photo of blue-eyed Raymond Hansen wearing a collar) on its television-listings page. The airtime was when kids presumably would be in bed, ten thirty p.m. Eastern time, nine thirty Central time, on a Monday.

Even before it was broadcast, "Eye of the Storm" was effusively endorsed by the National Education Association, which sent out a press release urging viewers not to miss the network program. In a press release, the executive producer of the ABC series, Arthur Holch, was extravagant in his praise for the documentary, calling it "a nonfiction drama, a real-life demonstration of those dark impulses in most of us. . . . Nothing we could have written or stage-managed would so effectively have combined the wholesome charm of these school children with the harsh fact that they too are susceptible to the ugly virus of discrimination."[36] In television's world of expected hype for any and all upcoming programs, Holch's comments were particularly noteworthy, signaling the network's endorsement not only of its documentary, but also of Elliott and the experiment.

On Monday, May 11, 1970, "Eye of the Storm" aired, narrated by veteran newsman Bill Beutel. The show was instantly hailed as a masterpiece. *Chicago Tribune* television critic Clarence Petersen wrote, "At the end, of course, she [Elliott] told them the truth. A little girl cried, so happy was she that the ugly game had ended. You will probably cry a little too."[37] James Doussard, the TV critic for the *Louisville Courier-Journal*, wrote, "Eye of the Storm is touching and beautiful; so is Jane Elliott, a teacher those kids in Riceville, Iowa, are lucky to have."[38] *Life*'s John Leonard, among the nation's most influential television critics, wrote a long, thoughtful review, which started, "For the third year in a row, Jane Elliott has introduced a little terror into the classroom where she teaches at the Riceville, Iowa elementary school." After describing the experiment, Leonard wrote, "All this is caught perfectly by the cameras. The faces of the children are astonishing. . . . [W]hen Mrs. Elliott ended the experiment, and with enormous relief the whole class joining in song, one little girl was in tears and one little boy was wholly absorbed in ripping apart his collar before flinging it into the wastepaper basket. . . . Unfortunately, not every elementary school is full of Mrs. Elliotts."[39]

Not every reviewer raved about "Eye of the Storm." Several raised the ethical issue of Elliott's and the administrators' authority in subjecting third graders to such an experiment. "I'm not sure what all this accomplishes beyond an experiment to be recorded in the *Journal of American Psychology* and if I were a Riceville parent I might question the wisdom of having my child's emotions tampered with to illustrate a lesson that should have been taught at home," wrote Terrence O'Flaherty, the television critic for the *San Francisco Chronicle*. O'Flaherty labeled the experiment a "stunt," adding, "I am not a psychiatrist—and neither, I suspect, is Mrs. Elliott—but I would guess that for every youngster who is taught compassion for the suppressed, there is another who rather enjoys his role as suppressor."[40]

Perhaps the harshest criticism came from Max Rafferty, the former California state superintendent of public instruction turned right-wing social critic, who lambasted the experiment as "hogwash." In his widely syndicated newspaper column, Rafferty wrote, "A teacher isn't hired by the taxpayers to plant her own ideas about political and sociological problems in the minds of third graders. She's hired to teach history and reading and mathematics to children who later on in life can use these and other skills to construct their own political and sociological philosophy as they may jolly see it. Neither is that teacher employed to frighten youngsters nor to torment them not to make them feel inferior, not for one day, nor for one minute."[41]

Once again, just as after *The Tonight Show* and the CBC documentary, Elliott was inundated with letters, positive and negative. A woman from Brooklyn, New York, suggested that her teaching methods were reminiscent of "the brainwashing system of Communism. I know because I lived under it."[42] Principal Brandmill also got complaints. "Oh boy—the harm done little children due to exposure of frustrated grade school teachers and this one really gets to go to the head of the class!" a woman from Chattanooga, Tennessee, wrote. "You surely need to see that she sees a psychiatrist. She really has something loose upstairs."[43]

Elliott took pains to correct those who called what she had done an "experiment." This may have stemmed from personal preference or perhaps out of fear of legal repercussions should a parent sue Elliott or the Riceville School District for subjecting their children to what had happened in Classroom No. 10, in spite of the signed waivers. In a letter following the broadcast, Elliott wrote Susan T. Mitchell, the executive in charge of licensing VHS tapes of ABC programs for sale, correcting the network's usage of the word "experiment."

"I'd appreciate having the word 'exercise' substituted for 'experiment' in the literature accompanying the film. This may sound like semantic antics to you, but I wasn't trying to discover how my students would behave under these circumstances. I wanted to acquire some insights into why people who live under these conditions behave as they do."[44] ABC complied.

In Riceville, all the TV show did was consolidate resentment. "Why are you concentrating on Elliott's classroom? There are interesting things going on in our rooms, too," one teacher told Vince Gaito, the ABC-TV crew's head cameraman, as he wandered the halls of Riceville Elementary during filming breaks.

"They hate you," Gaito reported back to Elliott after he'd interviewed several more teachers.[45]

After the show aired, Elliott received an unsigned letter with a Riceville postmark on the envelope, saying, "How much nicer it would have been if we in the Riceville Community School District could have rejoiced with you. . . .

But it was hard to swallow endorsing integration from a teacher who can't seem to find it in her heart to lower her head and speak to fellow teachers and school employees when she meets them in the school corridors! What's that old adage about practice what one preaches?"[46]

By now, though, Elliott wasn't playing to the locals in Riceville any longer. In Classroom No. 10, she hung a map of the United States and had her students stick pins in every state from which she, the school, or the class had received letters in response to the documentary. Forty-four states had pins in them by the end of the year.

So popular and acclaimed was "Eye of the Storm" that ABC rebroadcast it three times the same year it premiered. The documentary went on to win a George Foster Peabody Award, the Pulitzer Prize of television news; it also was honored at the Monte Carlo Television Festival, the only US TV program selected. Peters would go on to write a book, *A Class Divided*, about the experiment, published the following year.[47]

Elliott couldn't have asked for a better national showcase, better than either the Carson show or the CBC documentary. The following October, Elliott spoke to a group of teachers in St. Paul, Minnesota, at the behest of the state Department of Education. A multitude of other invitations followed.

Direct, in-your-face, and outspoken—just the opposite of what many approved of in Riceville—word continued to circulate that the third-grade teacher from Iowa was a fireball. She had something to say that was provocative and relevant to the times. "Eye of the Storm" had conferred on Elliott more confidence and authority. No longer content to teach just third graders, she wanted to teach the world.

It wasn't long before another invitation arrived, this one from the White House.

THIRTEEN

The White House

THE INVITATION WAS TO PARTICIPATE in the White House Conference on Children, and it arrived in the Elliotts' Riceville postbox with a return address that read simply, "The White House." Such presidential summits had been convened every ten years since 1909, and all the nation's heavy hitters in education had been invited to attend this year's decennial congress.[1] Some four thousand delegates were to descend on Washington, DC, to discuss everything kindergarten through high school. Stephen Hess, the conference's national chairman, wrote to Elliott, "Expect much excitement, few speeches, and no banquets. Expect to work hard with our forum chairmen in writing the final reports."[2] President Richard M. Nixon was scheduled to open the summit, even though his advisers had privately suggested that the audience of educators would likely be hostile. Many were angry over an assortment of issues facing teachers, from paltry salaries to outdated curricula. As the *Washington Post* put it, quoting a Republican official, "Asking this administration to hold a conference on youth is like asking the Kremlin to hold a conference on capitalism."[3]

The multi-ring convention was organized into twenty-four areas of inquiry. Elliott had been able to get assigned to a plum panel: she was one of twelve members of the "Children without Prejudice" forum. The panel's mandate was to "consider the consequences of adult behavior and actions upon the attitudes of children," as well as "to seek to identify not only how prejudice is acquired by children, but its impact on their healthy development."[4] This lined up nicely with Elliott's interests and drive.

Less than three years after Martin Luther King Jr.'s assassination, Elliott had rocketed from obscure Iowa schoolteacher to front and center of a burgeoning movement to demand change in how children were being educated about issues of race and discrimination. Forum 18, as it was called, would be ground zero for much of the conference. Issues of racism and equality had thoroughly infused the national education-reform agenda, and the conference was an opportunity to broaden the discussion from urban Black audiences to a larger arena of teachers, union leaders, legislators, academics, journalists, and national education policy wonks. The delegates from Forum 18 were charged with wrestling with these contentious topics, preparing recommendations, presenting them to the at-large delegates, and sending their report to President Nixon. What the president would do with the suggestions wasn't up to the delegates. No one expected much education reform, but at least the summit would provide a national platform to demand it.

The White House conference was a big deal, and scoring an invitation demonstrated Elliott's spiraling influence. "Eye of the Storm" had aired the previous spring and its reverberations were still being felt nationwide. After the show, Elliott had been invited to appear on *The Virginia Graham Show*, a nationally aired daytime talk show televised from Los Angeles, to discuss race and education. Elliott also had been a guest on an assortment of drive-time radio programs, including *Kennedy and Company*, carried on the ABC affiliate in Chicago. She was coming into her own. In her role as a rural schoolteacher with an unusual classroom experiment, Elliott seemed also to grasp what those in the national media wanted, and was able to deliver. She was a publicist's dream, but so savvy that she didn't need one.

With her invitation to the White House conference, Elliott had ascended to a national shrine of education innovators. Those invited were "the finest minds available from many disciplines and backgrounds," the summit's program touted. "Lawyers and educators, mothers and behaviorial [*sic*] scientists, doctors and administrators—these and others will explore together the worlds of all children, black and white, urban and rural, rich and poor."[5] She had come a long way from being the luncheon speaker at the Osage Rotary Club.

Whether by design or default, few in Riceville seemed to know much about what Elliott had accomplished. Perhaps they didn't want to know; perhaps they refused to acknowledge just how strategically Elliott had been able to position herself in the emerging national conversation on race. The only coverage Smitty Messersmith included about her in the *Riceville Recorder* was a sole photograph, published inside, of Elliott posing with Peters and the crew of "Eye of the Storm." The last thing locals seemed to care about was Elliott talking about eye color as a way to address the chasm between Blacks and whites in America. At home in Riceville, the other teachers continued to dismiss her. School administrators had grown weary of Elliott's requests to take time off for a speaking engagement, to respond to fallout from yet another classroom project, or to prepare for a journalist about to descend on Riceville Elementary to learn more about the classroom experiment.

When Elliott asked Riceville school superintendent Donald Johnston for a week off to attend the upcoming White House summit, Johnston glared at her, as though to ask, "What now?"

"*What* house conference?" a weary Johnston asked as though he hadn't heard her right.

"The *White* House conference," Elliott replied.

"The *what* house conference?"

"The *White* House," Elliott repeated with a degree of righteousness she couldn't hold back.

"Oh, *that* house. Well, I guess it'll be all right."[6]

Several months before the summit, delegates of Forum 18 convened a meeting in Chicago at the O'Hare Airport Sheraton Hotel to figure out the presentation they'd make at the DC conference. By now, "Eye of the Storm" was Elliott's professional calling card. The show radiated telegenic star appeal; it also succinctly conveyed the essence of the Riceville experiment under the imprimatur of ABC television.

At the time, pulling off a classroom experiment as racially charged and provocative as what Elliott had engineered in Riceville likely wouldn't have worked in many other settings. The experiment's stark proximity to Nazism probably would have made it too volatile for many urban or suburban school districts. And its frank acknowledgment of racism would not have been welcomed in many classrooms in the South and elsewhere. Experimenting on such young children likely would have met resistance; parents and school administrators might have stopped it before it began. Even in an isolated Iowa town, residents didn't like what she'd done. Elliott and her full-tilt personality, though, had been able to maneuver around local landmines for three straight years. Now, armed with Peters's well-received network documentary, she was about to take center stage at a presidential conference.

"Can you feature a hundred-and-sixty angry delegates all yelling at me?" Elliott wrote about the upcoming convention.[7] "Since fools rush in where angels fear to tread, I agreed to do as they asked," Elliott recounted, once again playing the modest Iowa card.[8]

In fact, what was to happen on December 15, 1970, at the ensuing White House conference was nothing short of stunning.[9] One hundred and eighty delegates had signed up to attend Forum 18's breakout session on racism and prejudice, to be held at the Sheraton Park Hotel in the Woodley Park neighborhood of Washington. While there were nineteen other steering committee members of Forum 18, the session belonged to Elliott. She claimed ownership of it outright.

As Elliott had done for the Canadian documentary, she brought with her armbands, which the blue-eyed (and green-eyed and hazel-eyed) delegates would be instructed to wear. Just so that everything would go according to plan, Elliott enlisted the help of several delegates on the Forum 18 committee to assume covert acting roles. Maurilio Ortiz, a junior high school principal from San Antonio, would act as Elliott's greeter; Piri Thomas, a Puerto Rican activist and author from New York, would play a security guard; and K. Patrick Okura, a Boys Town psychologist from California, would take on the role of enforcer and agent provocateur.[10]

"You've got blue eyes!" Ortiz gruffly noted without explanation as he handed an armband to each blue-eyed delegate signing in. "Put this on and wait outside!" The blue-eyed delegates were told to line up against a wall in a crowded hallway.

By contrast, Ortiz warmly welcomed the brown-eyed delegates and escorted them into a meeting room with comfortable chairs.

After thirty minutes of standing in the hallway, the blue-eyed delegates were allowed to join their brown-eyed counterparts but discovered that only half the number of chairs that were needed had been allotted. When someone asked if the hotel could bring more chairs into the meeting room, Elliott said no. She was firm about this. Blue-eyed delegates would have to stand.

By now, the delegates surely must have realized that Elliott was trying to pull off some kind of social-experiment stunt. This session was part of the conference's mandate, "Children without Prejudice," so the delegates had to have figured some ruse was underway. Those in attendance were clued-in educators, and Elliott's reputation by now had gone national.

That seemingly made no difference. Elliott, her trio of lieutenants, and assorted plants in the audience created a nonstop show. "The knowledge that it was only a game we were able to play did little to alleviate our mounting nervousness as we shifted uncomfortably under a barrage of standard, but to us new, abuse from the doorkeeper," wrote blue-eyed *Washington Evening Star* reporter Toni House, who posed as a delegate in the session that day. The afternoon newspaper in the nation's capital had sent a reporter to write a long take-out on Elliott's blue-eyes, brown-eyes session. Whether Elliott had anything to do with the reporter's assignment is unknown but she wasn't disappointed when she read about the unfolding experiment in the next day's newspaper.

Thirty minutes into Elliott's setup, one delegate up front, a plant, gazed at Elliott's face and shrieked, "*You* have blue eyes!"

"Yes, I do," Elliott calmly replied. "But I'm married to a brown-eyed man, so that makes it all right."

Flummoxed at how they were being treated, the blues grumbled among themselves, then caucused in a corner of the meeting room, and presented Elliott with a list of demands, which the browns promptly ridiculed. Pat Okura, acting in his role as enforcer and provocateur, announced that because of their subversive political action, the blues would have to pay by giving up their plastic zippered cases that contained the day's agenda. When asked why, Okura said that the blue-eyed delegates might be hiding knives in the packets. "Blue-eyed people can't shoot straight," he said. "That's why they always carry knives."

The blues responded by refusing to hand over the coveted conference portfolios, and when Okura and his cohorts forcibly tried to take the cases away, the blues, who had managed to secure seats, tucked the packets on their chairs securely under their butts.

"Okay. Let them keep them, now that they're sitting on them. That's the only part of their anatomy that can absorb any knowledge," Okura announced.

That comment turned the blue-eyed delegates even more hostile, and after a near scuffle, one blue-eyed woman led the rest of the blues in a rendition of "We Shall Overcome." Elliott had plants in both groups to act as musical provocateurs. The brown-eyed delegates tried to outdo the blues with their own performance of "Beautiful Brown Eyes," which drowned out the blue-eyed anthem.

All the while, Elliott kept railing at the blues. She was as obnoxious as she was insulting. "We hope YOU people can behave yourselves . . . YOU people will have to be quiet . . . YOU people get us some more chairs."

The blue-eyed delegates didn't know how to react to this pint-sized general. They caucused again, which prompted their brown-eyed counterparts to switch their hymn of solidarity to "God Bless America." The blues resorted by gathering in the front of the conference room and staging a sit-in.

At this point, a man burst down the aisle, shaking with rage. "Stop it! Stop it!" he demanded. "What are you people doing? We came here to talk about children without prejudice and look at what you grown-ups are doing!" It was unclear whether the interloper was a plant.

Whether or not he was, Elliott confronted him head-on. "Now, YOU go to the back of the room where YOU belong and stay there!"

As noon approached, Elliott hadn't let down her guard. She invited the brown-eyed delegates to adjourn for lunch, but told the blue-eyed attendees that they'd have to stay in the windowless conference room and that lunch would not be provided. When a blue asked why they wouldn't be able to leave, Elliott said, "Because you might vandalize the other areas of the hotel if you're allowed to wander off!"

This time Elliott had gone too far. The blues would have no more of the social-engineering experiment.

Dozens got up and tried to leave, at which point confederate Okura huddled with Ortiz and Thomas, and prevented them from exiting.

"Don't let them out! Don't let them out!" Ortiz shouted.

There was a mad dash for the door. The blues pushed past the three "security guards," crashed through the exit, and ran for freedom. Within minutes, a phalanx of real hotel guards showed up in response to the blues' complaints that they were being held hostage.

In the afternoon, after the break, the blue-eyed participants who hadn't had enough and hadn't left negotiated a neutral area in the hotel and refused to continue to participate in Elliott's session unless the brown-eyed delegates immediately forfeited their rights.

"It began to seem the 'game' would never end," House wrote in her powerful first-person *Washington Evening Star* story. "We tried reason. Some blue-eyes sank in their chairs in abject submission. We wanted out. A large blonde from Boston rose to lead us to the door. The doorkeeper blocked our way and we submitted to captivity."

By midafternoon, Elliott had made her point. She paused the experiment and asked the delegates regardless of their eye color their reactions to what they had experienced.

There had been no way for the blues to win. They were born losers and would stay losers for the rest of their lives, Elliott told the remaining delegates. If they protested, strived, or resisted, there'd be consequences. Whites would have it no other way. This is how it is in America, Elliott told those still in the room.

The experiment, even though it had been staged and manipulated by shills, had made an impact. The participants weren't third graders and they hadn't signed waivers to submit to an experiment of stacking the odds. But no one could deny the emotions it stirred; even though it had been prompted by theatrics, the experiment had touched a nerve.

"I knew you were wrong and I knew intellectually that I should try to do something to stop you," a blue-eyed woman announced to Elliott and the others. "But something inside me said, 'They're just going to do it to you anyway, so you might as well just sit here and take it.' So, that's what I did. I just sat there and took it."

The White House conference had been too pivotal a venue for Elliott to let human nature work its own course. In handwritten notes to herself on three-holed notebook paper, she had prepared a cheat sheet for the day:

- Place a stool pigeon in blue-eyed group to keep power structure informed of reactions.
- Plant brown-eyed people to initiate aggressive behavior if response fails to materialize. (May not be necessary.)
- Interrupt blue-eyed speakers.
- Call on brown-eyed people for most responses.
- I pledge allegiance to the flag of the United States of America and to the republic for which it stands, one nation, under god, indivisible, with liberty and justice for all brown eyes.
- Hold blues outside while browns are seated after breaks.
- Begin before all blues could possibly return. Blame their tardiness on eye color.

Elliott made additional program notes, including the option of playing "Beautiful Brown Eyes" as background music; having several brown-eyed delegates come in late and then demand that the blue-eyed delegates make room for them; label adjacent bathrooms free for brown-eyed delegates and pay for blue-eyed delegates. She also sought to fold into her speech reworked racist clichés such as, "Free, brown-eyed, and twenty-one"; "If I have only one life to live, let me live it as a brown"; "Is it true browns have more fun?"; "Eeny, meeny, miny, moe, catch a blue-eyes by the toe"; and "Last one in is a blue-eyed baby."[11]

To some, the experiment had been sophomoric and offensive, a way to show what many of these veteran educators already knew. "You white women go play your game," one delegate fumed. "You can jump in and out. Black children can't."[12]

In terms of the entire White House conference, by almost all accounts, the summit was a bust, just as had been predicted. It was wracked by dissension, which came to a head when at-large Black delegates demanded a vote to end the Vietnam War, hunger, and federal support of the supersonic transport program. A faction of the delegates physically tried to take over the conference podium during the final plenary session, but were rebuffed.[13] Many delegates wanted to convene a special session to address overarching national concerns of the educators, but that too failed. "We were so scattered and separated that there was no opportunity to think about children as a total group in the U.S.," reflected one of the other Iowa delegates, Ruth Anderson. "I really feel the only reason the conference occurred was because it's supposed to occur every 10 years."[14]

Still, Elliott had once again made a name for herself, this time in the shadow of the White House.

FOURTEEN

Trouble

BY THE TIME ELLIOTT RETURNED home to Riceville, trouble awaited her. This time, though, it wasn't as much from the locals as from a stranger from Colorado.

Elliott had received a disturbing letter from a sixth-grade teacher, Wilda Wood, from Pine Valley Elementary School, on the campus of the US Air Force Academy in Colorado Springs.

"Please convey my congratulations and sincere admiration to your delightful third grade class for their performance on ABC-TV's *Eye of the Storm*. They were superb!" Wood started her typed, two-page letter.

Then came the hammer.

"As I watched, I was repeatedly amazed at the similarities of another project widely publicized in 1965–1969." After citing multiple published stories about her own classroom experiment, during which Wood had divided her own students by the color of their eyes, Wood pointedly signed her letter, "Yours for more Creativity and Originality."[1]

Wood never explicitly accused Elliott of stealing her experiment, but she sure suggested it. Kentucky-born Wood, an experienced, twenty-year teacher, wrote that five years earlier she had designed an experiment to expose her sixth-grade students to a series of contrived racially motivated incidents for a period of one week. Wood called the experiment "Project Misery."

Wood's experiment was the felicitous result of a summer research project she undertook at nearby Colorado College under the tutelage of Morton Sobel, an administrator from the US Department of Education. Once she got approval from the elementary school principal and superintendent, Wood put the idea to her students and their parents for consideration.[2] They all signed off, and she began.

As the week progressed, day-by-day, the severity of discrimination increased. On Monday, half the class had to sit at an isolated lunchroom table; on Tuesday, select students had to ride in the back of the local bus (if they walked to school, they had to step off the sidewalk when someone came their way); on Wednesday, students were stripped of any duties that involved prestige, e.g., lunchroom duty, safety patrol, flag raising; on Thursday, half the class was denied use of new textbooks and required to use outdated texts. It was on Friday that Wilda Wood employed eye color as a means of discrimination: blue-eyed boys weren't allowed to engage with other students.

"I wanted to let the children know and learn what segregation is and what some of the problems are, not only in the South, but around the rest of the country," the fifty-one-year-old Wood had told a reporter for the *Boston Globe* in 1967, six months before Elliott had tried out the experiment in Riceville.[3]

There were marked differences between Elliott's and Wood's attempts to import racism into their respective classrooms. The Colorado version was more encompassing and involved children three years older than Elliott's students. Elliott's version focused solely on eye color; Wood limited discrimination based on eye color just to the last day. With Wood's experiment, there was a weeklong buildup. The children were programmatically introduced to arbitrary rank and privilege, culminating in the fifth day, when the blue-eyed boys were isolated based on their eye color. Wood also advised the administration, her students, and their parents about what was to happen. Nonetheless, the similarity between the two experiments was curious.

On the same day that Wilda Wood wrote to Elliott, another teacher at Wood's elementary school, Mary Carroll, also sent a letter to Elliott. This correspondence was more accusing. Carroll was outraged. She charged that Elliott had stolen the experiment from Wood, and demanded that Elliott credit the Colorado teacher for originating it.

"You deserve little praise for your efforts because you failed to recognize the originator of this plan to make children aware of the disadvantaged," Carroll wrote. "As you know, 'Eye of the Storm' was a duplication of the 'Project Misery' designed and used by Mrs. Wilda Wood. . . . Your failure to give credit to Mrs. Wood and her class for their efforts, initiative in planning, and implementation of idea was at best grossly unfair. . . . I feel we have a responsibility for integrity if we are to work with and to influence children. I sincerely hope you do some 'soul-searching' if you intend to continue in the field of education." Carroll wrote that she intended to file an ethics complaint with the National Education Association against Elliott.[4]

Roger Thorson, the principal at Pine Valley Elementary, joined Carroll in his indignation, and the two lodged a formal complaint with the NEA's Committee on Professional Ethics.

The NEA committee reviewed the ABC transcript of the "Eye of the Storm," and when it found that Elliott had never explicitly stated on air that she had originated the experiment, the committee ruled against censuring Elliott. The NEA's associate secretary for ethics, Donald H. Morrow, concluded that Wilda Wood's and Elliott's classroom activities could each be classified as educational experiments, both sharing a "concern that the children be involved in feeling the effects of discrimination." But there was no way to prove that Elliott had stolen the experiment from Wood, the NEA concluded.

In reality, it seemed unlikely that Elliott hadn't at least heard of Wood's experiment before launching her own. There had been an abundance of publicity on Wood and her Colorado undertaking on prejudice reduction. In addition to the *Boston Globe* account, both the Associated Press and United Press International ran extensive stories on Wood's experiment, carried in scores of newspapers nationwide, including several in Iowa and Minnesota. CBS's Walter Cronkite and ABC's Peter Jennings had picked up the story and aired segments on their evening news shows about Wood and the experiment she had implemented. Stories about Wood's "Project Misery" had also been published in a host of national education journals and magazines published for teachers.

"The experiences during Project Misery in Mrs. Wood's class were designed in such a way that the children actually felt discrimination by being segregated, denied privileges all other children have, or having some of their rights as citizens taken away from them," wrote principal Roger Thorson in the February 1966 issue of *National Elementary Principal*, more than two years before Elliott first tried her own version.[5] The magazine of the National Education Association, *NEA Journal*, in September of the same year also published an article on the Colorado experiment, as did another education magazine, *School Management*, in January. All cited Wilda Wood as its originator.[6]

The reactions that Wood got from her Colorado students turned out to be similar to those of Elliott's own third graders in Riceville. "At first, they were enthusiastic but, as the week went by, they became frustrated and quite irritable. By Friday there was no joking about it. They knew what 'second class citizen' meant."[7] The impact left the students more aware and considerate of everyone, Wood wrote.[8]

Whenever Elliott was asked about the origins of the experiment, she maintained that the idea had come to her from reading *Mila 18*, Leon Uris's classic World War II novel set in Poland during the German occupation.[9] When she heard the news of the King assassination on television on the evening of April 4, 1968, she said, she flashed back on the Uris book and spontaneously came up with the idea of separating her students according to eye color. Elliott said that she had read the Uris novel as an undergraduate at Iowa State Teachers College, and as a result "realized for the first time that eye color could be and had been used to determine whether people in a civilized society lived or died."[10] She later wrote, "Hitler was bent on founding a racially pure nation of Aryan people who were all going to be blue-eyed, blond-haired, and fair-skinned."[11]

Nazis surely practiced atrocities, but it wasn't in *Mila 18* that such savagery based on eye color was described. Further, the Uris book was published in 1961, eight years after Elliott had received her teaching certificate from ISTC. The claim that her experiment was inspired by the novel she maintained she read while in college could not have been true.

At other times, much later, Elliott said she learned the Nazis had conducted experiments based on eye color after reading two books about Josef Mengele, the notorious Nazi physician who oversaw experiments on concentration-camp inmates. Those books, *Mengele: The Complete Story* by Gerald L. Posner and John Ware and *The Nazi Doctors: Medical Killing and the Psychology of Genocide* by Robert Jay Lifton, were first published in 1986, eighteen years after Elliott first tried out the experiment.[12]

> I decided on the day after Martin Luther King was killed that I would do what Hitler did. I knew it worked for him, I thought it might work for me. I decided that I will pick out a group of people on the basis of a physical characteristic over which they had no control and I decided that it would be eye color. I didn't know for sure that that had really happened, I had read about it, I had heard about it and I had seen movies about it, but I wasn't sure until I read the book *Mengele* and also the book *The Nazi Doctors* and realized that, yes, indeed, this was true.[13]

Elliott never linked what she did in her classroom with Wilda Wood or any other teacher. "I didn't create this idea," she would say obliquely when asked about the experiment's origin. "I adapted it from Hitler and the people who were willing to go along with that insanity in order to stay alive."[14]

It might be that Elliott didn't know exactly where the idea that blossomed into the Riceville experiment came from. It could have been inspired by Wood, a general knowledge about Nazi experimentation, or articles about educational reform. It's conceivable that Elliott wholly fabricated the circumstances of her inspiration or that she embellished the homespun scenario of creating the teepee on her living room floor while watching TV news of the King assassination to make the genesis of the eye-color experiment sound portentous and media-worthy. No one knows for sure, except, of course, Elliott.

In fact, what Elliott did by separating her students according to eye color wasn't novel at all. Such efforts preceded Wilda Wood's experiment in a variety of iterations. Similar experiments had taken place across the United States during the mid-1960s and decades earlier. Many were antecedents to what Elliott was to do in Riceville, although Elliott certainly dialed up the voltage when it came to punishing and ridiculing children whose eye color she deemed inferior for the day.

When George Hanna, now a dentist in Cedar Rapids, Iowa, was in the sixth grade at Cedar Rapids' Erskine Elementary School in 1968, his teacher also separated his class according to eye color, with similar results. "One of my good friends (blue-eyed) really took his superiority to the extreme, so much so that another friend of ours ended up punching him in the nose at recess," Hanna recalled. He didn't recall the month when the Cedar Rapids experiment happened or whether it took place before or after Elliott tried her version in Riceville.[15]

When Keith Salvas, today an administrative staff aide for the Los Angeles Unified School District, was a student in 1966 at North Branch Parkway Elementary School in Springfield, Massachusetts, he recalled that his teacher separated his first-grade class into two groups and conducted the same experiment that Elliott was to carry out two years later. The blue-eyed children were seated on the "good" side of the room, next to the windows, and the brown-eyed students were moved to the "bad" side, next to the wall, Salvas remembered.

As in Riceville, the experiment made such a lasting impression on Salvas that, more than fifty years later, he maintains he's able to recall to an exacting degree what happened. Salvas remembers it this way:

One morning in class there was a knock on the door. When [the teacher] opened it, a few adult women entered. They split up and went desk to desk, starting from the front row, and began dragging kids while in their desks to one side of the room or the other. I was in the middle of the class, so it took a few moments before one of them reached me. She grabbed the sides of my desk-chair ready to drag me to one side of the room or the other. She looked into my eyes and for a moment froze. Then she said with a surprised voice, "Keith, you have green eyes!" She shook her head and in an almost flippant tone said, "Well, green is close to blue." And with that, she dragged me off to one side of the room.

That's when it became clear to me what was happening. The brown-eyed students were being grouped along the inside wall next to the building's central hallway and the blue-eyed children were being grouped along the outside wall, which was mostly windows with a great view of the outside playground.

At the end of the week, the school principal, Rebecca Johnson, who was African American, delivered a stirring speech in an all-school assembly about prejudice and skin color. As Salvas remembers, Johnson asked, "Would you judge someone because their skin is darker than yours? Would you judge me because my skin is darker than yours?" Johnson then extended her left arm in the air so the students would focus on her Black skin. Salvas did not know whether his class had been the only class that had undergone the experiment or whether the assembly had been the culmination of a school-wide lesson.[16]

In 2015, Salvas wrote Elliott about his eye-color experience, and asked whether she was aware of any precedents to her experiment. Elliott answered by saying, "Many people have contacted me to say that they had been doing the exercise before I did. I haven't been able to see any documentation of their efforts, but I hope that they got the same results that I did. I did know that Adolf Hitler had been using the eye-color exercise from 1933 to 1945 with undeniable effect, and I suppose that's where all of us who have been using it got the idea."[17]

The origins of such awareness experiments actually began even earlier. The blue-eyes, brown-eyes experiment, essentially an exercise in multicultural education, had its beginnings in the United States following World War I, with programs designed to highlight the value of immigrants.

One prominent proponent of such diversity was Rachel Davis DuBois, a teacher in Woodbury, New Jersey, who developed the so-called Woodbury Plan, a "good citizenship" curriculum, in the mid-1920s. DuBois went on to create a popular national radio series, *Americans All, Immigrants All* in 1938, broadcast on CBS.[18] Another proponent was the National Conference on

Christians and Jews (NCCJ), an ecumenical service group founded in 1927, which initiated Brotherhood Week, a kind of ethnicity-awareness program with classroom curricular lessons that took place annually the third week in February (the week ABC filmed "Eye of the Storm" in Riceville). As a pilot project, the NCCJ teamed up with administrators in the Springfield, Massachusetts, school district to launch what became known as the Springfield Plan, which turned into the nation's most comprehensive program to introduce public school students to multicultural education. When Keith Salvas's class was divided by eye color in 1966, he and his fellow students were subjects of an experiment that had been set into place years earlier when the Springfield Plan was first implemented.

In 1930, Springfield, a blue-collar city ninety miles west of Boston, had a population of fewer than 40 percent native-born whites while European-born immigrants made up 60 percent of the city's 150,000 residents. Led by innovative school superintendent John Granrud, with funding from the NCCJ and other philanthropic groups, Springfield turned into an early laboratory designed to train public school students to embrace cultural and ethnic differences. Programs highlighting interracial students, as well as students of different religions and heritages, were designed to "immunize" Springfield children against racial, ethnic, and religious prejudice.

Implementation of the Springfield Plan, under the aegis of the NCCJ, spread to twenty-two states and more than four thousand schools.[19] A plethora of articles and books detailed the program, spreading it further. By 1946, the architect of the Springfield Plan, John Granrud, left Springfield for Southern California, where his multicultural curriculum was to evolve into a youth leadership camp program called "Anytown, USA," at which provocative techniques were employed to increase fellowship between races and religions. Among the approaches still used at the teen retreats is separating students by eye color, and creating superior and inferior groups to simulate the impact of racism.[20]

Back in Riceville in 1971, as the next school year was to begin, Elliott prepared to roll out the experiment once again on a new class of third graders. Any national goodwill that Elliott had established never found its way to Riceville. Back home, locals continued to avoid Elliott at all turns. Gossip continued to circulate about Elliott, but this time it was more specific, about the origins of the experiment.

Dolores Steffen, the Riceville elementary school teacher who started teaching the same year as Elliott, remembered that she had read about Wilda

Wood and her Colorado experiment in an education magazine. Steffen said she may even have clipped the article from the magazine and given it to Elliott. Steffen said she and most of the other teachers at school assumed that's where Elliott got the idea.[21]

Pat Johnson, a former student in Elliott's class who today works in a commercial printing plant in Osage, said, "Mrs. Elliott wasn't the first to come up with the idea. I heard that she was talking to another teacher, who came up with the idea of brown eyes, blue eyes, but the other teacher wasn't going to do anything about it. And Mrs. Elliott ran with it."[22]

Others in town had their own theories. A Riceville farmer said that one of his own teachers at a one-room schoolhouse on the outskirts of town in the late 1940s had tried out a similar experiment. On alternating days, the teacher rewarded one eye-color group with chocolate milk and the other group with plain milk as a way to make children reflect about how random social distinctions were. "Everyone knows she stole that thing of hers," the farmer said.[23]

Was such discussion a case of jealousy, perhaps compounded by sexism, gossipy issues surrounding Elliott's family lineage, and Elliott's own chafing personality, along with the Riceville rumor mill gone viral—or was there substance to what the locals were saying? Could Elliott have stolen the experiment that forever would be attached to her?

FIFTEEN

Blackboard Jungle

JANE ELLIOTT CERTAINLY WASN'T THE FIRST INNOVATIVE teacher to rub Riceville locals the wrong way. The people of Riceville had their own ideas of what local teachers ought to teach, how they ought to behave, and just how far education ought to go in molding their children's minds.

In 1956, Paul J. Richer, the son of a Mason City automotive dealer who sold Hudsons, Studebakers, and Nashes, was a garrulous twenty-one-year-old graduate of what was then called the State University of Iowa. Richer (pronounced RICH-er) had just won a national debate competition and had been elected to Phi Beta Kappa. He never planned on becoming a teacher, but one day saw a newspaper advertisement for a teaching position in Riceville and applied. Richer was promptly hired to teach English and social studies at Riceville Junior High at a salary of $3,350 a year.

Like Elliott, Richer was a bubbling cauldron of ideas. He was smart and well read. As a young, new teacher in Riceville, he quickly cultivated a cadre of devoted students. Many were so taken with Richer that they "followed him around like the Pied Piper," recalled a mother of one student. Richer encouraged students to call him by his first name, Paul, an informality no Riceville teacher had ever accorded pupils. Richer spoke Spanish, and during lunch gave impromptu Spanish lessons to anyone, whether they were his students or not. Since he drove fifty miles between his parents' home in Mason City and Riceville to teach every weekday, when icy winter weather made the commute treacherous, Riceville parents invited Richer to stay overnight in their homes.

As a teacher, Richer had a particular fondness for poetry. One day, a farmer's son volunteered how much he hated verse. "Why do I have to waste my time?" the student pleaded with Richer. "How's it gonna help *me*?"

This was just the challenge Richer was waiting for. "For a moment," Richer responded, "close your eyes and imagine you're seated at the plow."

Not wanting to be left out, everyone in the class joined in. Richer waited a full minute.

"Now, what do you see?" he asked.

For the next two weeks, Richer read aloud rhapsodic poems written by the entire class about rows of lush sheaved ears of corn, domed silos, and sun-bleached barns.[1]

Paul Richer was a pre-incarnation of Elliott, a caller in the continuum of time and place—in this case, 1956 and rural America. The two teachers' paths never crossed and they never met, but their stories share uncanny similarities. Both Richer and Elliott were wildly creative in and out of the classroom. Both tilted at windmills only they could see rising from fertile fields of plenty. Both made the Riceville locals uneasy, and because of that, both paid a hefty price.

Like Elliott, Richer deviated from the prescribed course of instruction, as sure a way as any to court trouble within a school district. Richer was less interested in drilling students than letting their minds wander, the further the better. He augmented the required material with whatever he felt was appropriate and relevant. To the dismay of some parents, Richer introduced students to *Hamlet*, John Steinbeck's *The Grapes of Wrath* and *Of Mice and Men*, Lillian Hellman's *The Little Foxes*, and J. D. Salinger's *The Catcher in the Rye*. He directed a student production of *The Blackboard Jungle*, in which one of the characters stabs another with the staff of the American flag. Few of the locals had ever encountered anyone the likes of Paul Richer before.

Richer found his stage in the classroom, the students his audience. Teaching was a form of improvisational art, and Richer required his kids to engage fully. He encouraged them to share their opinions. If they had none, they needed to get some. Once students found their voices, Richer pushed them to defend whatever it was they said they believed in. He added topical issues to the junior high curriculum, which included subjects like crime, mental health, the nature of war, and Communism.

None of this would likely bode well for any teacher in any farming community in the northern plains of America in the mid-1950s. Like Elliott, Richer must have known what awaited him, yet he plunged in anyway.

In class, Richer talked about urban slums, juvenile delinquency, racial bigotry, and religious intolerance. He asked students to think about how each malignancy had been able to flourish in the richest country in the world.

Richer asked three questions: "What is wrong? Why? What can we do about it?" That Richer focused on negatives, rather than positives, baffled many in Riceville.

At first, it was the unit on Communism, introducing students to Engels, Marx, Lenin, and Stalin, that got Richer in trouble. The topic was not what many Riceville parents thought their thirteen- and fourteen-year-old children needed to be learning. But during the era of McCarthyism, spawned by the pugnacious US senator from the bordering state of Wisconsin, and the emergence of the Cold War, Richer figured differently. He thought a unit on Communism was essential material for every student.

That was only the beginning of the hole Richer was surely digging for himself. Richer questioned the district's long-standing policy of allowing students mandatory class-release time for religious training. For as long as anyone could remember, Riceville students were given two hours off every week to go to church for Bible study. Richer already had an impossible time squeezing in everything he wanted his students to learn within the allotted class time. Allowing them to leave school for two hours for Bible lessons had no place in a public school curriculum, Richer informed the students. This did not sit well with a number of people, including the local clergymen. It probably didn't help matters that Richer was Jewish.

The minister at the 150-member Riceville Congregational Church responded by accusing Richer of not believing in Christ and of being a Communist. Richer replied by having his students read the textbook *How the Great Religions Began*, copies of which Richer bought and paid for himself.[2] He had them study Islam, Buddhism, Shinto, and Judaism.

"When it came to delving into religion, I had the kids pick one, and besides being able to report to the class about that religion, they had to become a person who believed in that religion and report about the countries where that religion was practiced, prepare the food of that country and bring it to class, and get the clothing of the country and wear it to class," Richer recalled. "The kids were deeply involved. It was just terrific."[3] Such an interactive assignment sounded like something Elliott would introduce a decade later.

One of Richer's students happened to be the daughter of the Congregationalist minister Reverend William Bohi, Richer's chief accuser. Bohi was furious at Richer's impertinence, and a showdown commenced between the men. "Two different times he invaded my class, storming in, and screaming that I was the Antichrist, that I was the devil," Richer remembered.

The Reverend Bohi thoroughly defended his intervention in Richer's class-room. "This Richer was interested in a lot of fool things," Bohi told the *Des Moines Register*. Richer, he said, "talked to them about mental health. He had them write essays on 'my outlook on life.' Imagine asking seventh and eighth graders that. Then he went into Communism. I didn't want my daughter bothered with things like that." The Reverend Bohi also objected to Richer's reading list, in particular *The Catcher in the Rye*, which Bohi called "a scummy book," as well as anything by Steinbeck.[4] Another Riceville parent, Mrs. Gordon Eide, joined the fray, complaining that Richer "tried to teach on a college level. He dealt with subjects too deep for his students."[5]

Ultimately, it was the dramatic play that Richer sought to stage in Riceville that proved to be his undoing. Richer wrote a one-act adaptation of *The Blackboard Jungle*, at the time a popular Hollywood movie, starring Glenn Ford, Ann Francis, and a budding actor by the name of Sidney Poitier.[6] The film's protagonist was first-year English teacher Richard Dadier (Ford), who tries out several innovative methods to engage students. Early in the film, Dadier is given two tips by a veteran teacher, played by Louis Calhern: "Don't be a hero," and "Never turn your back on the class."[7] Substitute farmers' teenage sons and daughters for urban thugs and the story line of a dedicated teacher bucking the system could have been Richer's own.

The climax of *The Blackboard Jungle* is a confrontation between two sets of students, one of whom uses the flagpole as a weapon to stop a fight. In an instance where reality mimics art, this is how Richer remembers what happened on the evening of the play's debut:

"The place was mobbed. It was in a gymnasium, with a little stage on one end. Everyone came. We were ready to go on. And suddenly the superintendent comes in, looking chagrined. With him was the head of the American Legion. The superintendent said the American Legion head wanted to speak with me.

"He said, 'You can't do the play like it's done. You're desecrating the American flag.'" The two men told Richer he had to remove the flag from the play's final scene. They suggested the students substitute a wooden pole used to open windows instead of a flagstaff.

"This play belongs to the students," Richer told the men. "If these kids think it's appropriate to remove that scene from the play, then that's what'll happen. It's their play, not mine."

Richer stepped outside while the superintendent conferred with the students, who were getting ready for the curtain to rise. The audience was growing restless, expecting the show to go on. The program was already fifteen minutes late. Members of the audience had seen the superintendent slip behind the stage and had heard bits and pieces of a heated exchange. It turned out that the scene unfolding just beyond the reach of the audience's eyes was the stuff of real drama.

The student actors told the superintendent that any administrative meddling in the play would be unacceptable. "The kids said, 'That's the biggest scene in the play, you can't do that! You can't remove the flag! That's what the play's all about—freedom!'" Richer recalled.

The superintendent was adamant. No flagpole would be used as a weapon.

Given such an ultimatum, the students took to the stage and informed the audience that the show would not go on. "People were hollering and shouting, and finally everyone just went home. I told the kids how proud I was of them," Richer remembered.

The shutting down of the play proved to be curtains for Richer. After twenty-seven weeks, Richer said he wouldn't teach in Riceville the following year. Riceville was a town full of "ignorance, bigotry, and intellectual narrowness," he told the *Des Moines Register*.[8]

The school board did not appreciate Richer's characterization and reacted by preempting Richer's public resignation and firing him on the spot during an emergency closed session. Richer demanded an open hearing, which was denied. The school board president, Dr. Thomas Walker Jr., responded by saying, "There was very little point in having an open hearing merely to satisfy him [Richer] and to drive still more wedges in this community conflict." Walker labeled Richer "a brilliant chap, very intelligent. But he is a crusader, a reformer." In the board's letter terminating Richer, Walker wrote, "Your obvious disrespect of administrative authority manifested by your unwillingness to cooperate . . . and your defiant attitude toward the school board makes it mandatory to terminate your services."[9] Walker cited Richer's lack of attendance at faculty meetings, his nonmembership in the Iowa State Education Association, and an attitude that resulted in Richer's lack of involvement in community activities.[10] All was subterfuge. The real reason was the school board couldn't tolerate Richer's independence.

Richer responded by labeling Riceville "Main Street," a reference to Sinclair Lewis's scathing 1920 novel, portraying a small Minnesota community Lewis called Gopher Prairie. Gopher Prairie was a thinly veiled portrait of Lewis's own hometown of Sauk Centre, 250 miles northwest of Riceville.[11]

Richer accused the people of Riceville of having "an intense respect for yesterday, a complete disdain for today, and a rigid denial for tomorrow." He cited the locals' lack of appreciation for anything new or anyone different. He characterized the Riceville schools as a "place of sleeping souls" in a story he wrote for the national magazine, *Pageant*.[12]

The day after the school board fired Richer, several students staged a walk-out. They posted signs and banners around Riceville. One read: "Christ was crucified, why do you crucify Mr. Richer?"[13] But it was a battle already lost. Richer urged the students to return to their classes. "Walking out won't do you or me any good," he told student protesters at a local café, who put away their signs, perhaps having learned a lesson about bucking the local power structure.

After the *Des Moines Register*'s star reporter at the time, George Mills, wrote a long Sunday front-page account on Riceville and Richer, the story went national. *Time* rewrote Mills's story, labeling Richer "the most contro-versial figure in town," adding, "Last week, with Richer out of the way, it was hard to tell whether he or the town has paid the heavier price."[14]

In *Pageant*'s lengthy ten-page story, the magazine's editors asked, "Was it an incident peculiar to Riceville, Iowa, or could and would the same thing happen in Anywhere, U.S.A.? Are P.T.A. groups, school superintendents and principals, and parents really searching for the inspired teacher, or are they satisfied with the mediocre one who never deviates from the regulation text-books? How much leeway should the teacher be allowed? Was the teacher in question really inspired? What were the enormities he had committed in the eyes of the community that brought about his firing?"[15] Switching some of the specifics and the time frame, the same questions would be asked about Jane Elliott.

Both Richer and Elliott were education reformers and renegades. Both craved the spotlight and were keenly adept at using the media to their advan-tage. Richer occasionally talked about himself in the third person, a practice Elliott would also employ. Other similarities between the two were their unorthodox teaching methods that roiled locals. "I plead guilty to the accu-sation that Richer's classes were the noisiest in the building," Richer told *Pageant*, sounding prophetically like Elliott. "Enthusiasm ran at a fever level. We kept busy, not workbook busy, but practical project busy."[16]

As was to happen with Elliott, hundreds of Iowans weighed in on what became known as the "Riceville Episode." Richer became a flashpoint around the state. As with Elliott, there seemed to be no middle ground when it came to Richer. Stacyville resident Ralph Beland wrote the *Des Moines Register*, saying that by terminating Richer, the Riceville school board had "treated Mr. Richer ever too gently."[17] Floyd resident Mrs. T. V. Jacobson wrote, "If we could find one teacher like him for each county and pay $7,500 or better, it would be well worth it for our future in education."[18]

Like Elliott, Richer was capable, competent, and confident. "I was full of myself, and I don't think it was bad. I didn't place any limitations on myself," he would recall. "The kids had a sense that a lot of good stuff was happening inside the classroom."

Until his firing, school officials warned Richer that he was courting trouble. "The principal and superintendent would tell me to be careful, don't overdo it. 'Are you following the curriculum?' they'd ask. I'd respond by doing absolutely everything that was in the curriculum, and then twenty other things besides what was required." It turned into a balancing act Richer couldn't maintain. Nor did he want to.

With Richer out and Riceville reset to normal—at least until Elliott would appear—the way one observer assessed the local tempest was to compare Richer to the great river seventy-eight miles east: "Like the Mississippi, he has great potential when he is kept within his banks," *Mason City Globe-Gazette* farm editor Bill Webb wrote. "Perhaps the error that Riceville made was not to take the proper measures to see that Richer stayed on course, for once the water is over the banks then there is no way to control it."[19]

By the time Richer had arrived, Elliott had already gotten her start in teaching outside of Riceville, and it would be eight years before she would start teaching third graders in her hometown. By then, Richer had left Riceville and had set out on his own outside Iowa.[20] But in terms of place and personalities, the sagas of Elliott and Richer would be nearly identical.

To fill Richer's open teaching position in Riceville, the school board hired Sydna Shoemaker, the wife of a Lime Springs Chevrolet dealer, who was active in the local Order of the Eastern Star, the women's component of Freemasonry. When Elliott arrived in Riceville to teach third grade in 1964, fire and brimstone Reverend Bohi still lived in northeastern Iowa, but had been called to two other rural churches, in nearby Linden and Elma. Dr. Thomas Walker Jr., the school board president who oversaw Richer's firing, still lived in Riceville, although he no longer sat on the board. As befits any rural town where nearly everyone is connected in ways small and large, Dr. Walker was the physician who had delivered Jane as an infant at the Jennison family farm.

There were differences between Richer and Elliott, the most obvious being their genders. Richer was viewed as assured and cocky; in Elliott, such characteristics were seen as arrogant and bitchy. Surely that double standard was partially in play in the reaction Richer got in Riceville compared to what was to befall Elliott. Another difference between the two teachers was that Richer wasn't married. He had no children. When locals in Riceville arose in fury against Richer, there was no community backlash directed at his family members, just at Richer. This was not to be the case for Elliott.

Students gathering around Jane Elliott, 1970. Photo by Charlotte Button.

Brian Saltou. Photo by Charlotte Button.

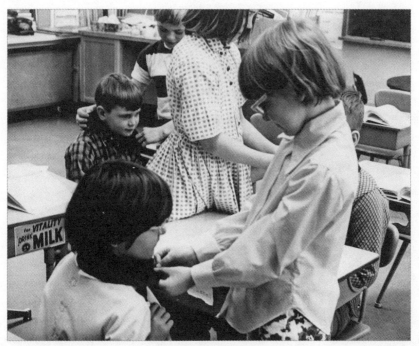
Students affixing collars on each other. Photo by Charlotte Button.

Newsman Bill Beutel interviewing Jane Elliott. Photo by Charlotte Button.

Students sitting around Jane Elliott, 1970. Photo by Charlotte Button.

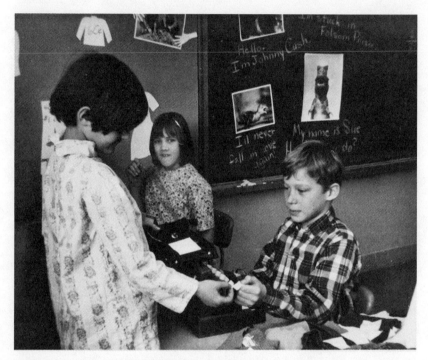

Room No. 10 store. Photo by Charlotte Button.

Sandi Dohlman. Photo by Charlotte Button.

Jane Elliott calling on students. Photo by Charlotte Button.

Rex Kozak. Photo by Charlotte Button.

Donna Reddel. Photo by Charlotte Button.

John Benttine. Photo by Charlotte Button.

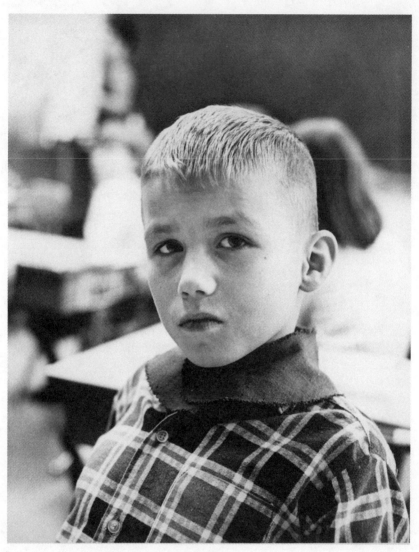

Roy Wilson with collar. Photo by Charlotte Button.

Filming of "Eye of the Storm." Photo by Charlotte Button.

Jane Elliott on *The Tonight Show*. Photo by Charlotte Button.

Jane Elliott on *The Tonight Show* with Johnny Carson. Photo by Charlotte Button.

With and without
collars. Photos by
Charlotte Button.

Student self-portrait without collar and with collar. Jane Elliott Papers, Iowa Women's Archives at the University of Iowa Libraries.

Student self-portrait with collar and without collar. Jane Elliott Papers, Iowa Women's Archives at the University of Iowa Libraries.

Student self-portrait with collar and without collar. Jane Elliott Papers, Iowa Women's Archives at the University of Iowa Libraries.

Jane Elliott, 2005. Photo © Layne Kennedy.

Riceville Elementary School. Photo © Layne Kennedy.

Downtown Riceville. Photo © Layne Kennedy.

SIXTEEN

Spooner

TWELVE YEARS. THAT'S THE SPAN of time between when Paul Richer and Jane Elliott each ran afoul of the Riceville locals. For Richer, the town outcry was over quickly. For Elliott, it would trigger a seismic wave that would last a lifetime. Richer's and Elliott's moments of strife happened at distinctly different stages of their careers. Richer, twenty-one, had just graduated from college; Elliott, thirty-five, had been out of Iowa State Teachers College for fourteen years. Richer had been a brand-new teacher from out of town; Elliott was a near-veteran teacher who was a Riceville native. Richer's career lay before him; Elliott's had already taken off.

There was little the locals could do to bring her down.

But that didn't mean they wouldn't try.

Elliott had an abundance of ambition, a dubious trait in Riceville, where about all that was required was to stay put, moderately prosper, go to church as regularly as anyone pleased, and beget a thriving family. Such a prescription was especially true for women, and particularly true for Elliott, the daughter of two ne'er-do-wells, opinioned Lloyd Jennison and his increasingly eccentric wife, Gie.

From her lonely perch in Riceville, Elliott was fashioning a national profile based on a contentious experiment that she had seemingly stamped as her own. Without the experiment, Elliott knew she'd be just another country schoolteacher among endless rows of corn somewhere over the rainbow.

Whether or not she had originated the experiment wasn't as important as the public perception of its ownership, and by now, the experiment was de facto Elliott's. The blue-eyes, brown-eyes experiment and Elliott were one and the same. It had been the engine that had taken her from *The Tonight Show* to CBC to ABC to the White House conference. Elliott might not have seen the elephant, but she had seen New York, Toronto, Washington, DC, and a sizeable swath of the Midwest because of the experiment. In less than three years, she had done the near-impossible. Elliott had succeeded in being recognized nationally on issues of children, racism, and prejudice, all from an outpost in a farming town with not a single Black soul for miles and miles. Elliott found herself fielding media inquiries as an expert, if not daily, then weekly, corresponding with a widening circle of admirers and allies from across the nation, participating in as many educational workshops and symposia as she could.

In 1971, she was part of a $76,000 grant from the US Department of Health, Education and Welfare with ninety other educators from twelve Iowa school districts. During a workshop in Iowa City, as had become her practice, she didn't identify herself as the seminar leader. At the session, Elliott sat hunched with the other teachers, and when no one got up to lead the session, she abruptly stood and demanded that all the blue-eyed attendees sit on the floor in the back of the classroom while the brown-eyed teachers remain in their chairs. No one quite knew what to make of this unnamed teacher issuing orders. Elliott never identified herself as the workshop leader. When she didn't back down, accusations started flying. Several teachers responded by making paper airplanes and tossing them at Elliott. When she persisted, they tried locking her out of the classroom.[1]

If some of Elliott's motives all along had been to get noticed, it was working. Word spread. Stories about her appeared in the national media. Slowly and with purpose, Elliott started broadening her niche, branching out from kids to adults. Soon, she was appearing as a headline speaker at seminars held for employees at banks, utility companies, school districts, and government entities interested in importing the unconventional prejudice-abatement experiment, eventually to be placed under the umbrellas of multiculturalism; antibias train-ing; and diversity, equity, and inclusion. Elliott had created a traveling show on all issues pertaining to race, which played to groups who'd listen and pay her. Considering America in the 1970s, this was a horse worthy of any wagon.

"I wanna see where all this is gonna go," Darald used to say, chuckling, shaking his head in disbelief at how far his wife had already traveled.[2]

As her success burgeoned, the reaction in Riceville grew testier. Elliott was still employed full-time as a third-grade teacher, and even though most locals hated that she continued to import the experiment to Riceville Elementary, there wasn't much they could do other than pulling their kids from her classes. Many found the experiment unacceptable and morally wrong.

By 1970, Dinsmore Brandmill had retired as principal, and Leonard Crawford, a forty-seven-year-old principal from an elementary school in small Ringgold County in the south-central part of the state, had taken over at Riceville Elementary. Neither Crawford nor new Superintendent Dean Weaver had many options when it came to neutralizing Elliott. She ostensibly couldn't be fired or transferred. No administrator relished telling her anything. She did pretty much whatever she wanted at Riceville Elementary.

Not to be overlooked was the memory of Paul Richer and what he had taught Riceville. The school board wasn't about to repeat that episode by getting in the way of yet another creative, hard-to-manage teacher. Demanding that Elliott disband an experiment that had garnered national acclaim posed the likelihood of shining a spotlight again on Riceville, and that was something no one was foolhardy enough to want to risk. Stripping Elliott of her authority in the classroom might placate many in Riceville, but it would surely be an issue she would turn to her advantage. Directing Elliott to pack up the experiment could turn into the cause of another hullabaloo. By now, she had amassed a roster of national endorsers, and she wouldn't be hesitant to leverage their support on her behalf. At least, that's what locals opposed to her feared. Elliott had placed the administration, teachers, parents, and residents over a barrel of their own making.

Riceville teachers and parents continued to register complaints about Elliott with Crawford, Weaver, and the school board. But such protests went only so far. The new principal didn't care to intercede. Crawford was loath to discuss Elliott or her experiment. He mostly chose to ignore her.[3]

That Elliott believed in herself and what she was doing despite the deluge of local hostility was testament to her self-preservation. She was an evangelist for the good she told supporters she was convinced she was creating one student at a time. She knew that the experiment was destined for greater glory than rural third graders. Jane and Darald both understood what Riceville had to offer, and they both knew that with Jane's smarts and tenacity, she could go places far beyond Mitchell County's Highway 9.

As she accepted more and more speaking engagements, occasionally taking a day or two off from teaching, Elliott's presence usually preceded her. She found herself both a draw and a celebrity. Along with her came the darting eyes that led to her practiced drop-dead stare; her crooked, wagging index finger; her inviolate certitude; her quick, assured repartee. She was the Iowa schoolteacher with the stamina to go eyeball-to-eyeball with anyone, Black or white, male or female, young or old.

The farther she got from Riceville, the greater the spring in her step became. For once, Elliott was able to thrive without apology. She had run laps past the locals. Away from Riceville, she became anyone she wanted: performer, prognosticator, philosopher, preacher, all wrapped into one inextinguishable presence.

With each invitation, Elliott began bringing home honoraria that, put together, were substantial; some speaking fees amounted to thousands of dollars, excluding travel and per diem expenses. This was another cause for locals to cluck.

Her detractors stored her supposed moonlighting jackpots away as ammunition to be used down the road. "I remember her telling me, 'You know, June, I make more now in a weekend than I make in a whole year teaching,'" recalled June Judge, a retired teacher in nearby Plymouth and the daughter of former Riceville Elementary principal Dinsmore Brandmill. "I laughed because she was telling the truth, but that would probably make some people uncomfortable."[4]

It did. "She didn't go and speak out of the goodness of her heart," recalled Jerry Markham, a former Riceville High science teacher ("I was the entire science department"), who also was the track, basketball, and volleyball coach. For a while, Markham and Elliott had classrooms next to each other and they knew each other well. "There were financial rewards for her. Here was someone who was making big dollars. She was making more money with three or four or five of these diversity deals than she was making as a teacher."[5]

For the locals, just as rampant as the gossip about the bankrolls of cash Elliott was supposedly hauling in was static about what she was saying on the speaking circuit. Word back home was that it wasn't beyond her to embarrass Riceville, calling rural Iowa a place where racism was not only tolerated but welcomed. No one actually knew if she ran down Riceville in her out-of-town lectures, but almost everyone was sure she did. To the locals, once again, Elliott was violating a cardinal rule: speak ill of cities all you want, but never countenance malice toward home—God's little acre.

"She looked down on us," recalled former mayor Walt Gabelmann, who ran the local livestock auction hall, as well as writing his weekly column in the *Recorder*. "She told me she was going to make it [the experiment] a national thing. I told her she could have all the publicity you want, but that she was dealing with human lives. I told her I couldn't imagine anything good coming out of this thing. My thinking was that she was playing with matches, and once the fire got started, she didn't want to put it out."[6]

Whether appearing on national TV or being interviewed by a journalist who had traveled from the big city (whenever an unfamiliar car was parked outside the Elliott home), Elliott wasn't shy. She was blustery or direct, depending on your point of view. When locals ran into her at the bank, pharmacy, or post office, and couldn't pull an about-face in time, *and* were foolhardy enough to bring up just about anything, Elliott would often take them apart piece by piece in full view of everyone.[7]

Where were her manners?

To a tight-knit community where outliers had no place, Elliott was an annoying, irritating splinter stuck in everyone's fingertip.

The locals had had enough. It was time to turn the tables, to teach *Elliott* a lesson.

The first target was the Jennison Hotel, the downtown dining room and inn that Darald and Jane owned and her parents now operated, where Smitty Messersmith had first heard about the experiment.

Seemingly overnight, the Jennison Hotel became the site of a community-wide boycott. No one formally organized anything—that's not the way small towns operate—but business at the hotel dining room nosedived. On the day before the ABC documentary, Lloyd and Gie Jennison had served forty-five dinners. The following Sunday, two people showed up. Holding their heads high, locals walked past the Jennison Hotel's front door and headed down the block for Elwood Pettitt's café.[8]

There was always the possibility that the shift in patronage could have been due to the Jennisons' food or service. Lloyd and Gie weren't the best cooks and servers; everyone in town knew that. The sudden drop-off might also have been a response to the diners who continued to eat at Jennison's, who by their presence supported Elliott. To no one's surprise, Elliott said there was only one reason for the disappearance of business: Lloyd and Gie "had raised the town's 'nigger lover.'"[9]

If any of the locals thought shutting down her parents' restaurant would motivate Elliott to moderate her behavior, they were mistaken. If anything, it made her more resolute. A civil war had formally commenced in Riceville with Elliott on one side and almost everyone else on the other.

Elliott continued separating her third graders in Classroom No. 10 by eye color, no matter how many dagger eyes she got. No way was she going to back down now. To Elliott, that her parents would have to close the Jennison Hotel dining room was collateral damage. "I was honestly naive enough to think (believe, hope?) that once the people in the community realized how great the learning had been and how important the concepts were that they'd be proud and impressed with what was happening in this little rural community rather than being angry and threatened," she would write. "Wrong again!"[10]

Elliott had to know that it was just a matter of time before the locals would go further. The week after Elliott returned from the White House conference, fourteen-year-old Sarah confided in her mother that her best friend had said that Elliott must have planned on having sex with men on the trip because the friend had seen a douche bag in Elliott's suitcase. And since Elliott would be in Washington, DC, she logically would be having sex with Black men, Sarah recalled her friend telling her.

One particularly nasty rumor suggested that Darald wasn't the biological father of two of the Elliotts' four children. The whispers multiplied and morphed. Sarah heard them and so did Brian, as did scores of others in town: Elliott must have been sleeping with Black men because Sarah and Brian had darker complexions than the other kids in Riceville.

Gossip seldom ends with its intended targets. Rumors pick up speed, change direction, and repurpose themselves, often at the expense of those most vulnerable. Being the children of any schoolteacher in town comes with baggage. Because Brian, Sarah, Mary, and Mark were Jane and Darald's children, they had to contend with additional slings. Elliott wasn't just the strict, no-nonsense teacher who took no guff from kids, she also had made a name for herself by accusing just about every person in Riceville of being a racist. At least, that was what people around town said. That, together with the town's certainty that Elliott was bringing home stratospheric sums of money with her big-city speaking engagements, made life daunting for the Elliott children.

When Sarah, Jane's older daughter, was in junior high school, rumors started circulating about her, too. When Jane asked at a parent-teacher conference how she might stop the mean-girl gossip, the teacher's response was, according to Elliott: "You should have thought about this before you did that eye thing."[11]

While in Washington, Elliott had bought for Sarah a denim purse. Sarah loved the purse, took it to school the next day, and placed it on a shelf in the girls' bathroom while she went into one of the stalls. When Sarah came out, she said she found the purse's straps had been cut off and someone had taken the lipstick from inside to scrawl *Nigger Lover* on the bathroom mirror.[12]

Sarah didn't place blame on her classmates for their alleged malicious behavior, but instead on her mother. "I hated my mother for a long time. When your mother took away all your friends, and when she took away all of

Brian's friends, it's hard to get over." Sarah said she can't remember how often she was told, "You're a nigger lover! You're a nigger lover!" The only retort she could come up with was, "No, I'm not! No, I'm not!"[13]

It was Brian who took the brunt of the bullying. Until he left Iowa after high school, Brian got into so many fights that he lost count. He was picked on mercilessly, although many of the altercations he ended up in were at least partially his own doing.[14] He was not a good student; he was dyslexic, and often posed a disciplinary problem in the classroom for his teachers. As he got into his teenage years, he developed an affection for alcohol, marijuana, and other drugs.

Brian and another student gave lip to the hulking high school shop teacher, who grabbed Brian by the collar and slammed him and the other boy against the wall.[15] It was one of scores of incidents that were to leave Brian scarred for the rest of his life.

"I woke up one morning and I was one of those 'nigger-lovin' Elliotts,'" he recalled, either accurately naming why he became the target of predators or choosing what was most convenient. Perhaps it was both.

"*Bamm*! Shit happened to me that I don't even wanna fuckin' remember. I got no fuckin' childhood to speak of. I learned to run real quick. I can smell tension. Eventually, you get addicted to that adrenaline. Well, it ain't a rush when you're fourteen fuckin' years old! It's not something you wanna get used to. Running from fuckin' class to class. And then running from school to home. Running as fast as you can. You learn how to get around places without being seen. It was like being on a goddamn hot LZ twenty-four seven.[16]

"Yeah, I got a lot of goddamn pent-up anger. People say you're supposed to let it go. Well, they didn't live through what I lived through."

Brian eventually would leave Iowa to work on a series of oil-drilling rigs, becoming an operating engineer for heavy construction machinery, and after that, a farrier in Washington State. The trauma he sustained as a youngster was indelible. "I've tried to put this thing to sleep for fuckin' fifty years, but you can't. I had high school guys beat on me when I was in junior high. Principals throw you around. Tear your fuckin' shirt right off of you and then throw you in a room for the rest of the day 'cause you're cutting up in class. None of that shit happened to the other guys around me."

The impact stayed with Brian. "I don't trust people. I don't trust people at all. I stay away from people who don't want to be around me. That was most anybody. Just get high. Stay away from everything, everybody you can. Just git gone. Hell, why put yourself through that torture daily? It took a long time to figure that out."[17]

The way Jane saw it, Brian became the local punching bag for one reason: because she was his mother. On three separate occasions, she said, teenage boys beat up Brian while chanting "nigger lover, nigger lover, nigger lover!" When he lined up to get on the school bus in the morning, she said, the driver slammed the door in Brian's face, laughing as he sped away.

"I came home from school one day to find Brian, bruised and bloody, beaten and bashed," she recalled. "'What in God's name happened to you?' I asked. Seems he'd been chased home from school for a couple of weeks by several high school guys in their car. On this day he hadn't hurried fast enough and a carload of five high school kids caught up with him. Three brave boys jumped out and beat him up while the other two stayed in the car, one to drive and the other to serve as a watchman to avoid getting caught."[18]

From Brian's point of view, the escalating violence amounted to nonstop terror. "'There's that nigger-lovin' Elliott!' Then you'd hear the motor rev and brakes squeal, and man, it was on! I just hit the brush. Looking back, these guys were punks, like coyotes running in packs. In the locker room one night, I got the living shit beaten out of me. Two, three on one. Nowhere to go. 'Fuckin' nigger lover!' Take cover!

"Who the fuck wanted to go to school? It was like fuckin' throwing Judas to the lions. Fuckin' gladiator class was all it was. When you're surrounded, there ain't no place to go. Every break between class, I was fistfighting."

When Darald called the parents of Brian's chief adversary, the father told him, "Your son got what he deserved." Overhearing this, Jane yanked the phone out of Darald's hand and demanded to speak to the boy's mother, who, Jane recalled, said, "You should have thought of this before you did that eye thing." It had become a familiar refrain.[19]

The Elliott kids were victims not just because they were Jane's kids, but also because they were seen as carrying a hefty dose of "attitude," too. Undoubtedly, the shade they threw stemmed from a bunker mentality that Jane and Darald had instilled in their four children. Instead of ducking, the Elliott children came out swinging, especially Brian and Sarah, the two oldest kids. Like their mother, both could be combustible and combative. No way were they going to be pushovers. Having Jane as their mother made them fight harder. How could they show their faces around the dinner table if they had backed down from a confrontation earlier in the day?

There are at least two sides to most skirmishes. One of Brian's many scuffles was with an unlikely opponent, Tammy Bill, a fellow student at Riceville Elementary (whose third-grade photograph is on the cover of this book). Bill, from a family of fifteen brothers and sisters whose father was a farmer, said that Brian often provoked fights with other children by invoking his mother's name. "Every time, he'd push someone down, he'd come back with, 'My mom, she's a teacher!'"

Once, when Brian shoved two of Bill's younger siblings, she recalled, "I had had enough. So, I ran after him and he ran into his house. I was so angry that I went in and dragged him out and beat him up. I really hit him. His mother called my folks. Mom told me, 'Just make sure he's not in his house when you hit him.'"[20]

In 1971, Jane and Darald pulled their kids out of the Riceville schools and moved to Osage. The move meant that the Elliott children would now attend Osage schools and that Jane would commute to and from Riceville to teach every day. Darald eventually took a job managing the Red Owl grocery store in downtown Osage.

Four adolescent kids brand-new to a nearby, competing school likely would have added to any family's problems. Whether Osage was a better place for the Elliott children than Riceville was something no one could know, but particularly for Brian and Sarah, it surely signaled the end of the Elysian life they once knew.

Rick Sletten, whose mother worked with Darald as a cashier at the Red Owl, remembered a time when Brian limped into the grocery store after yet another brawl. "Brian was never going to back away from a fight, that's for sure. I used to sit in the back with him and his dad, and Darald would be saying, 'Brian, you maybe should have walked away.' But that wasn't his nature. He wasn't going to walk away. After a while, you sorta get tagged. You've been in more than a couple of fights, and it's gonna go to fists. Diplomacy wasn't a strong suit for any of the Elliott kids. A debate can go to a fistfight pretty fast. I don't know if you could be a child of Jane and Darald's and *not* have a strong opinion."[21]

Older, stronger boys, pent-up resentment, and illicit drugs stimulated bravado that could turn deadly. One Saturday evening in April 1976, when Brian was seventeen, he was hanging out with friends Gary Chrencik, twenty, and Randy Wagner, nineteen, in an area southeast of Osage called Orchard Blacktop, where locals raced cars. Chrencik got out of the car and dared Wagner, who was driving, in a pedestrian game of chicken. Wagner revved the engine, and before anyone realized what might happen, Chrencik, one of nine children, was dead. Wagner had slammed into Chrencik, who died of massive head injuries, said a Mitchell County sheriff's deputy. The sheriff's office did no more than a routine investigation, and criminal charges were never filed against either Wagner or Brian.[22]

Another time, Jane and Darald's second-youngest child, Mary, and a friend drove from Osage to Riceville for a wrestling meet and a carload of teenagers spotted her. "They chased me and my friend until they could catch us and push us down in someone's front yard. We were screaming, when another car stopped and honked. It scared them enough so they ran away. I know they recognized me because they mentioned the 'nigger-lover's kid.'"[23]

Mark, the Elliotts' youngest, didn't escape taunts, either. "I didn't get invited to birthday parties after the exercise," he recalled. Mark said his fourth-grade schoolteacher announced to his whole class, "We mustn't blame Mark for what his mother did."

"I was embarrassed and bawling my eyes out in front of the other eight-year-olds. I also used to hear, 'What can you expect from a family like that?'"

Mark said he lost almost all of his childhood friends. He credits his mother, the experiment, and local reaction to both for that. "Do you know what it's like to have twenty-five, fifty, a hundred people who hate you, not based on what you do, but because of something I never did?"[24]

While everyone in the Elliott family claimed ownership of the family's dog, Spooner really belonged to Brian, whose bed he usually slept on. Spooner was a schipperke, a wiry, black, sheep-herding dog with no tail.

One day, Spooner went missing.

When Spooner didn't show up at the house by evening, Darald and Brian drove around town calling out Spooner's name. Darald had a hunch about what had happened, but said nothing as he continued cruising neighborhood streets while Brian shouted out Spooner's name. As Darald made a turn on Eighth and Pine, they found Spooner.

Spooner's lifeless body lay on the side of the road. Darald knelt down, scooped Spooner up, put him in the flatbed of his truck, and drove to the town veterinarian, who examined the dog, and concluded that he'd been poisoned. Maybe Spooner had licked some antifreeze, rat poison, or farm pesticide. The vet really couldn't say.

It turned out that a neighbor had poisoned Spooner. "He used to brag about poisoning dogs because they used to shit on his lawn," Sarah would say years later. "Mom said it was just to be mean, but we know it was because Spooner belonged to the town's nigger lover."[25]

"Everyone knew Spooner was poisoned," Brian recalled. "Everyone in town knew it and we knew who did it, too."

One onlooker to all this disruption was Brenda Church, the attorney who moved back home to Riceville. "There always was a lot of talk about how screwed up her [Elliott's] kids were as teenagers," she said, then, perhaps parsing her words, "I can say I don't believe her children lived in a happy home."[26] Karen Schofield, who graduated from Riceville High in 1971, has her own take. "She was a *really* harsh teacher. She was harsher than she needed to be. That kids picked on her son, I think, made her meaner. If your son gets bullied at school, and people don't like him, you're not gonna like the town."[27]

That the Elliott kids encountered trouble perhaps was to be expected, however cruel, wrong, and unfortunate it was, considering the time, place, motivation, personalities, and sentiment. That several of the Elliott children weren't saints complicated the issue.

Elliott liked to lodge blame, but never seemed to accept responsibility for her actions or those of her children, some locals said. They argued that Elliott often exaggerated or fabricated accusations to garner support outside of Riceville with a ready corps of supporters and journalists on the lookout for a black-and-white story of heroes and villains.

What stood out among those in Riceville and Osage was Elliott's automatic response to events that seemed to star her or her family as ready-made victims. Everything that happened to them *always* was race-based. Everything that befell them stemmed from the blue-eyes, brown-eyes experiment. It seemed too pat, too simple to many who knew the family.

A variation of that equation came from a local woman who didn't want her name used because she said she feared some form of rebuke from Elliott or her children. "*Why* would anyone continue doing that experiment knowing that it would subject her children to all this violence? Why *wouldn't* she stop doing what she was doing? If her children *might* have benefited? Why *not* stop? Why not back down, *just a little*? What kind of mother does such a thing to her children?"[28]

That was a kind of specious extortion that Elliott wouldn't entertain. If any of the violence or threats of violence directed at her family was actually perpetrated to get her to discontinue the experiment, well, that tactic wasn't about to work. Not by a long shot.

Of course, no one could say that if Elliott had packed up the experiment, all would have gone back to normal, either. That was just as unlikely.

SEVENTEEN

A Blind Spot

BY THE FALL OF 1977, nine years after she had first tried out the blue-eyes, brown-eyes experiment on third graders, a teacher's vacancy opened up at Riceville Junior High. Elliott applied for the position and got it. Still committed to the experiment, and not having been ordered to stop by anyone in the school administration, Elliott wanted to try it out with thirteen- and fourteen-year-olds. Peer-pressured, hormonally turbocharged teenagers might need the experiment even more than their younger counterparts.

With so many large families in and around Riceville, many students had siblings who had already gone through Elliott's third-grade class. If they hadn't, they certainly knew friends who had. The experiment and Mrs. Elliott had become one and the same to Riceville students. If they got assigned to her class, they'd undergo the experiment. Separating students according to eye color was what happened when Mrs. Elliott was your teacher.

Each year, parents marched into the principal's office and demanded that their children be taught by someone other than Elliott. Some years, as many as a third of students' parents put in for transfers; other years it was just one or two. Elliott blamed the parents' actions solely on the experiment, but for many, it was something else. To many, Elliott came across as demeaning and caustic. She played favorites in the classroom, students complained. Some parents said that unless their kids were destined to become doctors or rocket scientists, Elliott wouldn't have patience for them. Her standards were impossibly high. She demanded too much.

With or without her, Riceville Junior High in 1977 was a school beset with problems. Partially because of this, a new and energetic thirty-two-year-old principal, Steven Harnack, had been hired to help clean up the mess. Harnack was an easygoing and wry administrator who grew up on a farm in

Lime Springs, twenty miles northeast of Riceville. When Harnack arrived, what he found at the junior high would have been cause for alarm for any school administrator anywhere.[1]

During his first week, Harnack determined that the school was being undermined by a dozen boys he labeled "outlaws." Within the first two months, Harnack had expelled five, one of whom had pulled a knife at school. Longtime junior high principal Everett Berends, whom Harnack had replaced, was an alcoholic who used to go home at noon and return to school drunk. His wife, Helen, a teacher, was prone to frightening outbursts in class. During one year when she had broken her foot, Helen Berends used a baseball bat as a cane to hobble around class, as well as to hammer on desks if students crossed her. She had a penchant for whacking students on the heads with a plastic ruler. Students felt fortunate she had used the ruler.[2]

Another alcoholic teacher was Jane Groth, the organist at the Lutheran church, who kept a liquor bottle in her desk and used to come to school snookered. A rite of passage among students was how early in the day they'd be able to smell alcohol on Groth's breath. Harnack twice tried to fire her; the first time he was unsuccessful; the second time, he was able to demonstrate sufficient cause, and her contract was terminated.

Errant behavior among educators in Riceville went beyond coming to school drunk. Leonard Crawford, the elementary school principal, had been carrying on an affair with one of the school secretaries. The two eventually got divorces from their respective spouses, married each other, and moved to Humboldt County in the northwest of the state. In the junior high and high schools, two sets of teachers were carrying on extramarital affairs with other teachers; one was the softball coach and the other the football coach. Harnack was successful in getting the partner of each transferred.[3]

Word also started circulating about disturbing incidents taking place in the junior high boys' locker rooms, where Harnack initially discovered a kind of "grooming" going on. It started with older boys ordering younger boys to carry their gym bags. "'Do this. Do that. Tie my shoes,' knuckling and cracking them on the top of their heads," Harnack recalled.

That was just the beginning. "If the bigger guys didn't like somebody, they'd make your life hell. There was a lot of physical stuff. Guys got smacked around," recalled Bruce Fox, who had been in Elliott's third-grade class when she first tried out the experiment and was to graduate from Riceville High in 1977.[4]

After Harnack grilled several of the ringleaders, one confessed, which led to others admitting what had been happening in the locker room. When it got to "pop bottles up the ass, that's when the shit hit the fan," Harnack, now retired, said. Older boys would strip sixth and seventh graders to their ankles and descend on them. Rites of passage included dunking boys' heads in toilets and holding them underwater as they struggled to breathe. When Harnack confronted one of the school's coaches about the abuse, Harnack recalled being told, "Ah, hell, it happened to me! That's the tradition around here!"[5]

Sexual promiscuity was something else Harnack saw in and out of school, and the degree to which Harnack, certainly not a bluenose, witnessed it during the late 1970s made him wonder what he and his family had walked in on. Harnack found Riceville a veritable Peyton Place. One evening, he and his wife, Charlotte, went downtown to a tavern called Murph's that unbeknownst to them, had a reputation for "key parties." Patrons would drop their house keys into a bowl, pass the bowl around, and go home with the owner of whoever's key they'd fished out. "We were brand-new in town and after about a half hour at the bar, the topic started coming up about the keys. The parties were pretty popular for several years. Ten or fifteen couples would get together; even some singles were involved. Quite a few were parents of preschool kids." Another time, at a social event, a married couple approached Harnack and his wife and asked, "Who wants to join the key club?"[6]

Of all the challenges Harnack faced in his new job, though, Elliott proved the toughest. Harnack was a nonconfrontational yet tough administrator, but Elliott often pushed him for what seemed like endless personal exemptions. She demanded kid-glove treatment. She wasn't reticent about letting Harnack know what she thought of him as a principal and what she thought of other teachers. She'd volunteer that he was too easy on certain students and too hard on others. Few teachers burrowed under Harnack's skin because he was such a teddy bear. But Elliott did.

When she transferred to the junior high, glee reigned throughout the elementary school. "I'm damn glad she's gone. She's your headache now!" a veteran teacher announced to Harnack. The previous principal, Leonard Crawford, informed Harnack that Elliott was "100 percent trouble." As soon as Smitty Messersmith greeted Harnack in his first week on the job, Harnack remembers Messersmith asking, "So, how you gonna handle that witch?"

Harnack hadn't realized how pervasive Elliott's eye experiment had been when he arrived in Riceville. "If I had known what Jane had been doing, I would have stopped it. Flat-out stopped it with such young kids. I would never have allowed her to do this with third graders. I would never have let it get off the ground. I realize things go on in classrooms that principals have no idea about. But this went way over the line."

Harnack labeled the experiment "brainwashing." He said, "The kids buy into it wholeheartedly when they're that age. What she did wasn't right. She was the queen and the students were little paupers around her."

Under Harnack's administration in junior high, Elliott continued with a modified version of the experiment, one that he could tolerate. "I told her we'd have to get permissions or we're not going to do it. '*I'm* the person in charge,' I told her. I had one set of parents who said to me, 'My kid has to go through *that*? We'll keep him home!' They were adamant. They had two other kids who went through it and they had nightmares."

With Harnack as principal, buttressed by a stream of complaints from parents, the original experiment gave way to a broader class discussion about racism presided over by Elliott. That was something Harnack could live with.

But Harnack's interference ruffled Elliott. The era was ripe for diversity education in the private and public sector, and Elliott increasingly found herself juggling her Riceville teaching responsibilities, along with lecturing in and out of the Midwest, taking time off to give talks to corporate managers, government workers, professors, teachers, and college students. At these events, Elliott stepped up her role as a race provocateur. "I'm going to offend every person in this room in the first five minutes and frankly, I don't give a damn," she told an assembly of high school students in La Crosse, Wisconsin, at the time.[7] Another opener was, "I do what Hitler did."[8]

The polarity of opinion about Elliott as a teacher was stunning. There was never an in-between. She was doctrinaire. She was welcoming. She was cruel. She was encouraging. She was self-absorbed and egotistical. She was altruistic and compassionate.

At least one student complained that Elliott resorted to using physical tactics in the classroom. "If you were slouching, she'd take her knuckle and run it up your back," recalled Mitchell Laurren-Ring. "She did it until one kid started crying." (When asked about this, Elliott said it wasn't her knuckle, but her thumb.[9]) Yet despite that, Laurren-Ring remembered Elliott as "a great teacher. She had couches in her classroom so kids could just hang out and read. She was popular with many students; maybe that's why the other teachers didn't like her."[10]

At times, Elliott could resemble the Robin Williams character, John Keating, from the 1989 film *Dead Poets Society*. While some students were scared by her, others adored her and gravitated to her. She welcomed and embraced them. She courted outsiders, people like herself who, even though she was a Riceville native, found themselves at odds with the local establishment. Someone who felt such kinship to her was Bill Blake, the physician in Atlanta.

"I knew I was gay when I was eleven or twelve. That's one of the huge reasons why I knew I never could live in Riceville, why I knew I had to get out," Blake recalled. While Blake never came out to Elliott, it was she who helped make his life tolerable. "I was kind of strange for a lot of people in Riceville. Never, never would I talk about my sexual orientation with her, nor did she ever bring it up. In a way, maybe we were comrades of sorts."

Blake recalled that Elliott bought books she wanted her students to read. "Not just one copy, but ten, fifteen copies. Her classroom functioned like a library. She encouraged everyone to read, read, read as much as we could. She had an acronym—KIDS! 'Kids Interested in Doing Something!'"

Blake got so attached to Elliott that he'd show up for school an hour early every morning. "I latched on to her. She talked about things that no one else talked about. At least no one in Riceville." The two strolled together before classes. "When she spoke, she spoke with certainty, in absolutes. 'This is fact.' 'This is the way it is.' She pointed a lot. She'd shake her finger in front of you and she'd wrinkle her forehead. She was unapologetic about everything. The forcefulness of her personality caused problems. I was lucky enough never to be on the end of any wrath of hers. If people misbehaved, they got it. But she cared about us without a doubt. I'm sure of it. My mom didn't like her and my dad had a really bad opinion of her. One of my older sisters had a rough time in her class."[11]

To another junior high school student, Merri Cross, Elliott was, well, different. "She liked the smart kids. If you were smart, you got along great. She introduced herself the first day as *Ms.* Elliott. You just didn't do that kind of thing in Riceville. She said, 'You will call me Ms. Elliott! Not Mrs. Elliott. Not Miss Elliott. It's none of your business whether I'm married or not!'"[12]

Elliott nettled some students, among them Aaron Dvorak, who today teaches community-college courses to those who want to become power-line technicians. "First day, she was telling students that she is a superior person. She tells the students how she's been on Johnny Carson, that she's famous. I think some kids thought she was amazing because she said she was. But she was totally narcissistic. That was day one."

Dvorak said that the mention of Elliott's name today still makes his blood pressure spike, even though he was in her class almost four decades ago.

"She'd tell the kids that one teacher ate and ate, and that she'd never seen someone who could eat so much. She'd talk about how the other teachers were stupid. She degraded everyone she didn't like. She was way ahead of her time when it came to 'identity politics.'"

For a field trip, Elliott announced that she was going to take the entire class to see a popular movie at the time, *The Karate Kid*, which was showing at Watts movie theater in Osage. The class would first have a pizza party and then go to the movie, but for assorted reasons, Elliott had punished Dvorak and told him that he wouldn't be permitted to travel with the rest of the class. Dvorak complained to Harnack, who told Elliott, "You're either going to take everybody or you're not going at all."

Elliott responded by canceling the trip, explaining to the class that Dvorak was the reason. "I was having problems at home, and now I have my peers hating my guts because it was my fault that we weren't going to the movie." Dvorak went back to Harnack, and Harnack instructed Elliott that she'd take all the kids to the movie, including Dvorak. Dvorak remembered at the pizza party Elliott's eyes darting, then staring him down, and her warning him to "chew your pizza carefully!"

"And it wasn't in a joking way. I was actually scared that she was going to poison me! This sounds crazy, but I was scared out of my wits. My stomach was tied in knots for a year and a half. Junior high isn't an easy time for any kid, and she made my life miserable." Dvorak recalls that his sister, Rachel, four years old at the time, had heard her brother and parents complain so often about Elliott that she started labeling anyone she didn't like "Mrs. Elliott."[13]

Michael Blake, Bill Blake's older brother, never had Elliott as a teacher, but had a bizarre run-in with her, not in school, but at the Riceville Public Library.

To celebrate the fiftieth anniversary of the library, Blake, one of nine siblings, was asked by the town librarian, Margaret Duncomb, to display his artwork for a Sunday open house. Blake, who was to go on to receive a degree in fine arts from the University of Iowa, had just graduated from Riceville High, and was flattered to be asked to participate. He brought five eighteen-by twenty-four-inch drawings of classic nudes he had sketched with charcoal or graphite. Blake showed them to Duncomb, who was enthusiastic about the artwork and approved their display.

"It was my chance to do good for the community—and to show off," Blake recalled. Elliott also had a display at the library for the jubilee celebration, which included a montage of articles about her, including the invitation she had received for the 1970 White House Conference on Children.

"I came down to the library the next day and the place was filled with people. I was excited to see my work displayed, but as soon as I saw my sketches, my stomach turned. Jane had taped over all the 'naughty' bits. She had scrawled a large diagonal X across one of my drawings. I was furious.

"There was a huge confrontation in front of the whole town. Everyone was there. Jane's whole thing was she didn't want kids to learn about sex this way. I said, 'Well, how would you rather have them learn about it? By reading *Playboy*?'"

A standoff ensued. Eighteen-year-old Michael Blake stood nose-to-nose with forty-one-year-old Jane Elliott, and for several tense moments no one said a word.

Elliott blinked first and stormed out of the library, while the rest of the crowd, with Blake leading them, proceeded to a lemonade party to welcome the new pastor in town. Blake found himself transformed into a citywide hero. The locals gathered around him, congratulating him for standing up both for his art and to Elliott. "'You confronted the bitch, the woman we all hate! Good for you!' I was the talk of the town!"[14]

For Principal Harnack, he didn't believe that Elliott belonged in a school setting. She was too fixated on herself and what she had destined herself to become. "I remember saying once to a school secretary that Jane would have been a good mate for Hitler. I know the point she was trying to get across, but the way she did it, I thought, was totally unacceptable. You've got to have some compassion when you work with people. I'll come right out and say it. I think this lady has no compassion for anyone. It was all about Jane."

"I respected her much more than I liked her," recalled Jerry Markham, the science teacher whose classroom was next to Elliott's. "I don't think I ever would have gotten into an argument with her that I'd have won. So, what was the point arguing? I definitely would not have wanted to have her as an enemy."[15]

As the teachers at the elementary school level had done, the junior high teachers kept Elliott at a distance. They made a wide berth around her— unless they wanted to tease her.

In the junior high teachers' lounge, one male teacher who taught social studies used to jab at Elliott constantly. As Harnack recalled: "He'd ask, 'How are the colored people doing today, Jane?' And he didn't use the term 'colored people.' So, they'd go at it. Back and forth, and Jane would go wild!

It was a friendly-type thing. They baited her and everyone laughed about it. The other teachers would say, 'We got Jane's dander up again!' It was more fun than mean. And Jane, I think, enjoyed it. I did not feel it was done in a malicious way. The kids didn't hear what was going on, but they must have heard all the laughter coming from the teachers' lounge."

EIGHTEEN

Class Reunion

DURING THOSE TIMES IN THE TEACHERS' LOUNGE, Elliott was surrounded by at least one bigot playing to a half dozen or so other teachers who didn't have the guts to say or do anything but go along with the instigator. Perhaps the teachers' silence had as much to do with how much they loathed Elliott as it did with how much they enjoyed seeing her roasted, however abhorrent they may have found the language and the sentiment. Maybe it had to do with who was trying to bait Elliott. A case of grinning and bearing it. Looking the other way.

But just as reasonable an explanation is that by saying nothing, the teachers were giving their approval to what came out of the mouth of the educator who had referred to Blacks as "niggers." How difficult would it have been to have stopped such language among teachers in a public school setting, no matter who was saying it? No one said anything to shut the conversation down and censure the offender.

By saying nothing, of course, the teachers were guilty of allowing a racist teacher to speak as much for the school as for the city of Riceville. These were *teachers*, and as teachers, they were supposed to be role models. They were supposed to *teach*. Harnack had fired teachers who were drunks; he had transferred teachers who had carried on affairs. Was using the word *nigger* day in and day out while laughing about it any less offensive?

Change the location from the teachers' lounge to the boys' locker room. Change the racist language to sexual assault and call it "boys being boys." Was what happened in the teachers' lounge that different in principle? No one had the decency to do anything to stop a fellow teacher from acting despicably. Perhaps some kept quiet for fear of being labeled an ally of Elliott.

The covey of teachers seemed to have enjoyed—or at the least, tolerated—the racist razzing, even though such language was unacceptable anywhere in the United States by the early 1980s, including rural Iowa. No one stood up to the Riceville teacher who taunted Elliott when he used the word "nigger." No one said, "Enough! Stop the bullying! Stop using such words!" Instead, the teachers smiled, chatted, packed up their lunch boxes, and walked back to their classrooms for another afternoon of spelling, math, and American history taught by those who had just partaken in their own exercise of racism.

No wonder Elliott had such a near-impossible time comporting herself. If her fellow teachers spoke this way in the quasi-public space of a teachers' lounge, then what were they saying about Blacks, Jews, Asians, or Hispanics in their own homes? What were the locals saying at the grain elevator, at Andy's Mini-Mart, Pettitt's, the hardware store, the Riceville Bowl, in church, at the Hang Out, or Murph's?

If nothing else, such behavior gave Elliott a degree of sustenance, a reason to continue her self-appointed mission to change Riceville, and by extension, Iowa, the nation, and ultimately, maybe even the world. Starting with children was the way. Maybe from their children parents would pick up wisdom. "God Bless America," the anthem Riceville students sang each morning, went only so far. Children were the change agent. Who else was going to bring to the dinner table unspoken issues like racism, discrimination, and prejudice? Was Elliott the only one in Riceville who understood this? Was she the only one trying to do something about it?

At such times, Elliott sought consolation in the wisdom of the song "You've Got to Be Taught" from the 1949 Rodgers and Hammerstein musical *South Pacific* when one of the main characters, Lieutenant Cable, responds to a comment about racism, and suggests that children are taught by their family to hate and fear based on skin color and eye shapes before they are "six or seven or eight."[1]

What Elliott endured in the teachers' lounge wasn't the only form of insularity running rampant in her hometown. Despite all the gushing encomia that Midwesterners and much of the rest of America seem to lavish on the rural heartland, Elliott knew the truth. Yes, we are hardworking. Yes, we can be generous in spirit and deed. Yes, we are resourceful. But the views of many are narrow and provincial. We don't like big cities or the nerve that goes with them. We like it here just fine. What kept striking Elliott was the ceaseless congruity. The set pattern. The row after row, field after field. There was no room for anything or anyone different. Riceville was a remote enclave in a remote region in a remote state. This was how it had been for a hundred years and how it would be a hundred years hence.

Elliott allowed herself to consider the back biting gossip, the deficit of audacity, the unrelenting conformity during one of her early-morning walks before the school day started, before the other teachers would arrive. She liked to walk briskly. She needed to clear her head, to prepare for what lay ahead, to consider what tumult would invariably materialize to sidetrack her.

Thirteen-year-old Bill Blake had been one of her early-morning recruits. Every year there had been one or two. Smart youngsters who'd sooner or later realize that they'd have to leave Riceville to free themselves from the underbrush that would entangle them if they stayed. Elliott knew this from her own upbringing. Her father had told her so. "Git an education and git outta here!" She barely got the first and she still lived in the shadow of her father's farm, with its rock-hard, impermeable soil. Being ostracized wasn't new to her. Maybe that's why she had such a mouth. Not to offend, but to protect.

While driving home to Osage one evening, Elliott stewed—another awful remark, a lazy teacher, yet another run-in with Steven Harnack, the principal. Even before she had transferred to the junior high, Elliott would file away all the wicked thoughts about those she worked with, "particularly after some nastier-than-usual behavior on the part of my peers," she would write in a letter to her children. But she couldn't help herself. She'd allow herself to loiter in grisly, dark places. She'd go as far as to fantasize about "blowing the offender off the face of the earth." These were awful visions, Elliott knew. Such demons showed how enraged she had become. No one in Riceville wanted anything to do with her. Darald was a soothing husband. He listened and offered well-reasoned, practical opinions. But his everyday reality was groceries lined from floor to ceiling. When he had heard enough from Jane, he'd transport himself into his own world—a shop he had created behind the house, where he'd tinker with small engines. Darald didn't see the world the way Jane did, and that was fortunate. Jane brooded. Darald motored on.

Her grisly ruminations signaled many things, including a desire for at least a begrudging acknowledgment that perhaps she might be on the right path, that the experiment she had stuck with for sixteen years may have been worth all that it had cost her locally. The only admiration Elliott ever seemed to garner came in direct proportion to how far away she got from Riceville and Iowa. She found herself taking solace in Jesus's admonition, "Only in his hometown and in his own household is a prophet without honor. And He did not do many miracles there, because of their unbelief."[2] Or, more simply: "You can't be a prophet in your own land." It was a maxim Elliott repeated to herself, a mantra that grounded her, as well as reminded her of what she had set out to achieve for herself. Few in town would allow Elliott even a sliver of praise. To do so ran counter to the near unanimous community-wide condemnation of her. The people of Riceville had spoken.

"Several years after I'd been at the junior high I was walking the hall of the elementary building one afternoon and I saw one of those whom I had disposed of coming toward me," Elliott would write. "'What are you doing here?' I wondered in surprise. 'I thought I'd killed you.' I was saddened by my response in seeing her in the hall that day, but I was even more upset when I heard that one of those who had taken savage delight, it seemed to me, in the 'Dirty Tricks' game was dying. You see, I didn't feel any sympathy for her pain and suffering. I had so dehumanized myself where some of my peers were concerned that their agony was meaningless to me. I didn't rejoice in their misery; I just flat out didn't care."[3]

It was a constant, resolute me-against-them interior conviction that kept Elliott leashed to northeastern Iowa, even though she was traveling and speaking more and more to receptive audiences outside the state. Such engagements required her to take even more time off from teaching. She didn't think Steven Harnack would move to discipline her. No way was Elliott going to quit and give that particular pleasure to her fellow teachers or those residents of Riceville who loathed her. She'd stay as long as *she* wanted to stay. She had tenure, was a member of the local teachers' union, and unless she acted on some of her darkest homicidal fantasies, Elliott would likely have her job for as long as she wanted it, at least till retirement. Let them wheel her out when she was good and ready. And if she moved, where would she go? Iowa was the only place she and Darald had ever lived. It was home.

Elliott got a needed morale boost in the winter of 1984 when several former students who had been in her 1970 third-grade class, the one that had been filmed for the ABC documentary "Eye of the Storm," called to tell her they were planning a reunion. It had been five years since they'd graduated from Riceville High, fourteen since third grade.

Not one to pass up an opportunity, Elliott immediately called Bill Peters, the journalist who had put together the original television program.

"They're coming back!" Elliott told Peters.

Without asking who she was referring to, Peters responded: "We'll be there with a film crew."[4]

Peters first pitched a blue-eyes, brown-eyes reunion story to ABC, which turned down the idea. Old news, they said. The timing wasn't right. Peters wasn't working for ABC any longer, so he shopped the project and got a bite from PBS, the nonprofit public broadcasting network.

Peters and a television-production crew arrived in Riceville and began rolling on August 11, 1984, bright lights once again set up, cameras whirring, as eleven of Elliott's former third graders, now adults, reunited at Riceville Elementary, high-fiving and hugging each other.

Blue-eyed Russell Ring, the boy who had swallowed a pin in his excitement during the original experiment, had died in a car accident two weeks before high school graduation. Brown-eyed John Benttine, who had gotten into the fight with Russell on the playground during the first day of the experiment, had been injured in a car accident, lived with paraplegia, and could not travel. Of the remaining fourteen original third graders, more than three-quarters showed up: Julie Smith (now Julie Trampel), Donna Reddel (now Donna May), Sandi Dohlman (now Sandi Burke), Brian Saltou, Verla Buls, Roy Wilson (who slept in his pickup in the school parking lot after driving to Riceville from Missouri), Susan Ginder (now Susan Rolland), Sheila Schaefer (now Sheila Flaherty), Milton Wolthoff, Raymond Hansen, and Rex Kozak. Some were married and brought their spouses; one former third grader brought her baby.

The reunion started with everyone watching the original documentary. They laughed at the sight of themselves fourteen years younger. Boys in chinos, girls in dresses. Classroom No. 10 fossilized in time: the miniature desks; slate blackboard; Mrs. Elliott pointing, directing, questioning, scolding. Men and women, now in their early twenties, looking at incarnations of themselves as eight- and nine-year-olds. Elliott had been thirty-seven at the time; she was now fifty-one. Seeing the transformation was an uplifting, joyful experience, and with the PBS cameras rolling, it made for stirring television. Back together again, the former classmates had placed the children's chairs into a circle. It was Magic Circle all over again. Pizzui would have approved.

"I think every school ought to implement something like this program in their early stages of education," blue-eyed Raymond Hansen said about the experiment. "All your inhibitions were gone, and no matter if they were my friends or not, any pent-up hostilities or aggressions that these kids had ever caused you, you had a chance to get it all out."[5] The group nodded in agreement.

Others shared lessons learned that didn't have anything to do with skin color. Verla Buls, slender and tall, talked about discrimination against fat people. Rex Kozak talked about bullying. "I feel the same kind of emotion I had during the exercise when I see a bunch of bigger kids picking on a kid because he's little."[6]

The reunion was a controlled group. Not everyone showed up, and of those who did, their former teacher, Mrs. Elliott, was there once again to monitor their reactions, to approve or disapprove as she saw fit. Elliott was still the alpha-teacher. A normal jockeying of power among the former students—who was most successful, happiest, most attractive, most vocal, wealthiest—was in play, too.

But the reunion demonstrated, at least to Elliott, that the experiment had been a success. That she had done right, at least for those who had shown up.

After her former charges left, Elliott suggested to Peters that the experiment had served to provide the children with a sort of contract of decency that would last the rest of their lives. "What I would hope is that they will be able to say 'No' whenever a racist or sexist remark is made in their presence, to say, 'That's not true,' or at least to ask that such things not be said around them. I would hope that they might do more than just retain the new attitudes they have acquired, that they might actively resist random racism and discrimination in one way or another. If I'm right, they are going to have to make a decision at that point. 'Do I go along, or do I argue? Do I assert myself, or do I just let it go? Or do I join in?' At the very least, they're going to be confronted with the need to make a decision. Without the experience of the exercise, they probably wouldn't be aware that a decision was even called for."[7] It seemed that Elliott was sharing what she hoped would have happened in the Riceville teachers' lounges.

The reunion acted as a renewal for Elliott, considering all the personal history it had churned. "Constantly bucking the system does not win friends and influence people," she allowed to Peters. As for why she had become such a lightning rod in Riceville, Elliott conceded that she was "not the easiest person in the world to work with. I tend to be more than just a wee bit aggressive. I like to do what I think is best for students, and that doesn't always match the opinion of my peers. So teaching in the same school with me is not always the easiest thing in the world."[8]

Elliott pinned the local resentment on the whirlwinds that always seemed to swirl around her, which she usually had a hand in creating. This, of course, included the very interview she was participating in with Peters during which she was saying such things.

"It's difficult to see someone else get a lot of attention when she's doing the same job and getting the same pay as you are," Elliott reflected. "The fact that I've had less education than some of my fellow teachers probably didn't help, either. And while it's not particularly pleasant to be the object of resentment and jealousy from your peers, I can live with that and even understand it. What really bothered me was the hostility of some teachers that stemmed, not from jealousy, but from their own racist conviction."[9]

The PBS documentary, titled "A Class Divided" and aired on the network's *Frontline*, was introduced by Judy Woodruff and narrated by journalist Charlie Cobb. It debuted March 26, 1985.[10] The program sandwiched four segments into one show: film clips from the original "Eye of the Storm"; footage of the 1984 student reunion; shots of inmates at a maximum-security prison in New York, using the "Eye of the Storm" video as a discussion guide; and video of Elliott administering the experiment to Iowa prison guards and parole officers. The documentary was a mishmash of clips that seemed random and disconnected.

The last segment of the television show was the most explosive and disturbing. As Elliott had done in her classes, and at the Rotary Club luncheon and the White House conference, the correctional employees were manipulated and set up. At a sign-in table, they were split up according to eye color. The blue-eyed employees wore collars and were treated dismissively. Elliott picked on two blue-eyed employees and called them stupid and lazy. It was a put-on display of arrogance, ostensibly so the experiment would make an impact. The exchange was so over-the-top, it was cringeworthy. But not nearly as much as what was to follow.

During the closing minutes, Elliott put in a plug for herself and the experiment. "I'd like to see this exercise used with all teachers, all administrators. But certainly not with all students, unless it's done by people who are doing it for the right reasons and in the right way. I think you could damage your children with this exercise very, very easily, and I would never suggest that everyone should use it."

Then came the capper: "I think you could have training classes for teachers. Bring them in, put them through the thing, explain what happened, do the debriefing and then practice doing this until a group of teachers were able to do it on their own. . . . If I can do it, then most anyone can learn to do it. It doesn't take a super teacher to do this exercise."[11]

Elliott had turned the PBS documentary into a personal sales pitch. She was suggesting the creation of a corps of teachers trained to evangelize the experiment, and who better to lead them, but her.

After the airing of the documentary, Elliott received so many offers in response to her idea that she was able to secure the services of an agent and she signed with a speaker's bureau.

Once again, the issue arose whether Elliott could juggle her everyday teaching at the junior high with the multiple requests she was fielding for appearances and workshops. By fall, Harnack had issued her an ultimatum: "You need to make up your mind on what you want to do. You can't do both."[12]

To no one's surprise, the reaction around Riceville to the PBS documentary was wholly negative. Residents took offense at narrating journalist Cobb's opening description of Riceville as "a small farming community surrounded by cornfields. Its population is still under a thousand, and it's still all white and all Christian," even though that characterization was as true then as it is today.[13] Once again, locals looked at Elliott and the TV show as a slam on Riceville and an advertisement for herself. Elliott had used the documentary as a commercial to sell her services as a speaker and consultant while on the payroll as a Riceville public school teacher—at least, that's what her antagonists said.

This was just what they were looking for.

NINETEEN

───────

The Offer

IN THE AFTERMATH OF THE PBS DOCUMENTARY, one particularly lucrative offer came from Mountain Bell, about to become the mammoth telecommunications corporation known as US West, serving seven states and employing seventy thousand employees, with hubs in Phoenix, Seattle, Minneapolis, and Omaha. Executives at the communications company hired Elliott to create fifteen training sessions at its south Denver headquarters, essentially the blue-eyes, brown-eyes experiment for middle- and upper-management personnel. Elliott's dream of reaching overflow audiences of adults was about to become a reality.

With Mary and Mark still at home and Darald managing the grocery store in Osage, Elliott still felt tethered to Riceville. She was entering her twenty-second year of teaching in Riceville. Why couldn't she continue teaching *and* travel to Denver to administer the blue-eyes, brown-eyes experiment to US West's burgeoning multistate workforce? How could she turn down such a spectacular offer? It would make all she had endured back home worthwhile.

First, Elliott had to sell the idea to the school administration. She had gotten almost everything she had ever asked for, so why not this? Except for Steven Harnack, Riceville school administrators left her alone. They usually said yes, and then hurriedly walked the other way.

Elliott's solution was for her to hire a substitute teacher who would fill in for her whenever she'd be away overseeing the blue-eyes, brown-eyes experiment in Colorado.

It was worth a try. All she needed was to convince Harnack.

Easygoing Harnack listened. The plan Elliott laid out was to take fifteen days of unpaid leave that year, along with several days off a month. She'd prepare a lesson plan for a substitute teacher and she'd grade the homework her students would hand in during her time away.

Harnack knew better than to tell Elliott there was no way she could teach in Riceville and work as a diversity trainer 850 miles away at the same time. To Harnack, this was a scheme that sounded crazy.

Harnack mollified Elliott by saying he'd bring the matter to Norm Kolberg, the school superintendent who had taken over for Dean Weaver.[1] Harnack wasn't about to tell Elliott that she'd have to quit her teaching job to accept the US West offer. That would be Kolberg's call.

Before moving up to Riceville in 1977, forty-four-year-old Kolberg had been a principal and superintendent in Lytton, Iowa (population: 310).[2] An Iowa native with four children, Kolberg was a master fly fisherman who took weekends to try out his own hand-tied lures in nearby Minnesota lakes. He was well liked in Riceville and wanted to keep it that way.

When Harnack told Kolberg about Elliott's offer, Kolberg backed off from a confrontation. He didn't want to tangle with Elliott, either. He said he'd go directly to the school board for a decision.

Perhaps Harnack and Kolberg had something else in mind. Elliott's latest request might play in their favor.

Had she finally given the board a way to get rid of her?

If Elliott wasn't going to back down from the Mountain Bell offer—and she seldom backed down from anything—maybe she could be enticed to leave her teaching position. Getting Elliott to quit would be a coup. Neither Harnack nor Kolberg would directly involve themselves, but if the elected school board were to refuse Elliott's double-employment request, maybe she'd leave on her own. The marriage between Elliott and the Riceville schools could end in a neat separation, without any of the recriminations that had accompanied the Paul Richer debacle.

That next Thursday, in the *Riceville Recorder*, Smitty Messersmith, Elliott's nemesis, published the upcoming school board agenda, including a line item about her petition to take a leave.

That got the local teachers' association piqued. The Riceville Education Association served as the local teachers' union, negotiating teachers' contracts with the school board and ostensibly protecting their rights. An unnamed Riceville teacher noted that unpaid professional leave was not included in the teachers' contract with the district. Because of that, the teachers' association could oppose Elliott's request. The teachers' union, normally the organizational ally of public school educators, was pulling a card from the bottom of the deck to force Elliott's hand.

When Elliott heard this, she turned livid. She told Harnack that the teachers' contract, which was supposed to protect teachers, was being used to penalize her. Elliott informed Harnack that the teachers' union could "put the master contract where the sun doesn't shine."

As a compromise, she countered to Harnack and Kolberg that she'd take 180 days of unpaid leave, but that offer never went anywhere.[3] Someone suggested that she donate a percentage of the money she'd be making in Colorado back to the Riceville schools as a gesture of goodwill, but Kolberg dismissed the suggestion out of hand.[4]

Allowing Elliott to keep her teaching job and take time off to work somewhere else was a political battle no one in Riceville was willing to champion. Kolberg wasn't prepared to support her, neatly basing his objections on the issue of fairness to all the district's personnel, not on Elliott's teaching abilities. "The other teachers didn't like her because she was innovative," Kolberg would say years later. "People didn't like her because of what she was doing. Many [parents] felt that their kids were being exploited. But I thought she was an excellent teacher."[5]

Several members of the school board weren't as keen on Elliott as Kolberg ostensibly was. They were elected officials (though few ever ran against an opponent) and all had heard complaints about Elliott for years. You couldn't live in Riceville, Stacyville, or McIntire, the three communities that made up the district, without getting an earful about Elliott, and you didn't need to be a politician to realize that Elliott's request for so much time off presented the school board with a headache—and an opportunity. Firing a veteran public school teacher without cause would be impossible, *but* turning down her request for time off might force Elliott's hand. It might provoke her to resign. Those who knew Elliott knew she wasn't going to turn down the US West offer. It was too much money and too much opportunity. To members of the school board, here was a deft solution to an intractable problem.

"I could see why the other teachers had problems with her," recalled one former member of the school board who asked to remain anonymous, once again because she said she feared recriminations from Elliott, even though these incidents took place more than three decades ago. "She had an arrogance about her. She thought she was better than anyone else. She was successful at making other people feel they weren't smart. If she had it in for you, you could have a rough time."

There also was Elliott's anti-Riceville attitude—at least as many in town perceived it. "When she became famous, she really backstabbed Riceville," was how the former school board member put it.[6]

The former school board member never mentioned Elliott's name, a habit of almost all of her detractors. Many locals carried on extended conversations about Elliott without ever uttering her name. To invoke "Jane" or "Elliott" seemed to be a sign of regard or support. Not intoning her name was to accord her the degree of disrespect many in Riceville seemed to believe she merited.

For years, the school board had been miffed by the myriad accommodations and exceptions that Elliott had taken. "Our board wasn't trying to get rid of her," the former school board official insisted, perhaps laboring the point too far. "We just didn't agree to give her any more time off because we'd already given her so much off already. We'd already given her more time off than we had given any other teacher. We didn't feel it was fair to the students or the other teachers to give her more."

Elliott ultimately didn't show up for the board meeting at which her proposal was discussed. Instead, she wrote a preemptive letter of resignation to be presented to the board if she didn't get her way.

Elliott's bid for unpaid leave went forward, as another former board member Leo Jordan remembered it, requesting one unpaid week off every month. Jordan said that he struggled with trying to accommodate Elliott, but couldn't see how it could possibly work. When the board refused the request, she had no alternative. Her resignation letter was tendered to the board in absentia.

Jordan recalled that he made the motion "with great reluctance" to accept Elliott's resignation, which was approved unanimously. "We made the only decision we could have made. Everyone was in agreement," Jordan said.[7]

And the deed was done.

By then, Elliott had come to embrace that her future lay outside Riceville, leading workshops with adults rather than classes with Riceville children whose parents were leery of almost anything that bore her name. The portentous vision that had come to her during her appearance on the Carson show was to become reality.

With the news that Elliott would be gone, the relief in much of Riceville was palpable. "I felt she exploited the kids to make herself grow financially,"

Harnack would say years later. "I always felt that Jane used the kids to better herself."[8]

Elliott was now free from the backbiting of Riceville locals and her fellow teachers. She'd now be able to take the experiment that had shaped her career anywhere, at least any place that wanted her to divide blue-eyed from brown-eyed participants to explore what preconceived notions might be exposed about skin color and an assortment of other biases.

In doing so, Elliott didn't remove herself from the fray of controversy and provocation. If she thought that she had faced disagreeable opposition while trying out the experiment on Riceville kids, then all she had to do was wait till she'd tried it on adults.

TWENTY

Unbound

JAN FINCHER WAS THE US WEST EXECUTIVE charged with rolling out the new program that would enlighten and educate managers about issues of diversity at the newly configured telecommunications company, headquartered in the Denver suburb of Lakewood. US West was on the national forefront of such corporate training exercises, which the company internally termed "pluralism experiences."[1] Fincher had the responsibility (along with another executive, Linda Guillory) to overhaul how US West managers would comport themselves with each other and with the public in an increasingly multicultural environment. Fincher had seen Elliott run a workshop while Fincher was manager of a Denver bank and, along with other executives at US West, decided to hire her to try out the blue-eyes, brown-eyes experiment as part of the new company-wide training.

Fincher knew what to expect. "It's a very emotional experience," she would recall. "It's a trauma. As many times as I saw it, I'd get emotionally involved. To be treated in such a dismissive way has a powerful impact."[2]

It was precisely that experience that Fincher and her colleagues agreed would become mandatory for all US West management employees to undergo. Enrollment in the workshops was tied to a monetary-reward system; if employees opted out, they would be financially penalized and would not be eligible for promotion. After the company's top personnel went through the pluralism training sessions, middle management would be required to enroll as well. The corporate goal was massive and ambitious: sixty-five thousand employees were to be trained by Elliott and by as many as three hundred newly hired facilitators.[3]

By early 1985, Elliott was flying regularly to Denver to administer the blue-eyes, brown-eyes experiment to US West managers. It proved to be a turning point in Elliott's career. The fundamentals were the same as in Classroom No. 10, but with adults she amplified her on stage persona considerably. As her sister Mary Yager had put it, Elliott "had a mouth," and during the US West workshops, years of pent-up frustration seemed to come forth from it.[4] Elliott marched around the DoubleTree Hotel auditorium, where the sessions were held, barking commands and ultimatums. To many in the workshops, she came across as extreme. Some called her sadistic.

After out-of-town US West employees checked into the hotel adjacent to US West's headquarters, they were separated according to eye color. Elliott came prepared with stacks of collars, which the blue-eyed groups would wear throughout the sessions. None of the participants ostensibly knew what was to happen. A code of silence among those who had undergone the experiment prevailed; previous workshop participants held back on divulging what was to happen. To help set the scene, as Elliott had done at the Washington, DC, conference, she tacked on the walls posters with a variety of reworked racist messages:

- *Is it true Browns have more fun?*
- *Let in one blue-eye and there goes the neighborhood.*
- *If I have one life to live, let me live it as a brown!*
- *If Blueys don't like it here, why don't they go back to where they came from?*
- *Would you want your daughter to marry a Bluey?*[5]

During the 1970s and 1980s, such workshops had gained popularity in and out of the corporate world. They would go by names such as team-building, large group awareness training (LGAT), consciousness raising, and transformative leadership.[6] Elliott's experiment, which could last one to three days, was at a glance similar to other such human-potential-movement workshops of the era, including Werner Erhard's est training, in that it focused on changing basic self-perceptions and behavior.[7] While the heart of Elliott's experiment was racism abatement, she began folding into her presentations issues of gender and age bias, along with prejudice based on conventional beauty standards. Somewhere along the line from Riceville to Colorado, Elliott had retooled herself as a New Age visionary.

The sessions were part improvisation, part scripted terror. Elliott hurled insults at workshop participants, particularly those who were white and had blue eyes. As academic Gregory Jay observed, her techniques were "unforgiving, sarcastic, and unrelenting. Her manner [was] . . . a far cry from the therapeutic, feel-good multiculturalism of many American workshops. Elliott want[ed] . . . her blue-eyeds to really feel the pain of discrimination and inequality."[8]

Anyone familiar with Elliott would have recognized the method: jabbing index finger, wrinkled forehead, darting eyes then full-faced scowl, the raised voice. She went full-tilt with naysayers. She stared down anyone who disagreed with her. She accused participants, many of whom already felt vulnerable in a corporate setting far away from their home cities, of shocking allegations. As her third graders had done in Classroom No. 10, the US West employees were forced to sit while Elliott wielded all the power. One difference was that her students this time were adults. Another was that she turned up the voltage until it shot into the red zone.

In most workshops, there were indelible moments of joy and tears, affirmation and recrimination, hugging and screaming as Elliott choreographed the intense sessions, choosing who would be her victims and how long they'd remain in the hot seats she had ignited and stoked. Elliott praised and punished at her own discretion.

One employee who underwent the closed-door experiment at the US West complex in the mid-1980s was Judy Swinnerton, an engineer who had been so impressed with the sessions that she left her technical job with US West and became a diversity trainer. "It was harsh, but I think if you've grown up entitled, it's probably one of the first times that you experience where you're not getting automatic respect. It was really life-changing. I was angry, hurt, not understanding what was going on. But, boy, having gone through that experience, it opens you up and helps you understand what other people go through on a daily basis."[9]

Everyone took something deeply visceral from the sessions since Elliott's style was so aggressive and personal. For Swinnerton, that moment came when Elliott told the assembled participants: "You may not be a woman, you may not be Black. But if you're lucky, you're going to get old. And then you're going to experience some of what I'm talking about."[10]

No longer a third-grade teacher, Elliott had transformed herself into an omniscient and messianic leader who had the answers to an assortment of society's ills. Without the shackles of jealous teachers, skittish administrators, or protective parents, Elliott went about the corporate training sessions with near obsession. She took to inflicting gut-wrenching, emotional pain on participants. Some workshops went horribly awry.

For Julie Pasicznyk, the experience was devastating, creating such a negative impact that she still carries scars more than thirty years later. Pasicznyk, who had been working for US West in Minneapolis, was hesitant to enroll in the training at the Colorado facility, but was told that if she wanted to succeed as a manager, she'd have to attend. Pasicznyk joined seventy-five other employees for a several-day session that went from nine to five each day.

"Right off the bat, she picked me out of the room and called me 'Barbie.' That's how it started, and that's how it went all day long. She had never met me and she accused me in front of everyone in the room of using my sexuality to get ahead. She accused me of sleeping with my bosses because that's the only way women like me get promoted. She said I'd gotten by on my appearance all my life."

"Barbie" had to have a Ken, so Elliott picked from the audience a tall, handsome man and accused him of doing the same things with his female subordinates. She went after "Ken" and "Barbie" all day long, drilling, accusing, ridiculing them.

"People left crying," recalled Pasicznyk. "Or they just sat in their seats crying." To many, it seemed like Elliott's goal was to break the employees. "It was all so vicious, so assumptive, so not true and hateful. She was self-righteous and cruel. She clearly picked on the people she had resentment for just based on appearances. It went beyond the pale. It was like someone had slapped you in the face and kept slapping you. She wouldn't stop."

Since attendance was compulsory, employees were on the company clock, and because completion of the sessions was tied to promotion, there was little participants could do except take the bullying.

"I had a roaring sound in my ears. I've had the same feeling just a few other times in my life. It's when horrible things have happened. It's a rushing, roaring sound that won't stop," Pasicznyk recalled.

To Pasicznyk, Elliott seemed to delight in tormenting those in the session. "It really was about abuse. I think she found an outlet where she could cloak her cruelty in a 'lesson.' You can't be that good and that effective at cruelty without having something wrong with you. She's one of the two or three worst people I've ever met in my life. I really pride myself on being empathetic, on seeing the good in people, not inflicting any pain. She came across as evil. It's stunning that she could get away with that."

Elliott may have been ahead of a dawning era of intimidation, threats, and belittling for personal and political advantage, Pasicznyk said. "I don't think it's any different from what's happening in politics right now. You start calling people vile names and assigning to them thoughts and behaviors that aren't their thoughts and behaviors. It's all made up and it's awful. It's so awful that it shuts you down. It shuts down conversation. You're so appalled by it, it just takes the words right out of your mouth. You can't believe what's happening. It's so incredible, you just sit there."[11]

For Sandy Juettner, another former US West employee, whose heritage is Native American, French, and Norwegian, the experience was just as traumatic. Juettner attended a three-day workshop more than thirty years ago, and, like Pasicznyk, she remembers it as though it happened yesterday. As with Pasicznyk and others, Juettner retains such a scarring memory that she instinctively avoids mentioning Elliott's name.

"The people in the brown-eyed group were supposed to pick on the blue-eyed group and hurl insults at them. There was one woman in the blue-eyed group, and her daughter had recently died from cancer. I don't know how she found out about this, but she also discovered that the woman was a smoker. So, she honed in on that and told this woman that it was her fault that her daughter had died of cancer. She went on and on, hammering this poor woman. The woman was beside herself. She was hysterical. She was crying and was inconsolable, and she wouldn't let up. She kept on her all day."

Elliott's version of "Ken" for this workshop was a white Vietnam veteran. "She said he was a 'baby killer.' That, because he had been in Vietnam, he had killed babies. It was unconscionable. This wasn't about racism. It was about how cruel she could be. It was uncontrolled cruelty. She wouldn't stop."

In a subsequent debriefing session, Elliott tried to explain to Juettner and others that she was simulating what Black people experience every day because of pervasive, institutional racism. What Elliott had done was exaggerated, she allowed, but its purpose was to beat home her point. Her secondary goal, Juettner remembered, was to see how long the blue-eyed group would take the mistreatment before getting up and walking out. Or how long the privileged brown-eyed participants would allow Elliott to continue. Or how either group could tolerate such behavior before standing up to her. By doing nothing, they were implicitly endorsing Elliott's methods.

For most participants, though, confronting Elliott was impossible. The participants were getting paid to be there and finish the workshop; they were all supposed to be on the same corporate team. No one had advised them of the game's rules. If they came to the defense of a bullied coworker, Elliott would go after them. If they stormed out of the room, she'd mock them mercilessly to their backs. There was no way to win. It was a doomed-from-the-start, survival-of-the-fittest contest with Elliott holding all the power. Tossing a life preserver to a fellow employee meant Elliott would throw you overboard.

The last day of the session made Juettner the most uncomfortable. Elliott chose Juettner and two other women to be representatives of different races. During the session "when anyone had questions about racism, they'd turn to *us* for answers. It was embarrassing and humiliating and simplistic. There was a forced sisterhood between the three of us. I'd never been treated like that and had never been isolated like that. It was twisted and creepy."

To Juettner, the workshop failed miserably. "I didn't expect the company I trusted to put me through something like that. I felt like a pawn. I felt used and ashamed." In retrospect, Juettner said she believed Elliott "liked being the bully. Rape is too strong for what she did. But I was abused. I was emotionally abused. I felt trapped. She manipulated us. It was an unbelievable breach of trust. It was obscene. I don't like to talk about it and rarely do."

Several months after the session ended, Juettner was required to attend a follow-up workshop, which, when completed, would entitle her to the promised salary bonus. "I said, 'I'm not going. Keep your money.'"[12]

With each session, Elliott seemed to ramp up her anger and hostility. She became less focused on the workshop's goal of illuminating racism, and more intent on insulting and goading participants. As Elliott had done with Pasicznyk and Juettner, she'd hurl wild characterizations at participants she'd never met before. She'd badger them, barking out irrational commands. "There was one guy who was forced to be on his knees in the room," Pasicznyk remembered.[13] Elliott had used the same tactic back in Classroom No. 10.

Jan Fincher, who had started the program, ultimately developed grave reservations about what she had unleashed. "When I think back at that time, I'm almost horrified that we allowed and condoned the bullying," she recalled.

> I don't think we could do something like that today and get away with it legally. The thinking at the time was that it would be bullying for a short period of time, then we would talk about what had happened. Every session I went to was intense. I remember how I felt, and it was terrible being a part of it. The ad hominem attacks made no sense. I recall people crying. At the time, we thought it was having a positive impact. We did it. I think about it—what was the cost and what was the payoff?[14]

If workshop participants complained about what went on behind closed workshop doors, they'd get their knuckles rapped. It was best just to keep your mouth shut. Two would-be US West trainers filed a federal lawsuit against the company in 1992. A federal court initially ruled in their favor, but in 1995, a US Court of Appeals in Denver reversed the lower court's decision in US West's favor. The higher court ruled that "such workshops, by their very structure, are intended to cause the participants to lay bare the most bitter, bigoted, offensive, and often savage interpersonal confrontations and feeling that can arise. . . . The participants come expecting this and the possibility of bruised feeling to themselves and others."[15]

The court's ruling didn't mean, though, that such experiments were acceptable business practices. In December 1988, Fincher and R. Ann Jaramillo Welter, whose title with US West was manager–pluralism education, let Elliott go. The company's diversity-workshop program would continue, Fincher and Welter wrote Elliott, adding that in the coming year, the company would run 63 three-day workshops and 450 pluralism sessions. "This ambitious effort is necessary in order to effect the cultural change we need, to make this a truly pluralistic corporation."

But the US West executives wrote that Elliott's services would no longer be needed.[16] "It is always a pleasure to tell people about the successes we have had working with you," they concluded without elaboration.[17]

By now, Elliott had been able to leverage her credentials at US West to attract a multitude of consulting jobs. She also joined the lucrative college lecture circuit. Elliott was the go-to authority on all topics racial, especially after a racist incident was featured in the daily parade of news and journalists needed an explanatory quote to put the event in context. It made for an effective, synergistic marketing campaign for a consulting and lecture business with Elliott at its center.

TWENTY-ONE

Oprah

DURING THE SPRING OF 1986, Elliott's name caught the attention of an assistant producer of a local Chicago television talk show who invited Elliott to try out the blue-eyes, brown-eyes experiment on live TV. The assistant producer worked for a rising, charismatic entertainer, thirty-two-year-old Oprah Winfrey. The show hadn't gone national yet, but Winfrey was already a star. Her nascent TV career had included hosting *A.M. Chicago*, and that show had gone from third to first in local market share in its first month. More impressive was that the mega-talented Winfrey had been nominated for an Oscar for best supporting actress for her role as Sofia Johnson in the 1985 Steven Spielberg film *The Color Purple*.

Elliott said yes to the invitation, and two weeks later, took Winfrey's studio audience through an abbreviated, lite version of the experiment. To Elliott, the show was a rousing success. "It was terrific!" she would write. "People got angry. They got confused. Some became withdrawn. Some understood. Some didn't understand. Some said it was unfair. Some enjoyed it. Oprah helped. Many learned."[1]

Winfrey evidently agreed, and invited Elliott to appear again four months later, just after her show had gone national and was on the verge of becoming an American institution.[2] Right from the beginning of Show #01144, titled "A Study in Prejudice," when Winfrey faced the cameras, she seemed animated about what was to unfold. "In just a moment, you're going to see a unique learning exercise in prejudice, which has never been attempted on national television before," Winfrey told viewers, barely able to contain her enthusiasm. There was a sense of urgency, even history, in Winfrey's voice.

The freewheeling episode could go awfully wrong. It was a risky career move, more for Winfrey than for Elliott. Winfrey was about to showcase on national television a risky guest who would conduct a live experiment on unsuspecting subjects, based on the polarizing topics of race and racism. It could turn into a disaster—or a bold attempt to harness the power of television for good, as envisioned by the medium's newest superstar. It might turn into both.

Elliott brought her usual grab bag to the studio: hand-drawn posters and a stack of cloth collars, which she instructed Winfrey's audience members with blue, green, or hazel eyes to wear. From the outset, Winfrey and Elliott seemed in sync. No one in the studio audience ostensibly knew that they would become subjects of an experiment about racial prejudice. The TV audience at home was let in on the secret early on, as Winfrey in sotto voce explained backstage what to expect. The setup was reminiscent of *Candid Camera*, the old Allen Funt TV show in which a trick was played on a hapless innocent caught on camera as clued-in viewers at home waited for the gag to unfold.

Wearing a blue sweater vest, a long-sleeve blouse buttoned to her chin, a floppy bow, and oversized gray-framed glasses, Elliott sat on the TV studio stage, facing Winfrey's audience of seventy-five people. Elliott did not project the persona of a kindly third-grade teacher. She looked more like a stern women's prison matron.

"In twenty years as a teacher," Winfrey started out by asking Elliott, "what is the most important thing that you think you've learned?"[3]

The snare had been set.

Elliott scanned the audience from left to right, then replied straight-faced, "The most shocking thing is the inability of blue-eyed people to achieve academically."

This had to be a joke. A dozen audience members tittered nervously. But when neither Elliott nor Winfrey followed with a punch line, apparently it wasn't. No one seemed to know what Elliott had in store for them.

"How many brown-eyed people find that amusing?" Elliott snarled at the almost all-white female audience.

No one answered. They seemed too scared to reply.

A woman in the first row raised her eyebrows. Another woman sitting in the third row grimaced, shifted her shoulders, and rolled her eyes, as though to say, "Well, *this* ought to be interesting!"

Elliott pushed the experiment forward. "One of the things you learn early on is that blue-eyed people aren't as civilized as brown-eyed people. They aren't as smart as brown-eyed people. They aren't as clean as brown-eyed people. Blue-eyed people don't take learning seriously."

Playing along, Winfrey asked Elliott interview-style, "And what do you base this on?"

"I have watched them in the classroom for twenty-five years. I have watched them in major corporations all over the United States for the last year and a half. I have watched the way they behave and I have seen the kinds of things they do and the kinds of attitudes they display." Elliott was dead serious.

Then, skipping a beat, Elliott jumped the shark. "Blue-eyed people are violent," she announced.

Gazing out at the audience, Elliott spotted a pretty, blue-eyed, blond woman in her late twenties, wearing a periwinkle-blue sweater and khaki skirt. The woman seemed giddy about being in the national show's audience. She was beaming.

"This cutesy-pie in the fourth row back," Elliott said, pointing her index finger at the woman. "You get lots of this with blue-eyed females. You get lots of playing the cutesy-pie game. '*See me, I'm cute!*' She has lived her life being *cute*. If you're blue-eyed and female, all you have to be is *cute*. And then when you get on the job, you use your sex to get what you want. If someone comes on to you, you accuse that person of sexual harassment!"

It was a replay of what Elliott had done to Julie Pasicznyk at the US West workshop. Several members of the TV studio audience audibly gasped.

Winfrey nodded and said nothing. Roaming the audience Oprah-style, microphone in hand, Winfrey took a call from a viewer at home, who gleefully said, "I have to agree. I'm a blue-eyed woman and I have two brown-eyed children and one green-eyed child. From the beginning, my brown-eyed children were much smarter, walked earlier, talked earlier. They were faster. I . . . agree with her in the difference between blue-eyed and brown-eyed people."

When the caller volunteered that she herself had blue eyes, she proceeded to apologize. "I'm not an achiever," the caller explained, the verve in her voice dropping. "I have friends who are brown-eyed and they have achieved better than I have."

Winfrey said nothing, but took another call on air, this time from a woman who said, "I'm blue-eyed. And I think this is ridiculous!"

The blue-eyed audience members responded by clapping wholeheartedly, apparently unaware that they were being duped.

"I'm not stupid and I'm very, very clean. I take one or two showers a day," the caller added.

"She probably *needs* one or two showers a day!" Elliott sneered from the studio stage.

What was happening? No one in the TV audience seemed to know.

A third caller weighed in. "I'd like to say, Jane is absolutely right. Blue-eyed, white people are arrogant, think they know everything, got everything, and anything they say goes. That's it. You're right on the money, honey!"

By now, the confusion and discomfort in the audience was palpable. A blue-eyed woman in her early twenties raised her hand and volunteered, "The richest man in the United States has blue eyes," seemingly disputing Elliott's theory about brown-eyed superiority.

"Does that tell you something?" Elliott barked back. "The fact that he is a male is one of the reasons he has the power and one of the reasons he had the wealth. And when you get to be fifty-five, watch and see what that blue-eyed, richest man in the world thinks about you as a female."

Elliott suddenly stopped.

"What do you have in your mouth?" she asked, glowering at a blue-eyed woman in the front row. For an instance, Elliott was back in Classroom No. 10. "You have to watch these blue-eyed people! They're constantly chewing."

Once again, the studio audience shifted uncomfortably.

Winfrey took another call from a woman who said she had green eyes, to which Elliott trumpeted, "a bastardization of the races!"

A green-eyed man in the audience stood up. He was tentative at first, but found his footing and asked Winfrey what this guest was trying to prove by making all these baseless assumptions. Winfrey said nothing, looking toward Elliott for an answer. "I don't have to respond to *him*!" Elliott bellowed, practically spitting.

Winfrey took a deep breath, not knowing what she had hatched, then broke for a commercial.

Back live, a blue-eyed woman in the audience backed the green-eyed man, proclaiming, "People are people. I don't see people as Black, white, or brown. I never categorize people."

The statement seemed just what Elliott had been waiting for. "That person is either blind or stupid," Elliott declared. "I think color is extremely important. The fact that you have to say to yourself, 'I just see people as people' is a racist comment!"

One of the few Black women in the audience rose and motioned to Winfrey, who stuck a microphone under her mouth. "You all seem to forget now that *we* are the superior people in this room! If you do not like what you are hearing, then you can get up and walk out the door! You got that? And if you don't get up and walk out the door, you need to shut up because *we* are in control in this room right now! *We* got nothing to listen to from you. So, shut up, sit down, be good little boys and girls!"

The woman's manifesto sounded as though it had been spun from *Network*, the 1976 Paddy Chayefsky/Sidney Lumet film that begot the rant, "I'm as mad as hell and I'm not going to take this anymore!"[4] Winfrey didn't know how to react. She rolled her brown eyes and went to another commercial break.

Back in the studio, it was time. Winfrey asked Elliott to come clean.

"Look," Elliott said, softening just a bit, "the amount of melanin in your eyes does not make you a better or a worse person any more than the amount of melanin in your skin. What we did here this morning is totally irrational. It is an experience in racism. You can pick out a group of people. You give them characteristics. You can make them behave the way you expect them to. And then when they live down to your expectations, you can say, 'See, I told you so. You're just as dumb as I told you they were.' We have done it with Blacks, females, Indians, the handicapped. You can do it very easily. You can change people from what they really feel and into what you want them to be within fifteen minutes. All it takes in this country is to have the majority-group people reinforced for behaving like racists. It's happened before in this country and it will happen again."

Winfrey responded by taking another call on air, this time from a woman who said her blue-eyed son was much more mature and smarter than her brown-eyed daughter. "I think this lady's a quack," the caller proclaimed.

Some people out in TV Land had been taking Elliott seriously.

Indeed, Oprah's show with Elliott could have turned into a disaster of monumental proportion, akin to Orson Welles's 1938 radio broadcast of *War of the Worlds*.[5] Tens of thousands of viewers might have come away believing that what Elliott had said about eye color was true. That brown-eyed people *are* smarter and more civilized than blue-eyed people. They had heard it on TV, so it had to be true.

Winfrey looked alarmed, sensing a catastrophe in the making.

"Caller, did you hear what we said earlier? This. Is. An. Exercise, caller! Everything we've said for the past thirty-five minutes is *not* true! Blue-eyed people are *not* inferior to brown-eyed people!

"Did you *get* that?"

The caller squeaked a response.

Shaken, Winfrey cautiously threw the show over to Elliott for the payoff. "People want power. And they'll do whatever they can to get power and to hold power. *That's what racism is about, people*! There is nothing wrong with having blue eyes. There is nothing wrong with having brown eyes. There's nothing wrong with being Black. We do not have a Black problem in this country, folks. The problem is your reaction to Black. The problem is your reaction to people's differences. The problem lies not in the person who is different."

As Elliott began to wind down, members of the studio audience fully realized they'd been punked. What's more, Winfrey had allowed shills into the audience to help.

The angry woman who had laid down the Black Power screed got up once again, and announced that she was a hired actress. "It felt good because she [Elliott] told us to make them feel uncomfortable," the woman said, now giggling to the audience.

Winfrey confessed that when her staff had canvassed for audience members for the show, they had sought viewers who were new to Chicago since she didn't want people who might have seen the earlier program when Elliott had appeared and tried the experiment locally for the first time. That would have blown Elliott's cover.

As the show's credits rolled, the episode wrapped on an "all's well that ends well" note, with Elliott's closing: "We have lived in the land of epidermis too long in this country."

Over and out.

Elliott was to appear on *The Oprah Winfrey Show* three more times over the next six years. The trio of appearances tracks a smooth, then strained, then rocky relationship between Winfrey and Elliott, ultimately leading to a split between the two. Elliott's bluster and Winfrey's mission of racial equality seemingly mushroomed to a level where the two clashed to a point of no return.

Elliott's next appearance, on June 16, 1992, wasn't to try out the experiment again, but to deliver an excoriating rebuke to three white parents whose children were dating nonwhites and who admitted on air that the dislike of their children's partners was based solely on ethnicity.

As Elliott saw her role that day, she was to act as a surrogate for Winfrey. "'Oprah's a Black female,'" Elliott remembered one of the show's producers telling her backstage before she was to go on. "'*She* can't say those things. It will look like she's pushing her own agenda. But *you* can.'"

As Elliott recalled, the producer took out a sketch pad, and with a marker, wrote Elliott's name, circled it, and drew an arrow from the show's first quarter to the end.

"Say whatever you have to," the producer instructed Elliott, understanding her to be giving Elliott permission to say anything she wanted on the show.

"How much control is Oprah willing to give up?" Elliott recalled asking.

"Don't worry about that. Oprah wants this to happen. You go to it!"[6]

Elliott came out twenty-three minutes into the hour-long show, and it would be a performance few viewers would forget. From the moment she took to the studio stage, Elliott eliminated all discussion. She launched into a monologue, taking over for Winfrey and the other guests. She refused to allow Winfrey to get a word in edgewise. Elliott had effectively gagged Winfrey, the monarch of talk shows. One indelible shot showed Winfrey staring at Elliott, her eyes wide and her mouth agape, before the camera cut away.

When Ron, a white father who objected to his daughter dating a Hispanic man, tried to explain himself, Elliott raised her hand and proclaimed, "White males aren't accustomed to listening, so *you* listen!"

Among the items that Elliott brought onstage in her grab bag this time was a Mercator projection map, the US-centric world map that has hung in American classrooms for a century. Elliott pointed to the map, precariously propped on a three-legged easel, and declared it to be "a flat-out lie, people. This is a visual image that teaches a lie." She said that teachers ought to use a more geographically realistic map, the Peters projection map, which she then displayed as though she was lecturing to her third graders at Riceville Elementary.[7]

Elliott covered a multitude of topics in a meandering monologue, which included prostate and cervical cancer, love, ageism, condoms, justice, violence, and "flesh-colored" Band-Aids, crayons, and pantyhose. She talked about threats to her life, curing racism ("If you can learn it, you can *un*learn it!"), and the human race's common genealogy ("You all have the same great, great, great, great, great, great, great grandparent back there 280,000 years ago, and she was a Black female!"). None of what Elliott said addressed the topic at hand—white parents angry that their kids were dating outside their races or ethnicities. Of course, in a larger sense, it did. But the audience didn't seem to make the connection and most appeared to be scratching their heads.

For her next appearance on *Oprah*, Elliott reprised the experiment. It did not go over as expected. Winfrey had on her hands a full-fledged revolt.

Several audience members ripped off the collars Elliott had directed them to wear and stormed out of the studio.

Elliott changed several features of the experiment this time. Earlier in the day, with cameras trailing her, Elliott had invited brown-eyed audience members to go upstairs in Winfrey's studio building, while the blue-eyed audience members were instructed to remain downstairs, where Elliott declared all blue-eyed studio guests must pin the cloth collars around their necks.

"And what if I don't wear it?" one blue-eyed man asked.

"And what if we put you out of the building?" Elliott replied.

The man shrugged and put the collar on. Others got up and left.

Cameras followed Elliott walking upstairs, where the brown-eyed audience members were lounging in comfortable chairs, sipping coffee, and munching on donuts. One brown-eyed woman asked why her blue-eyed friend hadn't been allowed to join.

Elliott showed no patience for either her or the question. "You're outta here!" she exploded. "Go be a bluey!"

Per Elliott's setup, the blue-eyed audience members were crowded into an interior hallway while the brown-eyed guests enjoyed first-class treatment. Out of earshot of the blue-eyed guests, Elliott filled the brown-eyed audience members in on what was about to happen and asked that they play along. She then paraded them past the blue-eyed women and men, standing in the hallway, to the TV studio. As prompted by Elliott, the brown-eyed audience members had big, wide smiles; some exchanged high-fives as the blues hooted at this in-their-face display of brown-eyed privilege.

Elliott led the brown-eyed guests to the best seats. Once all were seated, their blue-eyed, collar-wearing counterparts were directed to side-view, inferior chairs. By now, several more had removed their collars. One blue-eyed man said, "We don't have to put up with this," and marched out of the studio.

Winfrey appeared backstage and clued in the home audience. "This show is a very important lesson in racism," she said, lowering her voice for dramatic effect. "It may make you angry. But no matter how angry you get, I encourage you to please don't turn the channel because its purpose will be revealed before the show is over. The idea is to see how easy it is to be taught to hate. What color eyes do you have? It really doesn't matter. Just as it doesn't matter what color skin you have. But I want you to watch as my guest convinces this audience that blue-eyed people are not as smart as brown-eyed people, just as a lot of Americans have been convinced that people of color are not as smart."

Winfrey then introduced Elliott to the studio audience, and instantly, those who were wearing collars booed in unison.

A blue-eyed woman stood up. "She was rude! She called us names!"

A blue-eyed man said, "She told me to shut my mouth when I was in line. She said, 'Close your mouth. Shut up!'"

"'You put that green collar on or you're outta here!'" a blue-eyed woman said Elliott had told her.

Just in the nick of time, a man rose and announced, "You people, look. I had a girlfriend in school who was blue-eyed. She was so stupid, she always was copying off of my papers. These people were so rude and so noisy today, we couldn't hear ourselves talk. It was ridiculous!"

This caused even more consternation, which Elliott fanned by saying, "If you don't like it here, why don't you go back where you came from," pointing to those sitting in the side seats in the audience.

At which point, this subscript appeared at the bottom of the TV screen for viewers at home:

Jane Elliott

Teaches race relations

When Winfrey pointedly asked a blue-eyed man wearing a collar why he was sitting on the floor, Elliott shot in, "He was told to sit there because these people multiply like flies."

That was followed by someone from the studio audience shouting to Elliott, "What color are *your* eyes?"

"My eyes are blue. That's the reason I know what *you* people are like!"

Just before a commercial break, Winfrey whispered from offstage to the at-home audience, "Remember this is just an exercise in racism. You know what the studio audience doesn't. But as you watch, don't let yourself be fooled."

In case they hadn't gotten the message, Winfrey repeated it when the show resumed. "Remember, this audience doesn't know that they are part of an exercise on racism. My guest has told them that blue-eyed people aren't as smart as brown-eyed people, and amazingly, as you're seeing, some of the people are starting to believe her. We all know eye color has nothing to do with intelligence, just as skin color does not make a group of people superior or inferior. That's the point."

Back in the studio as cameras rolled, Winfrey fired up Elliott by reminding her that several blue-eyed audience members had removed their collars.

"I want 'em out of here!" Elliott roared. "The rule in this room is you wear the collar or you leave. In this society, the rule is, 'Do it the white way or get out!' If this is going to be real, Oprah, they need to put their collars on or leave!"

Once again a superscript warning for home viewers flashed on the bottom of the screen:

This is an exercise in racism

A shill in the audience stood up. "I have a blue-eyed daughter and people look at her and they say to me, 'She's beautiful, but she has blue eyes.' Those big blue eyes. She's ostracized because of those blue eyes. I mean she stands out."

Enough.

A woman wearing a collar, who said she was a retired teacher, couldn't stand the performance any longer. She said for thirty-six years she had taught her students lessons in "kindness and understanding."

Before she could finish, a Black man interrupted her. "Does that mean that you will let me date your daughter because I have brown eyes?"

Elliott took the back-and-forth as her cue. "People of color have been on earth longer than white people have. That's a fact! You need to be aware of that! You need to be careful about mixing the races as far as eye color goes!"

Again the message on the screen flashed:

This is an exercise in racism

"You blue-eyed people are this angry over an hour of discomfort," Elliott growled to the audience. "Now, that should tell you something!"

Another woman wearing a collar rose. "We're angry about the attitude. The anger isn't deep-seated. It was because of *her* attitude and the attitude of the staff building up a prejudice," she said, pointing to Elliott.

"You know nothing about my attitude!" Elliott shot back.

This was turning ugly. Winfrey needed to step in. Just before the next commercial break, she whispered to home viewers, "Okay, here's the part you've all been waiting for. When you come back, we're going to tell this audience that they are a part of an exercise on racism. We'll see how they react."

As though they hadn't figured that out yet.

"When you walk into a store as a Black man and everyone starts to clutch their purses because you come in the store, you don't know it until you feel it," Winfrey started. "So that's why we put the collars on you. We apologize for doing it to you under these circumstances. But do you feel it?"

Elliott added: "If a Black male refused to follow your orders, or your husband's orders, or your father's orders on the street, you wouldn't see that as being highly principled. You would see that as being an uppity nigger. You wouldn't even want him to go through your neighborhood at a certain time of night because of the color of his skin. I know what this is like."

Those in the audience might have bought some of the tutorial, but by now they had heard enough.

A blue-eyed woman in a red polka-dot dress pointed at Elliott and nearly in tears said, "I'm totally appalled. I don't want you to sit there and judge me or my friends if I'm not that way. Don't *you* tell *me* that I'm that way!"

The audience erupted in applause.

The spotlight now shifted to Elliott, as she explained herself with sharp, rapid-fire accusations. "We good white folks have talked about eliminating racism in this country for one hundred years, but we haven't done it. Make no mistake about it. Change your behaviors. Change the words you say. Change the things you think. You are in charge of what you think and of what you do. If you think we aren't all racists, you are mistaken. In this country, if you are white, born, raised, and schooled in the United States of America, you were born, schooled, and raised to be a racist. That's what education in this country does."

Winfrey chimed in by asking a blue-eyed man in the audience why he had removed his collar. "I revolted against this whole experiment. I felt the frustration. My mother and father taught me to be totally tolerant." As a retired teacher, he said, "I treated all my students alike."

Elliott couldn't let this self-congratulatory riff go uncontested. "How many of you believe he treated all students alike?"

The audience responded in thunderous applause. Winfrey broke for a commercial.

After the break, Winfrey announced that more members of her audience had gotten up and walked out. "They were so pissed off. They couldn't stand it any longer," she said, punting to Elliott.

This is a new reality for us white people. White people do not live in the same reality as people of color do. We think because we have all these freedoms, everybody else has them, too. That isn't the way it is, people!

There is no place to go in this country where there isn't racism. How many of you women, when you get tired of sexist behaviors directed at you, can leave? None of you. Because there's no place in this country where there isn't sexism. How many of you know a gay or a lesbian person who is real tired of the treatment we're giving them? People, we've lost 150,000 people to AIDS in this country. Now think about that. People who are gay are being blamed for AIDS. We're calling AIDS a gay disease. And we're letting people die of it because we don't approve of their sexual orientation. If it can happen to gays today, and it is, it can happen to so-called heteros tomorrow. It can happen to blondes tomorrow.

Back from the break, the audience could not bear to hear more. It wasn't Elliott's message; most in the audience seemed to agree. It was Elliott's rage.

A blue-eyed woman stood and said, "That, that . . . woman," pointing toward Elliott. "I'm grateful you're not teaching any longer and you're doing talk shows because I would hate to have my child being taught by someone so angry as you are."

Another woman: "The experiment's over and you haven't even cracked. You are just a hostile person!"

Elliott seemed unfazed. "Neither of these women is telling the truth. That's what racism does to you. It makes you tell things and interpret things in ways that didn't happen."

A man stood up: "I'll never know what it's like to be Black. And you'll never know what it's like to be white," he said, nodding at Winfrey. "But all we can do is *try* to understand each other. But it sounds like she's [pointing to Elliott] saying she already knows what everyone feels."

Everyone looked toward Winfrey, mostly, it seemed, because by this time they couldn't stand the sight of Elliott. "The exercise was meant to show what racism feels like," Winfrey said. "It was not a personal attack on anybody. Jane does not feel personally any of the things that she has said about blue-eyed people. Do you all 'get' that?"

Seemingly exhausted, Winfrey pointed to Elliott for a final word.

"I'm not prejudiced. Some of my best friends are blue-eyed."

If that was a joke, no one laughed.

"In the Torah, it says, 'It is not your responsibility to finish the task, but neither is it your right not to take it up.' We have a problem. You can learn about the problem by experiencing it for a few minutes."

Everyone exhaled together.

Elliott would later say about the program, "A number of people left that show absolutely furious and frustrated and puzzled and full of resentment.

Even after Oprah apologized to them for what we'd put them through. Even after we'd explained that it was an exercise, that it wasn't real, that it was temporary, that I didn't really feel that way about blue-eyed people. I was amazed, once again, at the inability of white folks to cope for an hour with a tiny taste of what people of color live with every day in this country."[8]

Elliott was to appear on the renamed show *Oprah* one last time, in December 1993, on a program about the hurtful language of racism. She was one of six guests who were asked about what white people should and should not say to people of color.

Introducing Elliott as one of the most provocative visitors to the show, Winfrey said, "She's always irritated with us for one reason or the other. Jane Elliott is one of the most controversial and outspoken guests to ever sit on our panel." Nodding to Elliott, Winfrey added, "You hold the record for the most hate mail ever on *The Oprah Show* every time you're here . . . so try to keep the record down today."

The discussion opened with the use of derisive labels. "'Nigger' is not okay," said one of Winfrey's panelists, speaking largely to an audience of whites, although two other guests onstage debated whether among Blacks the term was appropriate. Elliott ignored the thread and took control.

"You people aren't listening! You are not listening! Gimme a break! What you're really saying is, 'If you just get white, you'll be all right.' I'm sick to death of hearing, 'Let's have a color-blind society.' I'm really offended by hearing people say, 'When does it stop?' It's gonna stop when white folks decide to stop it!"

By the end of the show, Elliott may have undercut Winfrey one too many times. According to June Judge, who has known Elliott for half a century and talked with her about the show several years later, here's what happened at the conclusion of the 1993 program.

"Jane told us that she had really offended Oprah. And we all asked, 'What did you do?'

"Jane said that Oprah had turned to her and asked, 'Do you think we have come any farther in race relations since your first program?'

"And Jane answered, 'You shouldn't ask me! Number one, because I'm not Black. And number two, look around at your staff,' which was mostly white.

"Oprah gave Jane a dagger look. She wasn't happy at all with that answer. And that was that."[9]

At least, that was Elliott's take on why she was never asked to appear on Winfrey's show again, according to Judge.

Gemma Bauer, *The Oprah Show*'s spokesperson, dodged the issue when asked whether there had been a rift between Winfrey and Elliott. "As this appearance was over twenty-five years ago, we are not able to confirm any further details," Bauer declared. Then, in a pro forma wrap-up, she added, "The 'blue eye/brown eye' episode was an important show for Ms. Winfrey, and she considers this exercise as one of the top moments of the 'Oprah show.'"[10]

TWENTY-TWO

The Greater Good

FROM THE MOMENT ELLIOTT INTRODUCED the nation to the blue-eyes, brown-eyes experiment on *The Tonight Show* in 1968, teachers searching for innovative ways to introduce the thorny issues of race and prejudice into their class curricula started writing and calling her. What Elliott said had resonated with hundreds of thousands of viewers. Interest accelerated with the arrival of more and more media attention, which in turn carried notice of the experiment in Classroom No. 10 to many places, including America's universities and colleges. Soon, word of the experiment spread to administrators, as well as to professors of psychology and education. The experiment struck a resonant chord during the nation's urban unrest, along with the advent of social-psychology experimentation, particularly popular in the 1970s and 1980s.

The groundbreaking textbook *Prejudice and Racism*, written by James M. Jones and published in 1972, used by legions of college students, made mention of Elliott and the experiment.[1] Similarly, Stanford psychologist Philip G. Zimbardo praised Elliott in his 1975 seminal college textbook, *Psychology and Life*.[2] Media coverage of Elliott often quoted the nation's most famous child psychiatrist, Robert Coles, proclaiming that the experiment was "the greatest thing to come out of American education in a hundred years."[3]

Elliott was profiled by practically every major television journalist of the era, including Ted Koppel, Dan Rather, and Peter Jennings, who called her "one tough cookie" while citing Elliott as ABC News's "Person of the Week."[4] National Public Radio (NPR) did a lengthy profile on her in 2001.[5]

While Elliott has undoubtedly been a crusader for racial equality, whether the experiment she promulgated has made any appreciable dent in reducing racism is uncertain. There's no evidence to show that Elliott's techniques have made any impact in decreasing prejudice among participants. The only sure result of the experiment is that it gets people angry.

In 2003, Tracie Stewart, a social psychologist at Kennesaw State University in Atlanta, was the lead author in a study to gauge the efficacy of the blue-eyes, brown-eyes experiment.[6] Stewart used as her test case a workshop that Elliott conducted in 2000 with students at Bard College, a small, private undergraduate institution in Annandale-on-Hudson, in New York State. So as not to skew their findings, Stewart and her coinvestigators looked for Bard students who hadn't heard of the experiment or of Elliott. Once accepted into the workshop, participants signed informed consent forms: "You should be aware that the learning exercise may be a difficult experience for some. Participants will take part in group discussions during which they may be exposed to harsh comments and uncomfortable conditions. . . . If you have a medical condition that might be aggravated by stressful situations or feel that you should avoid stressful situations at the present time, do not sign up for this project."[7]

Elliott conducted the experiment, which started early on a Saturday morning and lasted eight hours. She followed her routine, sorting forty-seven participants into a blue-eyed (and green- and hazel-eyed) group and a brown-eyed cohort. The blues were crowded into a small, stuffy room with half the number of chairs as people, while the browns were served a full breakfast in a comfortable setting. Per her drill, Elliott prompted the brown-eyed participants to act rudely toward the other group when the two sections convened. She also gave the brown-eyed students answers to an IQ test she would administer to both groups later that day.

When the two groups merged, Elliott had the blue-eyed students, wearing collars, sit in the middle of the room while the brown-eyed group sat on either side as though they were observing the "inferior" group. She proceeded to criticize the blues. She had them stand one at a time and read derogatory passages denigrating blue-eyed people. She scolded their performances. When the browns outscored the blues on the fake IQ test, Elliott amped up her scorn of the blues. She picked a blue-eyed, blond woman for ridicule, announcing to everyone that she wasn't a natural blonde and likely dyed her hair. To another woman, Elliott commented about her "cute butt" and "bedroom voice." All the while, she encouraged the brown-eyed students to join in on the hectoring. The insults got so intense that two blue-eyed students started to cry. One got up and left.

The two groups broke for lunch, returned to debrief, watched the 1970 ABC video "Eye of the Storm," and ate hors d'oeuvres together in the late afternoon and then left, the experiment officially over. During the next four to six weeks, both groups were assessed by Stewart and her colleagues to see if the experiment had made any impact on their self-awareness of prejudice and racism.

The results were decidedly mixed.[8] The responses from the students mirrored what participants in the US West pluralism workshops in the 1980s had said. They noted a multitude of insults and pain shared by the participants, but minimal change in attitude. Among the student reactions:

- As a Blue Eyes, I was uncomfortable and on edge. I found myself easily angered by anything Jane Elliott said. I felt frustrated and helpless to stop her charade (she was good at her job).

- I feel some of it was unethical, however, there were so many positive responses I can only believe that the positive outweighs the negatives. . . . I've had a few nightmares, but this is typical . . .

- Makes people upset; doesn't change much; too negative for me.

- I felt emotionally LOW after the experiment [exercise]. I wanted to try to forget some of the things that were said or done on the day of the experiment, but I guess that's what made it so effective.

Stewart's thoughts today about the experiment are "proceed with caution." She said that the experiment may have a positive impact on reducing negative racial attitudes "in the short term," but any long-term benefits are negligible. Stewart no longer shows videos of Elliott in her undergraduate psychology classes because "there tends to be a greater focus on JE [Jane Elliott] herself than the issue of institutional racism."[9]

A larger, systematic review, published in 2009, that assessed the effectiveness of scores of anti-bias workshops and experiments summarily suggested that further study was needed. "We conclude that the casual effects of many widespread prejudice-reduction interventions, such as workplace diversity training and media campaigns, remain unknown. Although some intergroup contact and cooperation interventions appear promising, a much more rigorous and broad-ranging empirical assessment of prejudice-reduction strategies is needed to determine what works."[10] In other words, the social scientists weren't able to say that any crash course to modify racial prejudice works.

That hasn't stopped such experiments from mushrooming. In the wake of Elliott's debut, blue-eyes, brown-eyes experimentation spread in America's classrooms. Tens of thousands of schoolteachers had learned about the experiment in college classes, through Elliott's own presentations (she created a popular touring lecture series called the "Anatomy of Prejudice" in the 1990s), the popular media, and Zimbardo's classic textbook. Once in their own classrooms, teachers across the nation tried out their own variations. There's no way to know how many imported the experiment, in which states, with what directives, and how many students were affected, but it seems reasonable to estimate that thousands of teachers tried out the experiment in some iteration, and hundreds of thousands of students have been part of it. The experiment was too quirky, easy to try, and inviting to pass up during the dawning of an era when teaching cultural competency in the classroom would become mandatory.

In 1970, one elementary school teacher especially taken by the experiment was an idealistic, thirty-one-year-old educator by the name of Phyllis Watts, who had recently been hired to teach third grade at a private school in Brooklyn, New York, named Saint Ann's. Watts was an imaginative and innovative teacher in the same mold as Elliott. She sought to involve her students with nearly anything that pushed them to think creatively. She worked to bring the world to her classroom on the seventh floor of the southeast corner of Saint Ann's building on Pierrepont Street, just as Elliott was doing in Classroom No. 10, a thousand miles away. Like Elliott, Watts had a mascot that lived in the classroom's science station. Watts's was a lizard named Fred.

Bright and energetic, Watts had graduated Phi Beta Kappa from Radcliffe College, studying history and literature. She continued her studies at Brown University and received a master's degree in American Studies from New York University. She taught at Saint Ann's from 1970 to 1972.[11]

Saint Ann's was as different from Riceville Elementary as Brooklyn was from Riceville. Founded in the vestry of an Episcopal church, it was a nonsectarian K–12 school that became one the most progressive private schools on the East Coast, perhaps in the nation. Teachers didn't give students letter grades. Saint Ann's offered classes in puppetry, kite-making, and printmaking. From the beginning, Saint Ann's prided itself on being an unconventional arts-and-humanities gateway to elite East Coast private colleges and universities. Its roster of alumni today includes actors Lena Dunham, Jennifer Connelly, and Paz de la Huerta, fashion designer Zac Posen, and writer Sasha Frere-Jones. In a profile of its founder and director for thirty-nine years, Stanley Bosworth, *New York* magazine wrote, "Stanley used to tell people that he planned to turn out 10 percent of the nation's poets at his school."[12]

Saint Ann's was the perfect incubator for the blue-eyes, brown-eyes experiment. "'Find out where they are and take them as far as they can go,' were Stanley's words to me," recalled Phyllis. Watts (Watts subsequently got married and today goes by Aldrich). "He gave me complete trust and carte blanche."

Watts tried out the experiment in her third-grade classroom during the 1970–71 school year, just before the Christmas break. "I stumbled on an education article in some magazine and read a description of this experiment, and I thought, 'Here we are at the end of the sixties and terrible upheavals and great injustices . . . and Saint Ann's gave teachers a lot of their own discretion to challenge the kids.' I read the article and said to myself, 'Well, this is important.' I didn't even know her [Elliott's] name. One day, I think I told the kids, 'We're going to try something today. We're going to have a little experiment to start out with. It'll be different, and at the end of the day, we'll talk about it and see what happened.'"[13]

As Watts remembered, she arbitrarily divided her class of twenty-one students. She didn't use armbands or collars to denote the two ranks of children. She recalled that she didn't opt to separate students by eye color. "I didn't want kids to go home, peering into a mirror at their eyes and wondering," she said.

Instead, she created felt badges in the shape of fruits or vegetables that the children would wear on their chests. "I had apples for the privileged kids and zucchinis for the inferior kids. I wanted to use a vegetable that all the kids hated. The apples were bright and cheerful; the zucchinis were a dark and drab gray or brown piece of fabric."

The privileged children wearing the apple badges would have more time at the classroom's science center. They'd be the first to choose books for in-class reading. They could pick a partner to go to the bathroom with. In art class, they got first dibs on the color and type of construction paper they'd use for projects.

As soon as the experiment started, Watts noticed an immediate and unmistakable change in the children. "Some kids were swaggering, nudging someone else out of line. 'I have the apple badge. You're lesser! You gotta wait! That's the rules of this thing!' There was shoving. 'Hey, you better move out of the way. I'm first in this line and you've gotta go in the back! There were taunts, 'You're just a zucchini!'"

Watts was struck by how fully the children took to their new social status. "They role-played with their whole selves. What amazed me was how quickly these groups could form. How those in the same groups would associate only with each other. They took their assignment absolutely seriously. It reminded me of *Lord of the Flies*."[14]

After lunch, the children traded badges. "And they didn't hand over power easily," Watts recalled. "They didn't want to give up being first in line or first to get the new construction paper." By the end of the day, all the students had experienced being members of both groups. "In the afternoon we talked for a good hour. 'How did you feel?' 'How do you think Betty felt when you said this to her?' 'Betty, how did you feel when Jacques did this to you?' We had a really long conversation." It was Watts's version of Elliott's Magic Circle.

Watts never met or talked to Jane Elliott, but she found the experiment a useful way for her students to begin thinking about larger issues such as civil rights and racism. Unlike Elliott, she didn't talk about genetic inferiority as the supposed basis of the experiment "because I didn't know enough about it, and I didn't want to lie to them."

Watts taught at Saint Ann's for one more year, repeated the experiment, and then left the school. For her, the experiment "was very, very powerful," but she never tried it again.

Little did Watts know the profound and lifelong impact the experiment would have on at least one student in the class. To Kate Gladstone, the power that Watts gave half of the students and withheld from the other half was *real*. That skewed sense of inferiority and superiority has stayed with Gladstone for more than fifty years.

Gladstone was in Watts's class in 1970. She was a new transfer student to Saint Ann's and not quite eight years old. The way Gladstone, today fifty-eight, remembers the experiment is at dramatic odds with how Phyllis Watts recalls it, but that may be because for Gladstone, the experiment was an exercise in terror that has never left her. Gladstone recalls the experiment lasting as long as two weeks, not a single day, but this also may be due to the lasting trauma she said she believes it caused her.[15]

Gladstone has brown eyes, and as she remembers the experiment, Watts *did* separate students by the color of their eyes. Gladstone said there were no felt badges of apples and zucchinis, and all distinctions between the two student groups were based on eye color. Gladstone vividly recalls that each student had a chart placed in the front of the classroom, listing height, eye color, number of siblings. The way Gladstone recollects the experiment was that Watts encouraged children in the superior group to mock the inferior-student group. "The brown-eyed kids had to wait to go to recess or to the water fountain. The brown-eyed kids were served last at lunch. They were ridiculed if they got an answer wrong. Even if they got an answer right, a brown-eyed person couldn't possibly do anything right, and a blue-eyed person couldn't do anything wrong."[16]

Watts eventually reversed the roles, but for Gladstone, that reversal never registered. "During my entire time at the school until the ninth grade, people would pass me on the stairs and tease, '*Brown Eyes!*' or, '*Stupid Brown Eyes!*' Those two weeks of school reinforced for everyone the lesson that Karen [the name she used at the time] Gladstone was fair game." The taunting was exacerbated since Gladstone was a new student at a clubby private school where peer relationships had already been solidified.

"For me, the experiment never ended. You might say, 'Get over it!' But you wouldn't tell someone with an amputated arm, 'Get over it! Your arm ought to have grown back by now!' If the consequences are real, they're real. How do you expect this *not* to have an effect on such a young child? Some therapists have told me that I ought to have accepted that the experiment was based on the greater good it created, that it didn't matter what happened to one individual as long as the entire group was strengthened and comforted."

Gladstone volunteered that she was subsequently diagnosed with Asperger's syndrome and later with autism, diagnoses few clinicians were fully aware of when Gladstone was a child. She said the experiment was executed without regard to students' individual circumstances or any lasting harm it might cause. Certainly, Gladstone's teacher, Phyllis Watts, had no idea how the experiment might affect her. As Gladstone put it,

> With people with autism, when you teach them something, it sticks with them for life, true or false. If you teach a kid with autism that dinosaurs walk the earth, he's going to believe that dinosaurs walk the earth for the rest of his life. So, here I was for a solid week, a teacher teaching me that I was inferior and blue-eyed people get to run my life, and that blue-eyed people could do whatever it took to keep me a pariah. I was taught that that was right. For a kid on the spectrum who believes that, it has a lasting effect, and it was horrible.
>
> You can't say, "We'll sacrifice one child so that the show can go on, so that the greater number can benefit." But having a group benefit over the individual is as racist as anything that the experiment is supposed to stamp out. Nobody ought to be thrown under the bus. Unlike my classmates, I did not end up loving and believing in affirmative action. I was mangled by it. I can't have been the only one.

Gladstone, who today teaches calligraphy, reflected, "I *still* get nervous when I'm around people with blue eyes, even though I know it's not rational."

Kate Gladstone's mother, Renee, recalled that her daughter had a terrible time in the class. "It really did affect her for a very long time. It's only been in her later adult years that she seems to be able to cope better. She really has been through a lot of pain. I tried to slough off the things that bothered her, saying you're dramatizing it or you're making too much of it. I don't think I fully understood the effect that the experiment had on her. But it did seem to affect her in a very profound way. She fell apart."[17]

As for her daughter's autism-spectrum diagnoses, Renee Gladstone said, "Kate is very literal. She doesn't always see nuances. She takes everything word for word."

Renee Gladstone doesn't blame Phyllis Watts. "I believe that the teacher was following an experiment that was in vogue at the time. But I know that Kate felt it was a personal attack on her, and that everyone in the class was turning against her. She didn't have any social clues. She had no mechanisms to cope with it."

Jay McGovern, who had Elliott as a teacher in both third and seventh grades, is today a teacher himself, and he too cited problems with what Elliott did in Classroom No. 10. "The way she did it, she put people down," said McGovern, who teaches special education and is the wrestling coach at Lee's Summit High School, a suburb of Kansas City, Missouri. "Today, you don't ridicule or berate people to try to make your point. Back in the sixties, there wasn't that body of research."[18] McGovern said he believes the experiment to be destructive, benefiting few and ultimately empowering one person, the teacher. "I find it ironic that she sent kids home crying. If my daughter came home crying and said her teacher ridiculed her, I'd be angry. That's not what school is for, no matter how important the teacher thinks the exercise is."

McGovern said he sees the damage that the experiment could cause, especially among children at such an impressionable age. "Third grade is the last grade kids really want to go to school. They love it. It's a critical time. I wouldn't want someone putting that kind of stress on kids."

As for her methods, McGovern said, "She did a lot of things for show. She was antagonistic. She was saying, 'I know the way, follow me.' Everyone had to taste the tea. [As a teacher] you have to build. She was more interested in tearing down. When someone has a problem, you all pitch in. But Jane never collaborated."

Today, teachers still readily employ the blue-eyes, brown-eyes experiment throughout the United States, as well as globally. For many, it is an inspired and clever way to introduce the concept of discrimination and race to youngsters.

At Iliff Preschool and Kindergarten, a private school in Denver, since 2009 kindergarten teacher Mary Weberg has used a version of the experiment for five- and six-year-olds.[19] During a weeklong unit on Martin Luther King Jr., Weberg devotes one morning to the experiment. In addition to activities noting brown and white eggs, and mixing paint colors to match students' skin tones, Weberg then splits her students according to their eye color and goes through a "lite" iteration of the experiment.[20]

She vaguely recalls learning about Elliott's work while earning a degree in elementary education at the University of Illinois between 1977 and 1981, but has never met Elliott. Like other teachers who have tried out the experiment, Weberg notes, "how fast they [the students] adapt to the idea, but how long it stays with them after we're done isn't clear. A trusted adult tells them, 'This is how it will be' and these children take on a role and it becomes a truth for them."[21]

As happened with Kate Gladstone, some of Weberg's students don't realize when the experiment is over. "Many continue to take sides based on eye color. Their good friend is now the 'bad person,' the inferior, the lesser, the unequal. It's scary." Weberg said there have been students who "become incredibly outraged—the child who cries so hard at the table that he is unable to talk to me, or the child who knows what is going on and tries desperately to get her friends to 'stop playing the game.'"

As for its utility, Weberg said, "I believe that having feelings of sadness, unfairness, and anger is part of life. Teaching them that those feelings are valid is just as fair as teaching them that happiness and safety are valid. They will let me know through their words and actions if they are feeling unsafe or threatened."

Weberg's desire to promote diversity and equality among such young children is shared by other educators intent on introducing difficult historical topics to their students. No national standards exist on how exactly to address the horrors of slavery in a school setting, but there are myriad examples of ostensibly well-meaning teachers separating their students and making half the class "slaves" for a day, then switching those roles, so the other half gets the same experience the next day. The substance of such an experiment isn't substantively different from what Elliott did in Classroom No. 10 in Riceville.

Such "gaming" experiments can go beyond the pale. "Lessons designed to separate children on the basis of race have no place in New York classrooms, or in classrooms throughout this country," said New York Attorney General

Letitia James, whose office in 2019 conducted an investigation of so-called mock "slave auctions" taking place in New York City schools.

"It's never OK to recreate painful oppressive events, even in the name of education," Mara Sapon-Shevin, a professor at Syracuse University, told the Associated Press at the time, adding that teachers risk harming their students' sense of belonging, safety, and inclusion with such activities. "One would never simulate an Indian massacre or having Jews march into the ovens."[22]

For Tammy Bill Loecher, who was a student in Elliott's 1970 class, featured in the television documentary "Eye of the Storm," the experiment also left a lasting impact. Loecher, from a farming family of seven sisters and seven brothers, is still pained when talking about Elliott or the experiment, so much so, that, like many others interviewed, she avoids mentioning Elliott by name more than a half century after she left third grade.

"I think it was awful what she did to us," recalled Loecher, who maintains that Elliott used Riceville students as a "stepping-stone" to build a national reputation. Loecher said Elliott "still doesn't think she's done anything wrong. She didn't care how it affected us at all."[23]

Another approach today might be one of kindness and compassion instead of insult and shock, as described by Beverly Daniel Tatum in *"Why Are All the Black Kids Sitting Together in the Cafeteria" and Other Conversations about Race*. Detailing a discussion in which participants of different races talked about vexing racial issues, Tatum recalled one teacher telling her, "'It was such a rich conversation and it just flowed the whole time. It was exciting to be a part of it. Everyone contributed and everybody felt the energy and the desire.'"[24] While not as dramatic, such a method may be a newer, more compassionate way to look at healing the racial divide. Instead of an inoculation, it's an empathetic exchange of personal emotion, detailing how each person feels.

In 2009, Elliott took the experiment to Great Britain, where she performed it for a television documentary called *The Event* in London. There, the thirty participants were adults. Following her script, Elliott threw profanity-laced insults at the collared "inferior" group of blue-eyed participants. As during the experiment's last iteration on *The Oprah Show*, the experiment imploded. Many of the UK participants refused to tolerate Elliott's bullying, and walked out.[25]

The show hired two psychologists to stand in the wings during the experiment in case anyone needed intervention, as well as to provide a sports-style play-by-play commentary for viewers at home. One was Dominic Abrams, a professor of social psychology at the University of Kent, who today, more than a decade later, doesn't quite know what to think of Elliott or what she did. "She is a very strong personality and did not appear to treat challenge as anything other than a battle to be won. She certainly had no desire to engage with me as a psychologist (or indeed as a person), so other than her brusque manner toward myself and the production team (which may have been partly an extension of her character part for the day), it was difficult to gain a sense of what she might have been thinking or intending," Abrams wrote in an email.[26]

Guardian journalist Andrew Anthony was less sanguine. Writing about the British iteration of the experiment, Anthony noted, "Nowadays, grey-haired and mean-eyed, she's honed her shtick to that of a drill sergeant or prison commandant. She describes herself as the 'resident bitch for the day', and speaks to the blue-eyed contingent as though they were criminally stupid or stupidly criminal. 'Keep your fucking mouth shut,' she tells one smiling blue-eyed young man. 'I don't play second banana.' The performance suggests someone who would be a natural in a Maoist re-education camp: self-righteous, vindictive and unswervingly convinced of her case."

Anthony concluded that Elliott was "more excited by white fear than she is by black success."[27]

When pressed by the British documentary's moderator, Krishnan Guru-Murthy, "What do you think people are going to say the legacy of Jane Elliott is?" Elliott snapped back, "Don't care."

Guru-Murthy wasn't satisfied. "You must care! You're doing this to change behavior and make the world a better place. You must care!"

"Don't care," Elliott insisted. "What people say about me is of little importance to me. Did I make a difference today? Did I make a positive difference today in the area of racism? That's what I want to do."

At least one person back home in Riceville thinks that ultimately Elliott will be vindicated from any scorn. Dick Woodruff, a retired teacher in Osage, said, "Without a doubt, people thought Jane went too far. Maybe she won't be appreciated in her own lifetime, but eventually her due will come. Recognition happens over a period of time. Is a saint recognized in her own time? If they are, they're burned at the stake."[28]

TWENTY-THREE

The Dogs Bark, but the Caravan Goes On

TODAY, JANE ELLIOTT'S STATUS AS A TOWN pariah in Riceville has
not abated. If time heals all, then that clock never started ticking in northeast
Iowa. There are lots of reasons why locals still don't mention Elliott's name
in polite conversation, but leading the list is the persistent buzz around town
of the bottomless wealth they say she's accumulated through the experiment.
A librarian at the Riceville Public Library maintained that Elliott earns "roy-
alties" whenever anyone anywhere at any time uses the words "blue eyes,
brown eyes," even though the reporting and bookkeeping of such an enter-
prise would surely be an impossible task. Others insist with certainty that
when Elliott's not home in Iowa, she lives in a multimillion-dollar California
estate with a swimming pool and servants.[1]

Jim Cross, the editor of the *Mitchell County Press News*, looks at the issue of
Elliott's alleged wealth this way: "There's nothing to disclaim it. There's never
a defense. It's more like, 'I don't have to defend myself to you people for what I
did.' The sense is, 'I don't need to tell you that I *don't* own a mansion.' But every
time you speak, we know you're getting paid. You're not doing it for free."[2]

In fact, Elliott's Osage home is assessed at $93,000, and a former one-
room schoolhouse on her property at $54,000. Elliott owns additional prop-
erty in Osage assessed at about $100,000.[3] A three-bedroom house Elliott
owns in Riverside County's Sun City, California, where she spends winters,
backs onto an interstate highway. It's valued at $325,000, which considering
California real estate puts it on the low end of modest.[4] She chose the location to be close to her younger daughter, Mary, who lives in nearby Murrieta.
In reality, Elliott seems to have retained a lifestyle born from her modest
Iowa roots.

Her local notoriety was conferred official status when the city of Riceville's 245-page sesquicentennial history was published in 2005, and nary a mention of Elliott was made, though she's without question the most famous person in Riceville history, and certainly would be on any list of famous Iowans, living or dead.[5]

Cross, who served on the oversight committee of the city's publication, said, "The feeling was that she had taken advantage of the community, that she didn't represent a happy experience for the town." Cross said he fought to include Elliott, but was overruled. "I felt when the book was being done, we had to put her in because it would really be an injustice not to put her in. She had to be in the book. I posed it to the committee, who were all local people, and it was a quick consensus of no."

For the parade commemorating Riceville's sesquicentennial, Elliott wasn't invited, either. "People felt we would have eggs and rotten tomatoes being thrown during the parade and we didn't want that negativity coming upon the town for what was supposed to be such a grand celebration," said Cross, who was in charge of the celebration.

Nor would the local newspaper, Smitty Messersmith's old *Riceville Recorder*, likely run a story on Elliott, except perhaps her obituary. "Small-town people can make or break your paper. In the big picture, would it be worth it? What purpose would it serve? It would cause pain, suffering, bad feelings," said Cross, the *Recorder*'s former editor.[6]

In *A History of Riceville Community School (1875–2012): Shining Brightly after 137 Years*, published by the *Recorder*, Elliott does merit a page, which concludes neutrally, "Her study in racism has caused an array of responses over the years, and even now, almost 45 years after the study, people have strong opinions of her and the experiment she conducted, which brought a national spotlight to Riceville."[7]

Some locals support Elliott, but not many. "What she was doing rubbed people the wrong way," said Bill Diederich, the former principal of Riceville High, who lived at the Riceville Community Rest Home until his death in 2019. "She was a first-class, double-A teacher. She was ahead of her time. She came up with a brilliant way to explain something very complicated to little kids. It was a classic job of teaching."

Then why do so many people dislike her?

"Jealousy," Diederich declared. "She earned a lot of fame, and people weren't ready to accept that."[8]

Another Riceville local, Linda Ring Kinneman, said Elliott was simply too much to handle. "People around here are very often very critical and judgmental. I don't know if it's that they don't venture out very far into the world. Their little world is, 'Let's sit around and gossip about people.' If you want to fit in here, better not be way out. You're not going to fit into Riceville if you're outside the norm." A teacher's aide who worked with Elliott, Kinneman used to eat lunch with Elliott in the school cafeteria, "because the other teachers didn't want much to do with her."[9]

With Jane traveling as much as she did, lecturing and leading workshops, and husband Darald home and running the Red Owl grocery store, the sturdy, stolid Marlon Brando look-alike stood by his wife for almost sixty years. "When Darald said 'for better or worse' in 1955, he meant every word of it. He just didn't know how much worse it was going to get," Elliott reflected in 1997.[10]

Darald died in 2013 of multiple system atrophy, a degenerative neurological disorder that shares many of the symptoms of Parkinson's disease.[11] He was seventy-nine.[12] Jane stopped traveling for a while, then decided that returning to the lecture circuit would be the best salve for grief.

Elliott's father, Lloyd, whom she adored, died at eighty-one in 1990.[13] Jane's mother, Gie, with whom Elliott had an embattled relationship through much of her life, continued living in the hotel in downtown Riceville that Jane and Darald bought in 1963. She died in 2008 at ninety-six.[14]

So much local derision trails Elliott that some of her former students, those who support and defend her, have banded together in an attempt to control what is written or broadcast about her. Before deciding to talk to outsiders about Elliott, they demand to know what message will be conveyed through any media representation of their former teacher. Several hold out a kind of test that outsiders must pass before they will discuss her.

Raymond Hansen, who appeared in two of the television documentaries, balked at answering any questions about Elliott. The Rochester, Minnesota, attorney today won't discuss his former teacher or the classroom experiment without first posing a series of vetting questions to determine whether he believes "any good would accrue from my involvement."[15]

Similarly, Rex Kozak, another of Elliott's former students who appeared in the same two documentaries, won't discuss her or the experiment because, he said, "I do not see where there will be any value added to the betterment of society." Kozak, a former public school administrator, said if any money earned from such discussion were deposited in a local scholarship program, he might reconsider.[16]

Elliott remains as sharp-tongued, contrary, resolute, and opinionated as ever. She has updated her lectures to include a range of contemporary issues: the concept of race ("There's only one race, the human race"); the Black Lives Matter movement ("It's insane what we've been doing to people of color for the last 250 years"), white supremacists ("They're coming out of the woodwork"), persistent women ("'Bitch' is an acronym for 'Being in Total Control, Honey'"), former President Trump ("He is basing his political philosophy on writings of Adolf Hitler"), racism among white evangelicals ("Jesus did *not* look like the little Pillsbury Doughboy"), and oppression of Native Americans ("We call Native Americans 'savages' but it was whites who killed them and stole their lands"). Her most recent lectures mention COVID-19, as well as the LGBTQ and Latinx communities. Elliott hasn't given up her interest in public education, which is at the center of any presentation she gives ("We could destroy racism in two generations by changing what is taught in classrooms all over the United States, but first we'd have to change the level of racism among the teachers").[17]

For decades, Elliott has issued sweeping generalizations, including her oft-repeated declaration that all whites in America are racists. "If you are looking at a white person who was born, reared, and schooled in the United States, then you are looking at a racist," she told an audience at the University of Northern Colorado as far back as 1993. "Blacks aren't racist; they are only reacting to the actions of whites."[18]

During her lectures, tear well up seemingly on cue when she recalls the original experiment back in 1968 in Classroom No. 10. Her speaking fees today can reach as much as twenty thousand dollars per event.[19] She often travels business- or first-class with her older daughter, Sarah, who acts as a personal assistant and one-woman security detail.

Elliott often displays a kind of martyr mentality in her public talks. She frequently includes a passage that goes like this: "I know some of you would like to shoot me. Be smart, don't shoot me here because of what I do, because if you do, you might make a martyr out of me, and you might have to spend the rest of your life celebrating Jane Elliott Day once a year."[20] In Milwaukee, she told an interviewer, "I have been threatened with death lots of times. Now I say, 'Go for it, fool!' My husband died four years ago. Being with him would not be a bad thing for me. Living a worthless, useless life is much worse than dying."²¹ During another talk, she said, "I can be scared, but I won't be scared to die, or, at my age, of death. I'm fully aware that it goes with the territory. I think that living a cowardly life and having to play that game would be worse than death."²²

Robin DiAngelo, the author of *White Fragility: Why It's So Hard for White People to Talk about Racism*, attended a lecture Elliott gave in Seattle several years ago, and to her, Elliott "came across as rambling and a little unhinged." On-stage, Elliott referred to then-President Trump as "an abortion," which, DiAngelo said, drew a collective gasp from the audience.

DiAngelo recalled Elliott as talking in "stream of consciousness . . . at times—a sense of her being a loose cannon." But for DiAngelo, who is also white, Elliott remains a hero. "I am in awe of her courage. She calls people on their bullshit, whether they like it or not. She privileges interrupting racism over coddling delicate white sensibilities. I understand that her approach will not work for some and cause them to dig in deeper. But no approach will reach everyone and hers is very effective for many. We need the Jane Elliotts of the world. I have been in awe of her saying and doing what others (including myself) may be only thinking or dreaming of doing."

Elliott has never had much patience for those who disagree with her. "Jane's anger is understandable to me because she challenges racism and has had to face white denial, apathy, complicity, hostility, entitlement, superiority, and fragility day in and day out for years," said DiAngelo. "How could she *not* be angry in the face of that? I see her anger as a righteous and rational response to injustice."²³

When Elliott appeared with longtime Black activist Angela Davis at the University of Houston in September 2018, she hardly let Davis speak. Accustomed to being the center of attention, Jane steadfastly refused to give up the floor to Davis.²⁴

Elliott often refers to herself as "a faded Black person." When she spoke with actress Jada Pinkett Smith on her Facebook Watch show, *Red Table Talk*, in 2018, she said, "My people moved far from the Equator and that's the only reason my skin is lighter. That's all any white person is."²⁵ She concedes that as a white woman speaking about how some Black people might feel, she may be guilty of accusations that she's a charlatan and a poseur. "There are those Blacks who ask me what a white woman like me is doing talking about their experience, since I can't possibly know what it's like to walk in their shoes. Sometimes I'm accused of just running another white woman's game. Those are valid criticisms."²⁶

Elliott's relevance and popularity picked up in a big way following a late-May evening in Minneapolis in 2020, when a Black man, George Floyd, was killed in Minneapolis by white police officer Derek Chauvin, who knelt on Floyd's neck for more than nine minutes in front of a gathering of incredulous onlookers. The act, caught on cellphone cameras and transmitted worldwide, galvanized tens of millions of protesters globally, demanding an end to systemic racism.

Instantly, talk of the blue-eyes, brown-eyes experiment returned with a fury. Journalists scrambled to find someone to place into perspective the Floyd killing and massive protests that ensued. Experts on race were needed to "make sense" of what had happened, and once again, Elliott became a go-to authority on the racial divide in America. Elliott found herself in the middle of a media frenzy.

And just as had happened in 1968, she received a call from a producer at *The Tonight Show*, who wanted Elliott to talk about the blue-eyes, brown-eyes experiment, almost fifty-two years to the date when she had last appeared on the late-night program. This time, the host would be another likable funnyman, Jimmy Fallon.

Fallon's original headliner for June 1 was supposed to have been Lady Gaga, whose appearance had been timed to plug her new album, *Chromatica*, which had been released three days earlier. Along with Lady Gaga, Little Big Town, a Nashville country music group, also was to appear. But both were pulled in the wake of the Floyd protests, with Elliott, NAACP President Derrick Johnson, and CNN journalist Don Lemon hurriedly put in their place.[27]

Because of COVID-19, instead of flying to New York and being ushered back to Studio 6B in Rockefeller Center, Elliott was interviewed from her home via video hookup. Just as Carson had been when he interviewed Elliott on May 30, 1968, Fallon appeared ill at ease with Elliott and the subject matter. Apparently, no one had clued Fallon in that Elliott had once appeared on the show; at least, Fallon said nothing about her appearance a half century earlier. As with Carson, there was little repartee between Fallon and Elliott. Like Carson, Fallon looked as though he didn't know how to react to Elliott's practiced recitation of the classroom experiment.

Elliott talked with little intention of conversing; this time, it was Elliott who seemed to be presenting *The Tonight Show* monologue. Fallon took it all in, but looked spacey and shellshocked. Fallon did not risk interrupting. Jokes were for another time. The evening's backdrop was nearly as volatile as it had been in 1968. The noninterview fell flat, and after several nonstarters,

Fallon closed out the segment stiffly. "I cannot wait to see you in person. Thank you so much again." Fallon looked relieved. This time, Elliott had appeared for a little more than seven minutes.[28]

The *New York Times*, a month later, ran two stories on Elliott, first a Q&A, then a profile titled "The Return of Jane Elliott." In the first piece, published on July 4, Elliott said, when asked about cures for racism, that whites can start by acknowledging two issues:

> You have to realize what I do isn't hard work. What Black people do is hard work. I get paid for the work that I do. They don't get paid for taking this crap every day—they have to take it. They don't volunteer for it. It was forced on them. And second, white people need to stop referring to themselves as "allies"—as if we can make it all right. They need to educate away the ignorance that was poured into them when they were in school and realize that *they* are the reason everyone is so angry. I've been saying these things for 52 years.[29]

It was in the second *Times* story that Elliott related the local turmoil she and had family endured in the wake of the experiment. "I didn't know how this exercise would work. If I had known how it would work, I probably wouldn't have done it. If I had known that our four children would be spit on and their belongings would be destroyed, that they would be verbally and physically abused by their peers, by their teachers and some of the parents of their peers, because they had what that community labeled as an N-word-lover for a mother."

The piece ended in the way most popular media stories about Elliott end, with a muted, somewhat troubling, resigned note: "Ms. Elliott feels it was all worth it and says she has no plans of stepping back from educating people—not until every living person understands that the problem underlying racism in America is easy to identify and fix. . . . 'When am I going to quit? When racists quit,' she said. 'Do I have a job for a lifetime? I'm afraid so.'"[30]

Afterword

THE CASE OF ROBERT COLES AND OTHERS

JANE ELLIOTT HAS AMPLY DEMONSTRATED that she is an iconic cultural force to be reckoned with. She has lectured at more than three hundred colleges and universities. She has addressed audiences in just about every state in the nation, as well as in Germany, the Netherlands, Australia, Canada, Saudi Arabia, England, Scotland, and Northern Ireland. In 2016, she self-published a book, in the form of a letter to her children, titled *A Collar in My Pocket: Blue-Eyes, Brown-Eyes Exercise*.[1] A rhyming children's book, *Blue Eyes Brown Eyes*, which introduces the experiment and the concept of racial prejudice, was published in 2018.[2]

Elliott has created a series of training videos available through her website, including *The Stolen Eye*, which showcases the experiment in Australia with whites and Aborigines ("Watch the astonishing and thoughtful results of this exercise. A must-buy for Jane Elliott admirers"[3]) and *Blue-Eyed*, which allows viewers to sit in on the experiment with a group of Kansas City teachers, police officers, and social workers ("In just a few hours under Ms. Elliott's withering regime, we watch grown professionals become despondent and distracted, stumbling over the simplest commands"[4]). Other for-sale videos document Elliott conducting the experiment in Regina, Saskatchewan, and in Glasgow, Scotland.[5]

German filmmaker Bertram Verhaag wrote and directed *Blauäugig* (Blue Eyed) in the mid-1990s, a German-language documentary in which Elliott conducts the experiment (she speaks in English, but the narration is in German). Per her usual, she bullies participants; those who don't follow Elliott's directives are ejected by security guards.[6]

A made-for-TV movie, starring Susan Sarandon, was in the works in 1996, but nothing ever came of it. The production company, Shoelace Productions, owned by Julia Roberts, was to have produced the feature film, and a script was written, but the project never got off the ground.[7] A dramatic play based on the experiment, *Class*, debuted regionally in 2008.[8]

Despite her initial welcome, Elliott proved to be a difficult subject for me to write about. Once she realized that I wasn't going to reprise the default moralistic Disney story almost all other journalists had written about her, she closed shop. I was no longer welcome. She would have nothing to do with me.

By then, I had interviewed Elliott many times. I had spent months in Riceville, interviewing scores of residents. I had interviewed all of her children; I had interviewed Darald during my first round of reporting.

After her message on my office phone warning me about continuing, I plunged into the book. To a newspaper reporter turned book writer, all attempts at intimidation are invitations to dig deeper. I had a taste of what many people, in and out of Riceville, had warned me about.

Through years of researching Elliott, I found she does have a persistent habit of braggadocio. Some claims she has made about herself proved to be false. Before she shut the door on me, when I questioned her about the originality of the experiment, she backtracked and zigzagged. The accusing index finger appeared, as did her wide-eyed glare. Her explanation that the experiment came from Leon Uris's *Mila 18* proved to be either an error of memory or a tall tale. She sidestepped allegations that she had stolen the experiment from another teacher.

There was another question just as basic: Did that epiphany really happen on the evening of April 4, 1968, when Elliott said she was watching TV news reports of Martin Luther King Jr.'s assassination and the experiment in an instant sprang to life? Was it really the television news that had prompted her to let loose the experiment on the children in Classroom No. 10? Such a scenario surely made for the kind of story that journalists love. But was it true?

There were other aspects of Elliott's rise to fame that nagged at me. One was the endorsement she said she had received from famed Harvard children's psychiatrist Robert Coles, who, according to hundreds, perhaps thousands, of media reports, had called the experiment "the greatest thing to come out of American education in a hundred years." Coles is without a doubt the most famous and well-published child psychiatrist in the United States today and perhaps ever.

He also is one of my own models. I've read all of his crossover books about children and social culture, including his acclaimed five-volume series, *Children of Crisis, The Moral Life of Children, The Political Life of Children,*

The Spiritual Life of Children, and *The Moral Intelligence of Children.* In 2002, I wrote an essay for a groundbreaking magazine, *DoubleTake,* that Coles helped found. A MacArthur Award winner, Pulitzer Prize winner, and recipient of the National Medal of Freedom, Coles is a titan in the world of arts, letters, child development, and psychiatry. His endorsement carried immeasurable authority.

Initially, I was thrilled that Coles had given such praise to Elliott. Tributes that cast anyone's work in century-long blocks of time are unheard of in almost any endeavor. But upon fuller reflection, something struck me as fundamentally wrong about the quote. It didn't seem like it could have come from Coles, who rarely wrote or spoke in such absolutes. The *greatest* thing to come out of American education in a *hundred* years? I couldn't imagine Coles having uttered this. It seemed inauthentic, coming from him or really anyone with such a towering pedigree in the field of children's education.

Coles, at ninety-one, had virtually disappeared. In today's world of online footprints everywhere, he had vanished. Inquiries to Harvard's Kennedy School of Government and Harvard's College of Medicine, where the eminent psychiatrist is professor emeritus, yielded no forwarding address. Inquiries to Duke University's Center for Documentary Studies, which Coles help found, also proved inconclusive. No one seemed to have heard from Coles for years. His voluminous personal and professional papers are housed at two archives, the University of North Carolina, Chapel Hill, and Michigan State University, but inquiries to archivists at both institutions yielded no mention of Coles's endorsement of Elliott in their holdings.

I discovered that Coles has a son, Daniel, a pediatrician for Indian Health Services in New Mexico. I sent Daniel Coles a letter, asking whether he could contact his father and ascertain the veracity of his father's alleged praise about Elliott.

Daniel Coles responded a week later. In a telephone interview, he said he had talked to his father about the matter, and Robert Coles told him categorically he "absolutely never said this."

Daniel Coles said, "He is 100 percent certain that he never said or wrote this or communicated it in any way. It just isn't true. My father told me there is absolutely no way he ever said it because he doesn't believe it. There is zero room for doubt on this. It is incorrect." Daniel Coles added that his father is very alert and his memory is excellent. "He is quite certain on this point."[9]

This flew in the face of multiple instances where the Coles quote had been used to endorse Elliott. As far back as 1985, Coles was quoted as saying that the experiment Elliott popularized was "the greatest thing to come out of American education in a hundred years."[10] When she spoke in Meriden, Connecticut, that year, the *Hartford Courant* published the quote.[11] The same quote was reported in 1990, when Elliott spoke in New Jersey, as it was when she spoke in Sioux City, Iowa, November 27, 1999.[12] In 1991, the *Daily Iowan* reported Coles's encomium when she visited the University of Iowa.[13] The attribution was cited to promote lectures at scores of other institutions. In 2017, when she spoke at the University of Michigan, the *Michigan Chronicle* repeated the endorsement.[14]

This isn't to say that Elliott made up Coles's alleged comment; lots of erroneous statements get manufactured, mangled, and take on a life of their own. But that Elliott apparently never stopped this apparent misappropriation of Coles's name and alleged words is telling. If Daniel Coles was correct in saying his father never uttered or wrote such an endorsement, where did it come from, and how could Elliott have allowed such a falsehood to be used for thirty-five years?

There are other troubling instances. In the aftermath of the George Floyd killing, Elliott was featured on the September 2020 fold-out cover of British *Vogue* magazine, with the headline, "Activism Now: The Faces of Hope." Elliott's black-and-white photograph was prominently displayed alongside images of nineteen other global activists.[15] It was a coup of sorts to be featured in the world's most prestigious fashion magazine, in the largest issue of the year. Elliott was wearing a white sweatshirt, bearing a printed quote that looked identical to the one emblazoned on the sweatshirt she has worn for years as her uniform. When I heard Elliott speak at the Englert Theatre in Iowa City, she had been wearing a sweatshirt bearing what appeared to be the same quote: "Prejudice is an emotional commitment to ignorance," with the printed name of the author, Nathan Rutstein.[16]

But this time, on the cover of British *Vogue*, there were no quote marks around the sentence, and on closer inspection, the maxim read, "Racial prejudice is an emotional commitment to ignorance." This time, the source of the quote printed below the epigram was Jane Elliott. Rutstein's name had been excised.

It was a detail few would notice. But to anyone who had followed Elliott, such expropriation did not come as a surprise. As in the Coles instance, why would she have needed to do this? That is, if what appeared to be a misappropriation was one.

If there is any Rosebud to Jane Elliott, it's found in her children. In 1993, Elliott told filmmaker Bertram Verhaag, "It took me a long time to get over the feeling that I had done something wrong. . . . [But] if I had stopped, it would have been saying to my kids, 'When things get unpleasant, just stop what you are doing, just go along to get along.' That wasn't the message I wanted to send to them."[17]

The message that got through to her children was more nuanced and multilayered. Elliott's youngest child, Mark, who lives in nearby Osage, refuses to discuss his mother today, citing the potential of local upheaval (he has a job and a family of his own in the area). Elliott's younger daughter, Mary, moved two thousand miles away from Riceville to Southern California, and today is involved in online sales of Elliott's videos and other materials.

Perhaps the greatest personal anguish was experienced by Elliott's son Brian, who died of nasopharyngeal carcinoma in Snohomish, Washington, in 2018 at age sixty. In an interview with me three months before his death, Brian, a recovering alcoholic, said, he never let on who his mother was at AA or union hall meetings. "I'm proud of what she did. But I don't want it known. I don't brag about it. She's done a lot of good. But the guys I work with don't know because I'd be that 'nigger-lovin' Elliott all over again."

Brian's trusted boyhood dog, Spooner, was replaced by countless other dogs over the next five decades. "I've been around dogs my whole life," Brian said, conjuring up images of one of the few touchstones of trust he had during his peripatetic, hopscotch journey after leaving Iowa.

As for the impact of his mother's long crusade, Brian reflected pessimistically, "Stick your finger in a glass of water, pull it out, and see how much of an impression you make."[18]

The Elliotts' oldest child, Sarah, continues to serve as the keeper of her mother's flame. Sarah married a Saudi man in the mid-1980s in a mosque in Cedar Rapids, then moved to Saudi Arabia before returning to Iowa and eventually filing for divorce. She posts her mother's comings and goings on Facebook and Instagram. Active in progressive Democratic politics, she was an early supporter of Democratic presidential contender Bernie Sanders in the Iowa caucuses.

Sarah has ruminated a lot about her parents. "These two people loved each other so much! He could have given up on her every time he turned around. He could have walked out. Any other man would have because she was so hard to live with. And she was mean! She held that over him. He hung in there because he loved her. He didn't want to leave. He wanted to see how it all would turn out. He was the rock that held all this together."

Sarah was deeply influenced by her mother and still is. Supportive of her mother, she said she still wrestles to better understand her. "She's a bitch," Sarah told me, slowly and deliberately.

What was it like to grow up with Elliott as her mother?

> She wasn't easy. Harsh. Tougher than tough love. "What the hell is wrong with you!" she'd say to us. I would someday like to sit down with Martin Luther King's kids, and ask, "How did you do it?"
>
> This is a woman who needed attention from the get-go. She was the middle child in her family. She was the attention-getter. All the time. She's a complete narcissist. There's nothing wrong with it, unless you hurt people's feelings with it. She takes advantage of it, right up to a point, and then backs off. She is cruel. She does it with people who pay her. I don't know why it was she who was chosen. Was it the right time and the right place? Normal people don't seek attention the way Jane does. She loved it! It's the power.[19]

Elliott's star continues to ascend. After she appeared with Fallon on *The Tonight Show*, Oprah—or at least, her staff—came calling once again, despite how Elliott and Winfrey had seemingly disagreed after Elliott's last appearance on the show in 1993. This time, Elliott was profiled in Oprah's eponymous magazine. The article's headline didn't conform to Elliott's longtime demand to label the experiment an "exercise." The headline read: "Jane Elliott, Creator of the 'Blue/Brown Eyes' Experiment, Says Racism Is Easy to Fix."

Elliott made the case for reprising the experiment, but this time with a new wrinkle: her daughter Sarah would be taking over. Elliott's plug was an update of what she had done on the PBS documentary, when she floated the idea of educating an army of teachers to conduct the experiment, with herself as instructor in chief.

"I have a daughter who would be good at leading the exercise, so she's studying to do it. I also have three granddaughters who could lead it very well. Because they've listened to me a lot, they've learned some things that convinced them that a lot of what they learned [in school] is nonsense."

Elliott told the *Oprah* writer, Kieron Johnson, "White women have to lead the exercise, because people won't listen to Black women. Coming from a man, no one is going to put up with the kinds of things I say during the exercise. They'll take it from a woman. They'll take it from a *white* woman."[20]

Coda

ANDY'S AND THE VILLE

THE MEN START GATHERING at Andy's Mini-Mart at five in the morning. Almost all are farmers or truckers, stopping by for a cup of coffee before sunrise. On Fridays, all you can drink is free, paid for by a local plumbing-parts company. Tom and Steve Anderlik, the brothers who run the convenience store, are a popular pair, tossing Iowa-dry humor to anyone who pushes through the front door. Andy's is a 100-percent man cave. There's not a woman to be found, save for Roni Rae, Steve's wife, who bakes pizza and fries donuts, but she scurries around so fast that no one pays much attention to her. She skitters past three or four coveys of men dressed in Carhartts like a cat around grumpy dogs.

On the drive from Waverly, an hour south, no one is on the road except eighteen-wheelers chasing the waning night, pedal to the metal to get to the Minnesota state line by sunrise. There's a hazy, low-lying blue-gray fog gusting laterally across the wide-open plains. At Charles City, for miles and miles, a horizontal band of flashing lights in the distance stretches east–west, midlevel on the flat, gauzy, treeless horizon. Could be pulsating beacons atop cellphone towers or landing-strip lights carved from a cornfield. The scene is so spooky that the location could pass for a Midwest station of Area 51. On closer inspection, the shadowy, blinking lights are atop enormous wind turbines, elliptical vanes slowly moving currents of heavy, moist air. The turbines, the equivalents of thirty-story buildings, are strategically placed for miles—forty, fifty, seventy-five giant, whirling slot machines fanned out in a vast crescent formation. They're as foreign as Stonehenge must have seemed to medieval wayfarers awed by such a mammoth, incongruous sight.

A yellow, diamond-shaped sign, barely legible at this hour, indicates a silhouette of a vaulting deer with a terse advisory: "Next ten miles." Everyone in Iowa knows there's nothing to do when an errant doe or buck leaps in front of your vehicle. Does weigh three hundred pounds; bucks more. Swerving is the natural thing to do, but also a certain way to flip whatever it is you're driving and end up in a ditch. It's best to plow right through, holding on to your thumping steering wheel for dear life. This might sound cruel to a city slicker. But it's what Iowa drivers are trained to do. No one doesn't know someone who hasn't had a run-in with deer. Deer are everywhere. More these days than ever. So many, that counties pay hunters to thin the cervidae population every fall; bow-hunting season begins the first week of October. Deer invade vegetable patches, shopping malls, downtowns; some have even been known to walk into kitchens, open the refrigerator, and help themselves to leftovers.

At the turnoff for Highway 218 and the town of Floyd, the nose-twitching smell that started north of Waterloo gets denser and more pungent. This isn't an aroma that wafts, coming and going, depending on the direction of head-winds swooping in from Canadian provinces. It is a constant, steady miasma that, mixed with the early-morning fog, clings to nostrils. It's the olfactory welcome that girds the state's treasury of corn. The fetor largely comes from a particularly profitable agribusiness invention called a CAFO, which stands for concentrated animal feeding operation. Iowa has at least ten thousand such hog operations.[1]

The night gives way to a dusky-purple dawn. It's worth admiring; in fif-teen minutes, the light show will disappear and turn into full-fledged morning.

Andy's Mini-Mart is on Highway 9, which in Riceville is East and West Main Street, divided at the T of Woodland Avenue. From downtown, if you've driven past Immaculate Conception Church, Lindstrom Funeral Home, and the Dollar General, you've gone too far, on your way to Cresco.

"I stay out of all that," Tom Anderlik says. "No business of myself to say anything about her. She got family who live in town. She done what she did."[2]

"I never had her as a teacher," volunteers a lanky, full-bearded trucker in his fifties. "But I don't approve of it. I'll tell you right out, I'm conservative. Most everyone here is. I don't think anyone around here cares for her. No one *I* know."

"Gonna be a swap meet on Saturday!"

"UNI's gonna lose against Iowa this Saturday."

"They better lose, I got money on it!"

"What you been up to?"

"Gotta go to the dump today. They take an old TV?"

"It's the dump, ain't it?"

"What the hell you doin' these days?" asks a sixtyish farmer who, upon seeing another man in zippered coveralls and mud-caked boots, slaps him on the crown of his head in what appears to be a gesture of affection.

"Tryin' to stay outta trouble," says the slap's recipient, munching on the open end of a cellophane-wrapped oatmeal creme pie. The slapper rescues a lone slice of curled pizza languishing under a heat lamp.

Do we really have to be talking about Jane Elliott? seems to be the sentiment this dawning fall morning.

A man pulls out a red bandana and snorts heartily into it, producing a toot that for a moment silences discussion.

"Never had her, but don't like what she done," a man in overalls says. "I knew her. Went to high school with her, as a matter of fact.

"She stole the goddamn exercise. There's a reason no one don't give her no time of day. I went to a country school and the teacher did the same thing. One day she'd give the blue-eyed kids chocolate milk, the next day it'd be the brown-eyed kids. That's where she got it."

When asked to elaborate, the man replies, "I don't wanna get into it. But I'll tell you this. That family brought everything on itself. Every damn thing."

"Morning!"

"You goin' to work today?"

"Hell, no!"

For a moment, Tom Anderlik leaves the cash-register island, a fortress of lottery tickets, cigarettes, chewing tobacco, energy drinks, pep pills, and candy of all shapes and sizes. "Hey, first thing I gotta ask you, 'What color are *your* eyes?'"

"I'm a brownie."

"Then you're outta here!" Anderlik says, as though calling out a runner trying to stretch a double into a triple.

"You know there's a National League pitcher with one brown eye and one blue eye.[3] I wanna know what she would've thought of *him*. Coulda caused him a heap of problems if he ever had her as a teacher, doncha think?"

A ripple of chuckles. "I ain't saying anything about her. I'm staying clear the hell out of it."

"You oughta look into the destruction of the state of Iowa by the hog-agricultural business," says the trucker." They're destroying the atmosphere. That sulfur smell is wicked. You can't drink the water no more."

"I don't smell it," someone says. "Don't bother me."

A man in his eighties hobbles in, showing off his new hip replacement; he's as good as anyone to be teased.

"Fifty years ago, and people are still talkin' about her. You know who we talkin' about?"

"She still alive?"

"She was on TV. *The Johnny Carson Show*."

"Blue eyes?" teases another. "Mean anything?"

The man shakes his head.

"We're givin' you hints."

"Brown eyes?"

"Got any idea?"

"Oh . . . *That* woman!" the man says, shooing away the others as though clearing the air. "Don't get me started on *her*."

The men begin to thin by seven. Truck routes to run, chores to begin, farm equipment that needs fixing, fields and crops to be inspected.

Time to move to the breakfast club at the Ville (short for Riceville), which used to house one of two bars in town, where years earlier Steven and Charlotte Harnack were approached to join a swinging key party.

Monday through Saturday mornings, a breakfast club now convenes at the tavern: Geraldine Torney, Jean and Lee Breitsprecher, Jane and Harvey Mosher, and Lavonne and Wayne Klein. They're all about Jane Elliott's age.

Torney offers some Homestyle oatmeal cookies to the table as everyone sips coffee (although Lavonne Klein brought a tea bag and dips it in a china mug of hot water).

Here, too, Elliott is not a popular topic. There's a collective pause, a moment of reflection and contrition until Jane Mosher cheerily announces, "Well, I'm a Democrat!" which prompts several awkward smiles.

"Is Jane still alive?"

When assured she is, Lavonne Klein says, "I knew her and liked her. She was very bright and she was very brave because of the things she did. Anytime you do something like that, you can expect to get into trouble. And there's always jealousy."

Jane Mosher picks up the conversation. "Our son liked her. He said she was an excellent teacher. She made butter in school.

"She made it more interesting than if you just had to read the book, have the right answers, otherwise keep your mouth shut, go out and play at noon and don't get into fights."

Around the table, Mosher seems to be Elliott's staunchest defender. "She had a strong personality and some people were offended by that. The whole family had strong personalities."

Lee Breitsprecher used to have breakfast with Elliott's father, Lloyd Jennison, and he remembers Jennison saying, "If there's anything I hate, it's a basement that leaks." And Breitsprecher recalls responding, "If there's anything *I* hate, it's a roof that leaks!" Nods around the table in appreciation of Iowa weather and wit.

Jane Mosher recalls the day Smitty Messersmith, Elliott's old nemesis, died. "One day he come into the bank, says hello to everyone, was happy and joyous, walked out, went over to Pettitt's, and next thing you know, the ambulance was there."

"Coffee, anyone want coffee?"

"I still remember Jane with Johnny Carson on the TV."

"And you know what? He didn't intimidate her. A lot of people would have acted nervous. But Jane was just herself."

"Yep!"

"You knew she was there when she was there. Very dominant personality."

"Everyone knows her name, and hardly anyone knows mine!"

The discussion goes back and forth from Elliott to coffee-klatch members present and past.

"Lucille was doing her normal thing the day she died. She was baking."

"Was her health that good?"

"Well, if you knew Lucille, she was gonna bake come hell or high water."

"You never know, do you?" Jean Breitsprecher nods.

"We probably won't be around in two, three years," Jane Mosher says, to which everyone laughs a little uneasily.

Harvey, her husband, says, "I'll be going down to the university. Signed up to be a donor. They keep you for a year, take everything out, then send you back home. I don't know what they're gonna do with me. Nothing works right. But that's their problem."

. . .

Harvey's act is considered noble. An optimistic deed, one that suggests a degree of commitment to improving the lot of the next generation. Perhaps what Jane Elliott had in mind.

Elliott certainly had a bushel full of motives that fed her determination. Given a different set of circumstances, she might be sitting right here at the Ville, grousing with these Riceville stalwarts, discussing everything from the countywide porcine odor to whom to support for city council. Maybe if Elliott hadn't been so sure about what she figured needed to be done in Classroom No. 10 and beyond, she'd have created a life similar to that of the locals at the breakfast club this morning.

But I think not. Elliott had too much drive, provoked by a combination of anger, righteousness, and drive, for her to take a seat around the table. Getting even, sticking it to the locals, succeeding in a grand way, seemed as much a motive as any other for what Elliott did in and out of Classroom No. 10.

Some in Riceville couldn't tolerate that she was a woman who had achieved so much fame and recognition outside of being a wife and mother. Others were annoyed with her never-ending pronouncements that racism was alive and well in all-white Riceville, not to mention Iowa and America. Even the most forbearing locals would be hard-pressed to turn the other cheek, considering all the uproar Elliott created back home.

But if there was one error the locals made about her, it was to personalize the calumny Elliott seemed to direct at them. Elliott wasn't just casting shade on the locals. Her scope, like her ambition, was colossal. It had no limits.

If the experiment had never existed, Elliott's combustible, combative personality surely would have led to a disconnect with Riceville locals on something else.

The troubling question on the minds of anyone in Riceville who cares to think about it is this: Could Elliott have knowingly used Riceville's children as a way to catapult her own career from rural Iowa classroom to national, then global, stage? Were the children—and later, adults—pawns in a quest to make her famous?

Could she have *planned* it that way?

Her trajectory didn't just happen.

Could she have been that calculating and cagey?

What truly motivated Elliott to introduce an experiment to a roomful of third graders and to make two days last more than five decades?

Perhaps she was seeking an exit from what she envisioned would be her own humdrum life. She had something personal to prove, a game of one-upmanship amid a landlocked sea of naysayers who had looked down on her ever since she'd been born. What was it about her that seemed to require that she push the limits, shocking everyone—starting with children? Was it to make up for the shortcomings the locals had assigned her? Was it to make her father proud? Was it to get back at the locals and their sense of what it meant to be successful, particularly as a woman? Was it to show the other teachers in the chatty teachers' lounge how horribly wrong they were?

Classroom No. 10 was way too small for Elliott. Her dream was to teach *everyone*.

Perhaps Elliott was initially motivated for altruistic reasons, pure and simple. But once she saw the bounty of what lay beyond the endless rows of corn in Mitchell and Howard Counties, she was a goner, never to return the same.

ACKNOWLEDGMENTS

While Jane Elliott is a thoroughly public figure, until *Blue Eyes, Brown Eyes*, little had been written about the person behind the persona Elliott has spent more than fifty years inventing and nurturing. Her message, if not her presence, has been felt the world over, yet no one had ever set out to learn who Elliott really was and is. Nor had anyone except a handful of scholars assessed the impact of the provocative experiment that for a half century has been associated with her.

Below are the names of those who over the course of sixteen years confided in me to wrestle with these issues. All share (or shared) varying degrees of connection with Elliott. Each added something, large or small—a telling anecdote, canny observation, haunting recollection, sobering realization, a jarring impression. Most have (or had) known Elliott for years. Some were students whose worlds were changed the moment she stepped into Classroom No. 10; others were educators who befriended her or clashed with her. Many were family members, friends, observers, insiders, or bystanders who witnessed Elliott's arc from anonymous teacher to global celebrity.

I approached everyone the same way: without judgment, without preconceived notion. *Tell me what you know about Jane Elliott* is how I started each conversation.

Three people in Osage, Iowa, were particularly welcoming: Jolene and Steve Norbie, and Monte Kloberdanz. The trio provided robust conversation and a depth of knowledge about northeastern Iowa unmatched in Mitchell or Howard Counties. Former Riceville Junior High School principal Steven Harnack was a straight shooter, a veteran public school administrator who never blanched, even when our conversations veered toward the underbelly of Riceville. I enjoyed our chats around his kitchen table, particularly when his cat Bomber was listening in.

Katy and Ralph Campbell, long-standing supporters of my work, offered encouragement of what can be a lonely endeavor—sleeping on lumpy mattresses in rural motel rooms, then setting out to convince wary, taciturn farmers that I might be worthy of their time. The soft skin of my palm gave me away as soon as I shook their calloused hands. When I brought up Elliott, few wanted to talk; several looked me up and down, sneered, and walked away.

After all these years, they were still dismayed with what they perceived Elliott had done to them, their children, and to the city of Riceville. The last thing they wanted was for someone to give Elliott yet another megaphone. Just a handful of locals were sympathetic to a woman they believed had been wronged and was misunderstood.

I conducted interviews in two distinct phases—in 2004 and 2018–2019. The first round was essential to learn the early story of Elliott, her rise to fame, and the bitter, local consternation it caused. As I approached the second round of interviews fifteen years later, the voices were getting scarcer. Many of the Riceville locals I had talked to had died, which made the remaining voices all the more essential in affording me as complete a picture of Elliott as possible. The passage of time had given Riceville residents and others the chance to mull over Elliott's contributions and provocations, an ability to place her in fuller context. It also gave Elliott a second chance. For some, it meant a leavening of opinion. For others, the intervening years had hardened suspicion and distrust. The two rounds served another purpose: they showed Riceville locals that I was intent on telling the story right. *Oh, that guy. He's been working on that book forever. He's talked to nearly everyone in town*!

Teaching at the University of Iowa cut both ways. It afforded me proximity to Riceville; I was a three-hour drive away. It also had given me the opportunity to know the state intimately. I've visited each of its ninety-nine counties several times over. But it also gave residents one more reason not to talk to me. To many, Iowa City might as well be enemy territory. It certainly was foreign.

The state's agriculture university is Iowa State University in Ames. Iowa City, where the University of Iowa is located, is by and large the place for humanities (and a medical school). Strange things happen there. Higher education, especially that kind, is not always trusted by rural Iowans. It can separate children from their parents, and some ideas taught in Iowa City, well, what good are they when it comes to swine, corn, or bean yields? If locals were Hawkeye football fans, my affiliation might be enough to open the back screen door. But just a crack.

The list below includes those who shared their thoughts during both phases of my reporting. There were others who talked with me, but asked that their names not be attached to their comments. Some said it was because of potential reprisals in such a small town; others just wanted to fly under the local radar. For most, I think, it was because in a town as insular as Riceville, few wanted to take a public stand that others might disagree with. I understood this hesitancy. Many conversations ended with, *Please don't use my name. I'm afraid of what might happen.* Whether these were imagined or real redresses, I wasn't sure.

2004: Julie Kleckner Baird, Patty Bodenham, Holly Boggess, Sandi Dohlman Burke, Jean Clausen, Leonard Crawford, Jim Cross, Merri Cross, Gretchen

Eastman, Darald Elliott, Mark Elliott, Walt Gabelmann, Jeanette Mayer Goodale, Dr. George Hanna, Ray Hansen, John Hemann, Kim Reynolds Huemann, Kristine Kunkle Isaacson, Dianne Juhl, Steven Knode, Norm Kolberg, Mary Lou Koschmeder, Rex Kozak, Randy Krukow, Jeanette Goodale Mayer, Dale McCarthy, Jay McGovern, Kelly McGovern, Lavonne Moses, Al Moss, Sue Oulman Rawhouser, Penny Rickerl, Mitchell Laurren-Ring, Debra Anderson Roth, Tricia Bottolsson Rotta, Ruth Setka, Rick Sletten, Dolores Steffen, Debbie Hughes Sutton, Kerri Swancutt, Dorothy Wallace, Dean Weaver, Malinda Sunnes Whisenhunt, and Sharon Cummings Zobeck.

2018–19: Dominic Abrams, Phyllis Watts Aldrich, Ann Alves, Tom Anderlik, Bill Blake, Michael Blake, Jean and Lee Breitsprecher, Carol Lou and Adolph Brunner, Brenda Church, Daniel Coles, Bill Diederich, Joel Dorow, Martha Dorow, Aaron Dvorak, Brian Elliott, Sarah Elliott, Jan Fincher, Bruce Fox, Mary Elliott Gasteiger, Kate Gladstone, Renee Gladstone, Bonita Ihns, Pat Johnson, Leo Jordan, June Judge, Sandy Juettner, Linda Ring Kinneman, Lavonne and Wayne Klein, Sandy and Jerry Koenigs, Dennis Leard, Joanne Machin, Jerry Markham, Cathy Martin, Denny McCabe, Sarah McCarthy-Dougherty, Gail Messersmith Morris, Jane and Harvey Mosher, Mary Myers, Mary Noble, Jerry O'Donnell, Julie Pasicznyk, Wanda Patton Platte, Paul Richer, Vickie Bill Roethler, Brian Saltou, Karen Schofield, Kristian Schofield, Julie Smith Siemonsma, Judy Swinnerton, Nancy Moss Thompson, Richard Valenzuela, Mary Weberg, Dick Woodruff, Kay Worple, and Mary Yager.

Two journalism students at the University of Iowa, Rachael Hovde and James Kay, conducted preliminary interviews for me. Several scholars helped place Elliott's work in perspective. They include Elizabeth Levy Paluck and Donald P. Green, who have studied programs and exercises designed to reduce the incidence of prejudice; and especially Tracie L. Stewart, the lead author of an analysis of the efficacy of the blue-eyes, brown-eyes experiment as experienced by students at Bard College in 2002. Robin DiAngelo, the author of *White Fragility: Why It's So Hard for White People to Talk about Racism*, was illuminating and forthcoming. I appreciated her candor and honesty.

The Women's Archive at the University of Iowa Libraries allowed me access to boxes full of Elliott's correspondence, personal writing, newspaper articles, invitations, photographs, and program notes. My gratitude to Kären Mason, who conducted an insightful oral history with Elliott at her home on November 4, 2009. I also relied on William Peters's book, *A Class Divided Then and Now*. Gemma Bauer of the Oprah Winfrey Network supplied me with tapes of episodes of *The Oprah Winfrey Show* on which Elliott appeared between 1986 and 1993. Mike Hendrickson, my colleague at the University of Iowa, was my trusted computer guru. Friend and resident *Moby Dick* expert David Dowling was as usual a font of support.

Keith Salvas provided me with insight while delving into his own experience with a similar eye-color experiment that Salvas's first-grade teacher, Dorothy Johnson, tried out in Springfield, Massachusetts, in the mid-1960s. Lauri Johnson, a professor at Boston College, wrote an important monograph detailing the Springfield Plan, a precursor to the experiment, which I have cited. An incisive essay by Gregory Jay, a professor at the University of Wisconsin, Milwaukee, gave me insight into the concept of "whiteness studies" as a way to explore issues of racism and prejudice. Karen de Sá, a terrific reporter for the *San Francisco Chronicle*, was generous in sharing the background of her enterprising series of articles about Camp Anytown retreats. My gratitude also goes to deceased friend, George "Lefty" Mills, the legendary reporter for the *Des Moines Register*, who wrote about Paul Richer, the fired Riceville teacher; Mills died in 2003. Newspaper and magazine clips about Wilda Wood, a teacher in Colorado Springs, helped place into historic context the blue-eyes, brown-eyes experiment before Elliott tried her version in Riceville.

The State Historical Society of Iowa's microfilm collection of the *Riceville Recorder* was a valuable source of information, allowing me to transport into Riceville's weekly dramas from 1940 to 1980, and reminded me of the essential role that community newspapers provide. I relied on hundreds of articles from five additional regional newspapers: *Waterloo Courier, Nashua Reporter, Mason City Globe-Gazette, Osage Press-News*, and *Mitchell County Press News*. A particular thanks goes to Jim Cross, the former editor of the *Riceville Recorder* and more recently, the editor of the *Mitchell County Press News*.

The story of Jane Elliott proved to be complex and confounding. To tell the narrative truthfully required a commitment to uncovering and reporting facts, not relying on misstatements that had been repeated so often they had become accepted as canon. It was my felicitous pleasure to work with Niels Hooper, an executive editor at the University of California Press, who saw the importance and vitality of the story, and wasn't scared away.

Three reviewers, Pulitzer Prize winner Dale Maharidge; Jessica Bruder, the author of *Nomadland*, the basis of the 2020 Academy Award–winning film starring Frances McDormand; and Cornell University Professor of law and government Joseph Margulies, an authority on detention and torture at Guantánamo Bay Naval Station, were candid and fierce, everything a writer seeks, and for their prescient comments I'm indebted. Copyeditor Caroline Knapp improved the manuscript with incisive questions and comments. Their collective wisdom has made this a better book, and for that I am grateful.

NOTES

AUTHOR'S NOTE: THE SCAB

1. Wayne J. Urban and Jennings L. Wagoner Jr., "The McGraw-Hill Foundations of Education Timeline," *American Education: A History*, 3rd ed. (New York: McGraw Hill, 2004).

2. Philip G. Zimbardo, *Psychology and Life*, 10th ed. (Glenview, IL: Scott, Foresman and Company, 1979), 637–38.

3. For more information on the Stanford Prison Experiment, see Philip Zimbardo's website on the simulation, https://www.prisonexp.org/.

4. The Coles quote has been cited numerous times in the popular press, but its origin is unclear. See Afterword for more.

5. Author interview with Walt Gabelmann, July 13, 2004. Gabelmann died in the intervening years between my reporting trips, on December 14, 2008.

6. Stephen G. Bloom, "Lesson of a Lifetime," *Smithsonian*, September 2005, https://www.smithsonianmag.com/science-nature/lesson-of-a-lifetime-72754306/.

7. Rutstein, journalist, author, educator, and founder of the Institute for the Healing of Racism, died May 22, 2006. The quote is cited in Carol Rutstein, ed., *From a Gnat to an Eagle: The Story of Nathan Rutstein* (Wilmette, IL: Baha'i Publishing, 2008), 187.

8. Letter to author sent by Jean Clausen, July 1, 2004.

9. Fred M. Rogers, "It's You I Like," 1971, available at http://www.neighborhood archive.com/music/songs/its_you_i_like.html. Reprinted with permission from fre-drogers.org, January 21, 2021.

10. Shirley Jackson, *The Lottery and Other Stories* (New York: Farrar, Straus and Giroux, 2005).

11. Jane Elliott, voicemail to the author, May 1, 2018.

PROLOGUE: *THE TONIGHT SHOW*

1. The bulk of this chapter is based on author interviews with Jane Elliott, March 17, 2018; the April 18, 1968 and May 30, 1968 issues of the *Riceville Recorder*; and

Laurence Leamer, *King of the Night: The Life of Johnny Carson* (New York: William Morrow, 1989). For behind-the-scenes articles on Carson and *The Tonight Show*, see Sam Kashner's piece in *Vanity Fair*, "Theeeere's Johnny!" January 27, 2014, https:// www.vanityfair.com/hollywood/2014/02/johnny-carson-the-tonight-show; Kenneth Tynan's massive piece in *The New Yorker*, "Fifteen Years of the Salto Mortale," February 20, 1978, https://www.newyorker.com/magazine/1978/02/20/fifteen -years-salto-mortale; Stephen Cox, *Here's Johnny*! (Nashville: Cumberland House, 2002); Timothy White, "Johnny Carson: The Rolling Stone Interview," *Rolling Stone*, March 22, 1979, https://www.rollingstone.com/culture/culture-features /johnny-carson-the-rolling-stone-interview-45826/; Paul Corkery, *Carson: The Unauthorized Biography* (Ketchum, ID: Randt and Company, 1987); Henry Bushkin, *Johnny Carson* (New York: Thorndike Press, 2013); and Alex Haley, *The Playboy Interviews* (New York: Ballantine Books, 1993).

2. As quoted in Tynan, "Fifteen Years."

3. Author interview with Jane Elliott, September 24, 2003.

CHAPTER ONE: THE CORN

1. "Iowa Pork Facts," Iowa Pork Producers Association, https://www.iowapork .org/news-from-the-iowa-pork-producers-association/iowa-pork-facts/; Christopher Jones, "Iowa's Real Population," posted March 14, 2019, https://www.iihr.uiowa.edu /cjones/iowas-real-population/.

2. US Census Bureau, "QuickFacts: Iowa," population estimates, July 1, 2019, https://www.census.gov/quickfacts/IA.

3. US Census Bureau, "QuickFacts: Des Moines City, Iowa," population estimates, July 1, 2019, https://www.census.gov/quickfacts/fact/table/desmoinescityiowa /PST045219.

4. Farmland Information Center, "Iowa Data and Statistics," accessed March 2021, https://farmlandinfo.org/statistics/iowa-statistics/.

5. Author email with Monte Kloberdanz, May 25, 2019.

6. Author interview with Brenda Church, June 1, 2018.

7. University of Northern Iowa is Jane Elliott's alma mater; when she attended it was known as Iowa State Teachers College.

8. Author interview with Linda Ring Kinneman, August 24, 2018.

9. Author interview with Jerry and Sandy Koenigs, September 14, 2018.

10. Author interview with Dennis Leard, September 14, 2018.

11. Author interviews with Steven Harnack, former Riceville Junior High School principal, and Linda Ring Kinneman. The Harnack interviews took place January 24, 2018, November 19, 2018; the Kinneman interview took place August 24, 2018. Many Riceville residents and former residents corroborated these allegations.

12. Matt Stevens and Sheryl Gay Stolberg, "Steve King Asks If There Would Be 'Any Population' Left without Rape and Incest," *New York Times*, August 15, 2019,

https://www.nytimes.com/2019/08/14/us/politics/steve-king-rape-incest.html?searchResultPosition=1.

13. An oft-used expression of surprise or pardon, *Ope!* is used, for instance, after accidentally bumping into someone. Derived from the Norwegian, *Uff-dah!* is an expression that means anything from "my goodness!" to "ouch!" When arising from a chair, a person might intone *Uff-dah* while clutching his or her lower back.

14. Author interview with Karen Schofield, January 17, 2019.

CHAPTER TWO: DIRTY LITTLE BASTARDS

1. Jennison marriage certificate, August 25, 1927, on file with Iowa State Board of Health.

2. Jane Elliott with Susan K. Golant, "Blinded by Color: A White Woman Challenges the Racial Status Quo in America," undated manuscript and book proposal, p. 7, author's collection; other biographical material comes from Kären Mason, "An Oral History Interview with Jane Elliott," November 4, 2009, Jane Elliott Papers, Iowa Women's Archives at the University of Iowa Libraries; Jane Elliott, untitled manuscript dated "1968," Iowa Women's Archives at the University of Iowa Libraries; and author interview with Jane Elliott, March 17, 2018.

3. Author interview with Jane Elliott, March 17, 2018.

4. "Riceville Farmer Loses 52 Hogs with Cholera," *Waterloo Courier*, December 16, 1941, 14.

5. Author interview with Patty Bodenham, July 7, 2004. Bodenham died June 10, 2007, at age ninety-two.

6. From an undated typed sheet in the Jane Elliott Papers, Iowa Women's Archives at the University of Iowa Libraries; author interview with Mary Jennison Yager, Jane's sister, April 12, 2018.

7. Mason, "An Oral History Interview," 10.

8. Author interview with Mary Jennison Yager, April 12, 2018.

9. Author interview with Jane Elliott, March 17, 2018.

10. Mason, "An Oral History Interview," 15.

11. Mason, "An Oral History Interview," 11.

12. Elliott and Golant, "Blinded by Color," chapter 2, p. 4.

13. From a poster displaying the names and photographs of the Riceville High School Class of 1952, located in the hallway outside the school's gymnasium.

14. Author interview with Jane Elliott, September 24, 2003.

15. Author interviews with Carol Lou and Adolph Brunner, May 14, 2018, May 17, 2019.

16. Elliott and Golant, "Blinded by Color," chapter 2, pp. 4–6; Mason, "An Oral History Interview," 11.

17. Author interview with Mary Yager, April 12, 2018.

18. One student in the graduating class must not have shown up for photo day.

19. "Riceville High to Have 41 Graduates," *Waterloo Courier*, May 12, 1952, 7.

20. Riceville High School Class of 1952 poster.

21. Jane Elliott's Iowa State Teachers College official student transcript, Office of the Registrar, University of Northern Iowa.

22. Among other sources for information on the history of the show *Amos 'n' Andy*, see Melvin Patrick Ely's *The Adventures of Amos 'n' Andy: A Social History of an American Phenomenon* (Charlottesville: University of Virginia Press, 2001).

23. Mason, "An Oral History Interview," 43, 44.

24. For more information on Manly, Iowa, see William J. Maddix, "Blacks and Whites in Manly: An Iowa Town Overcomes Racism," *The Palimpsest* 63, no. 5 (1982): 130–37. Dunn was such a gifted tackle that he was named an All-American—a nearly impossible feat for an athlete who played at a small teachers' college, particularly one in the boonies of northern Iowa. He went on to earn a PhD in education from Michigan State University, and taught at State University College at Oswego, New York.

CHAPTER THREE: PIZZUI

1. Jane Elliott, unpublished letter/manuscript, formatted as a remembrance to her children, November 1986, p. 186, author's collection.

2. "Randall Teacher Gets Linen Gifts at Recent Shower," *Ames Daily Tribune*, February 18, 1955, 6; "Randall School Spruced Up," *Ames Daily Tribune*, August 29, 1952, 4; "Slater," *Ames Daily Tribune*, February 21, 1955, 7.

3. "New National Food Store Opened," *Waterloo Courier*, August 7, 1962, 16; "New National Store," *Waterloo Courier*, July 15, 2002, 5.

4. "1759 Corning Ave, Waterloo, IA 50701," Zillow, https://www.zillow.com /homes/for_sale/1759-Corning-Waterloo-Iowa_rb/, accessed February 2021.

5. "Six New Teachers at Riceville School," *Mason City Globe-Gazette*, September 8, 1964, 5.

6. "801 S Pine St, Riceville, IA 50466," Zillow, https://www.zillow.com /homes/801-Pine-Street-Riceville-Iowa_rb/, accessed February 2021.

7. "Hotel Management Change at Riceville," *Waterloo Courier*, September 8, 1963, 43; "Wanted!" *Riceville Recorder* advertisement, May 7, 1964, 5; author interview with Jane Elliott, March 17, 2018.

8. Author interview with Jane Elliott, September 12, 2003; Elliott, unpublished letter/manuscript for her children, p. 50.

9. William Peters, *A Class Divided: Then and Now* (New Haven, CT: Yale University Press, 1987), 18, 19.

10. US Bureau of the Census. "Negro Population, by County: 1960 and 1950," *US Census of Population: 1960*, Supplementary Reports, Series PC(S1)-52 (Washington, DC: US Government Printing Office, 1966).

11. Tim Jamison, "Grant to Document Waterloo's 'Smokey Row,'" *Waterloo Courier*, January 8, 2018, https://wcfcourier.com/news/local/govt-and-politics /grant-to-document-waterloo-s-smokey-row/article_571770a5-f708-551a-ba6e

-7c3c9d7d0b32.html; Amie Steffen, "Waterloo Race Relations Still an Issue 40 Years after City Report," *Waterloo Courier*, September 9, 2007, https://wcfcourier .com/news/top_story/waterloo-race-relations-still-an-issue-years-after-city-report /article_42d89ae7-9c4e-5048-9877-ad949bbfc893.html.

12. Author interview with Jane Elliott, October 19, 2003.

13. "Vietnam War Casualties from Iowa," The Virtual Wall Vietnam Veterans Memorial https://www.virtualwall.org/istate/istatia.htm, accessed February 2021; "Vietnam War U.S. Military Fatal Casualty Statistics," Military Records, National Archives, https://www.archives.gov/research/military/vietnam-war/casualty -statistics#date, accessed February 2021. The data cover US fatalities in Vietnam from 1956 through 1964. The first Riceville fatality was Air Force Captain Jerome Smith, thirty, killed October 2, 1966. Smith was a 1954 graduate of Riceville High School. Another Riceville fatality was Marine Lance Cpl. Stanton Setka, twenty, killed August 29, 1967. Setka was a 1965 graduate of Riceville High School. He was the son of Stanley and Ruth Setka; Ruth Setka taught with Jane Elliott at Riceville Elementary School. A total of 522 Iowans were killed during the Vietnam War.

14. "NE Iowa Election Results," *Waterloo Courier*, November 4, 1964, 9.

15. "Total Population for Iowa's Incorporated Places: 1850–2000," Iowa Data Center, State Library of Iowa, https://www.iowadatacenter.org/datatables/PlacesAll /plpopulation18502000.pdf.

16. *Riceville Recorder:* January 2, 1964; January 23, 1964; February 20, 1964; February 27, 1964; March 26, 1964; May 21, 1964; June, 25, 1964; July 9, 1964.

17. Kären Mason, "An Oral History Interview with Jane Elliott," November 4, 2009, Jane Elliott Papers, Iowa Women's Archives at the University of Iowa Libraries, 27, 28.

18. Mason, "An Oral History Interview," 27, 28.

19. Mason, "An Oral History Interview," 28, 29.

20. Mason, "An Oral History Interview," 29, 30.

21. Philosopher and educator John Dewey in 1938 wrote *Experience and Education*, in which he argued that the authoritarian knowledge approach of traditional education robs children of the thrill of discovery through participation. He advocated that schools must be social and interactive institutions, where students must be allowed to interact with each other in their learning as well as with the curriculum.

22. Mason, "An Oral History Interview," 34, 35.

23. M.K. Henry and S.G. Brickley, eds., *Dyslexia: Samuel T. Orton and His Legacy* (Baltimore: International Dyslexia Association, 1999).

24. Author interview with Sandi Dohlman Burke, January 11, 2019.

25. Author interview with Sandy and Jerry Koenigs, September 14, 2018.

26. Author interview with Cathy Martin, April 5, 2018.

27. Author interview with Bill Blake, August 2, 2018.

28. Erector Sets are a brand of metal-toy construction assemblies, patented by Alfred Carlton Gilbert and first sold by his company, the Mysto Manufacturing Company, in 1913. The sets are still manufactured today; see http://www.meccano .com/about.

29. Author interview with Ruth Setka, July 19, 2004.

30. Author interview with Dean Weaver, July 20, 2004.

31. Mason, "An Oral History Interview," 18; "Riceville Hopes to Bridge Two Eras," *Waterloo Courier*, December 26, 1976, 37.

32. Author interview with Mary Lou Koschmeder, July 16, 2004.

33. Mason, "An Oral History Interview," 32.

CHAPTER FOUR: ELYSIAN FIELDS

1. Author interview with Sarah Elliott, April 12, 2018; "Clubs in Area Are Keeping Busy," *Waterloo Courier*, May 4, 1964, 7; "Ada Y. Crum Observes Her 89th Birthday," *Mason City Globe-Gazette*, January 12, 1962, 15; "Mrs. Ada Crum, Riceville, Observes 90th Birthday," *Mason City Globe-Gazette*, January 9, 1963, 10; "Two Riceville Citizens Have Birthday Observations," *Waterloo Courier*, January 8, 1964, 15; "Hobby at Riceville Began with Gift," *Waterloo Courier*, November 11, 1962, 34; "Northeast Iowa Notes," *Waterloo Courier*, June 16, 1963, 48.

2. Author interview with Linda Ring Kinneman, August 24, 2018; "Fire Cleanup at Riceville," *Waterloo Courier*, October 21, 1974, 10.

3. The Watts Theatre was opened in 1950. The fourteen-acre Starlite Drive-In opened in 1947; see "First Drive-In Theater in Iowa Opens Sept. 10," *Waterloo Sunday Courier*, August 31, 1947, 3.

CHAPTER FIVE: FROM MEMPHIS TO RICEVILLE

1. "April 4, 1968: Martin Luther King Jr. Assassinated," ABC News, video, 6:28, January 15, 2010, https://www.youtube.com/watch?v=pi6NeuFr5Us&feature=player_embedded.

2. "April 4, 1968: Martin Luther King Jr. Assassinated."

3. "1968 King Assassination Report (CBS News)," CBS, video, 3:10, April 2, 2008, https://www.youtube.com/watch?v=cmOBbxgxKvo.

4. Leon Uris, *Mila 18* (New York: Doubleday, 1961).

5. Letter to Marilyn "Mickey" Alcorn, April 4, 1968, Jane Elliott Papers, Iowa Women's Archives at the University of Iowa Libraries. This and several other letters Elliott handwrote to Alcorn, her former college friend, are curious. The question arises of why Elliott would have kept copies of these letters, written by her and supposedly sent in the mail, in cursive and with a pencil. Perhaps they were never sent. Perhaps they were drafts of letters. Perhaps they were written after the fact. After Alcorn graduated from Iowa State Teachers College, she taught kindergarten at the Iowa Braille and Sight Saving School, then continued her education at the University of Iowa. She got married and relocated to Los Alamos, New Mexico, then to Silver Spring, Maryland, where she taught elementary school. Alcorn later moved

to Virginia and Florida. The college friendship between Alcorn and Elliott didn't hold. One of the author's research assistants, Rachael Hovde, tracked down Alcorn's whereabouts in Florida in early 2019. Hovde spoke to Alcorn's daughter, Ann Alves. The author interviewed Alves on February 6, 2019, who told him that her mother was not in good health, but said she would ask her mother about any recollections of Elliott. Alves told the author that, when asked about Elliott, Alcorn recalled Elliott as "arrogant," without further elaboration.

CHAPTER SIX: THE EXPERIMENT

1. The day's class events were re-created through a variety of sources, including author interviews with Jane Elliott; letters written to Marilyn "Mickey" Alcorn by Jane Elliott, contained in the Jane Elliott Papers, Iowa Women's Archives at the University of Iowa Libraries; Kären Mason, "An Oral History Interview with Jane Elliott," Iowa Women's Archives at the University of Iowa Libraries; Jane Elliott with Susan K. Golant, "Blinded by Color: A White Woman Challenges the Racial Status Quo in America," undated manuscript and book proposal, author's collection; William Peters, *A Class Divided: Then and Now* (New Haven, CT: Yale University Press, 1987); author interviews and email exchanges with eleven students who were present that day; author interviews and email exchanges with five Riceville Elementary teachers who were working at the school in 1968. The author interviews and email exchanges were conducted in 2004 and 2018–19.

2. The students enrolled in the 1967–68 class in the fall were Debra Anderson, Steven Armstrong, James Benttine, Vickie Bill, Dale Brunner, Byron Bucknell, Sharon Cummings, Bruce Fox, Jeanette Goodale, Sindee Hockens, Debra Hughes, Pat Johnson, Julie Kleckner, Steven Knode, Danny Lewis, Cindy Meyer, Alan Moss, Theodore Perzynski, Kim Reynolds, Ricky Ring, Dennis Runde, Nancy Schumann, Ricky Sletten, Lowell Sprung, Billy Thompson, Steven VanDeWalker, Julie Wilcox, and Teresa Wade. Carol Anderson was a transfer student who joined the class later in the year.

3. Author interviews with Dinsmore Brandmill's daughter, June Judge, June 18, 2018, and Bruce Fox, a former Riceville Elementary School student, January 25, 2019.

4. This specific recollection is from an online conversation between Jane Elliott and Angela Davis, at a symposium at the University of Houston Graduate College of Social Work, September 6, 2018.

5. Letter to Marilyn "Mickey" Alcorn, April 5, 1968, Jane Elliott Papers, Iowa Women's Archives at the University of Iowa Libraries.

6. Author interview with former student Bruce Fox, January 25, 2019.

7. Author interviews, via email, with Debra Anderson Roth, August 15, 2019, and August 2, 2004.

8. Author interview with Julie Kleckner Baird, July 15–20, 2004. Baird died February 3, 2008.

9. Author interviews with Rick Sletten, July 9, 2004, and February 5, 2019.

10. Jane recalled in her April 5, 1968, letter to Alcorn and in an author interview (October 26, 2017), the teacher as Helen Weaver, although a former principal, a former teacher, and several students interviewed said they found it impossible to imagine and believe that Weaver would have used such language. Weaver died October 18, 1996.

CHAPTER SEVEN: "DID SHE REALLY?"

1. Kären Mason, "An Oral History Interview with Jane Elliott," November 4, 2009, Jane Elliott Papers, Iowa Women's Archives at the University of Iowa Libraries, 39.

2. The actual quote is: "I am in blood / Stepp'd in so far that, should I wade no more, / Returning were as tedious as go o'er." *Macbeth*, ed. Kenneth Muir, Arden Shakespeare (London: Routledge, 1951), 3.4.135–37.

3. As quoted in a letter to Marilyn "Mickey" Alcorn, August 8, 1970, Jane Elliott Papers, Iowa Women's Archives at the University of Iowa Libraries. The date is unaccountable; it ought to be dated sometime during the second week in May 1968 when the experiment and its aftermath took place—unless Elliott re-created the letters after the event, and forgot to date this one letter correctly.

4. *Riceville Recorder*, April 18, 1968, 4.

CHAPTER EIGHT: "HERE'S JOHNNY!"

1. Events described in this chapter are re-created from author interview with Jane Elliott, March 17, 2018; Jane Elliott Papers, Iowa Women's Archives, the University of Iowa Libraries; and Jane Elliott, unpublished letter/manuscript, formatted as a remembrance to her children, November 1986, author's collection.

2. Letter to Marilyn "Mickey" Alcorn, May 17, 1968, Jane Elliott Papers, Iowa Women's Archives, the University of Iowa Libraries.

3. Letter to Alcorn, May 17, 1968.

4. Letter to Alcorn, May 17, 1968.

5. *Riceville Recorder*, May 30, 1968, 1.

6. The *Des Moines Register* ran the first statewide story on Jane Elliott and her classroom experiment, on page 1, Sunday, June 2, 1968, two days after Elliott appeared on *The Tonight Show*. The Associated Press followed the *Register* story with a seventeen-paragraph dispatch that moved on its national wire on July 12, 1968. The story was written by Celiene Nold with a Riceville, Iowa, dateline. Along with the story, the AP transmitted a photo of Elliott's students in the playground, some jumping rope and others on the swing set, as two children longingly looked on from the sidelines. The photo carried this cutline: "PLAYGROUND

OUTCASTS—To show third graders in a rural Iowa community with no negro residents how discrimination on the basis of color feels, Mrs. Darald Elliott of Riceville made brown-eyed students stand in restricted area while blue-eyed students enjoyed playground equipment and game of skip rope. Mrs. Elliott called the response 'frightening.'"

7. Author interview with Gail Messersmith Morris, November 15, 2018.

8. *Riceville Recorder*, May 30, 1968, 2.

9. Author interviews with Jane Elliott, October 21, 2004, and October 26, 2017.

10. Jane Elliott Papers, Iowa Women's Archives, University of Iowa Libraries.

11. "History," Warwick Hotels and Resorts, https://warwickhotels.com/history /, accessed February 2021.

12. Reminder notes on Warwick Hotel notepad papers and undated letter to Marilyn "Mickey" Alcorn, Jane Elliott Papers, Iowa Women's Archives, University of Iowa Libraries.

13. Author interview with Darald Elliott, October 21, 2004.

14. Letter to Marilyn "Mickey" Alcorn, undated, Jane Elliott Papers, Iowa Women's Archives, University of Iowa Libraries.

15. An example of this can be seen in the TV listings for the *Long Beach Independent*, May 31, 1968, 24.

16. Alex Haley, *The Playboy Interviews* (New York: Ballantine Books, 1993), 290–91.

17. Robert Metz, *The Tonight Show* (Chicago: Playboy Press, 1980), xiii; and Henry Bushkin, *Johnny Carson* (New York: Thorndike Press, 2013), 250.

18. See Joan Walsh, "49 Years Ago, Harry Belafonte Hosted the Tonight Show— and It was Amazing," *The Nation*, February 16, 2017, https://www.thenation.com /article/49-years-ago-harry-belafonte-hosted-the-tonight-show-and-it-was-amazing/.

19. As quoted in Kenneth Tynan, "Fifteen Years of the Salto Mortale," *New Yorker*, February 20, 1978, https://www.newyorker.com/magazine/1978/02/20 /fifteen-years-salto-mortale.

20. Author interviews with Jane Elliott, October 21, 2004, and October 26, 2017; Letter to Alcorn, undated.

21. Letter to Alcorn, undated.

22. Letter to Alcorn, undated.

23. George Langford, "Sox Win in 14th! Beat Twins 2–1, on Bunt by Aparicio," *Chicago Tribune*, June 1, 1968, 45.

24. Author interview with Jane Elliott, October 26, 2017.

CHAPTER NINE: BACK HOME

1. Kären Mason, "An Oral History Interview with Jane Elliott," November 4, 2009, Jane Elliott Papers, Iowa Women's Archives at the University of Iowa Libraries, 52.

2. Letter to Marilyn "Mickey" Alcorn, undated, Jane Elliott Papers, Iowa Women's Archives at the University of Iowa Libraries. The phrase was likely a reference to

westward-bound American settlers, who anticipated "elephant sightings" along their overland routes; when they saw none, they came away disappointed and disillusioned. For more on the phrase, see Gerald Conti's article, "Seeing the Elephant," *Civil War Times Illustrated*, June 1984, http://wesclark.com/jw/elephant.html; and B. A. Botkin, *A Treasury of American Folklore*, 1944, available at http://wesclark.com/jw/elephant_book.jpg.

3. Coverage of Elliott occasionally appeared in the *Riceville Recorder*, but never commensurate with her importance. When William Peters was to film "Eye of the Storm" in 1970 in Riceville, the local newspaper did run a photograph of Elliott, Peters, and the ABC film crew and an eight-line caption with the headline, "ABC Television Cameras in Operation This Week in RCS Elementary School."

4. Author interview with a former Riceville resident, who asked that her name not be used, May 21, 2018.

5. Author interview with JoAnne Machin, October 10, 2018.

6. Author interview with Jerry and Sandy Koenigs, September 14, 2018.

7. These alleged incidents come from Jane Elliott's March 17, 2018, recollection, and are contested. Many of those involved are deceased; several of those alive, when contacted, said they would not discuss their relationship with Elliott. John Dinger, Hazel Dinger's son, disputed Elliott's assertion. He said it was impossible, since to his knowledge his mother never played bridge.

8. Author interview with Jane Elliott, March 17, 2018.

9. Author interview with Jane Elliott, March 17, 2018.

10. For a sampling of such letters from supporters, see letters contained in Jane Elliott Papers, Women's Archives at the University of Iowa Libraries.

11. Author interview with Mary Noble, February 24, 2018.

12. Letter to Jane Elliott from Hazel Farus, Iowa City, May 31, 1968, Jane Elliott Papers, Women's Archives at the University of Iowa Libraries.

13. Letter to Jane Elliott, signed from "Eunice, Joe & Joey," June 3, 1968, Jane Elliott Papers, Women's Archives at the University of Iowa Libraries.

14. Letter from Jane Elliott to Mrs. William Turner, Worcester, MA, June 5, 1968, Jane Elliott Papers, Women's Archives at the University of Iowa Libraries.

15. Letter to Jane Elliott, from Mrs. D. R. Thompkins, June 3, 1968, Jane Elliott Papers, Women's Archives at the University of Iowa Libraries. The letter was addressed to "Mrs. Jane Phillips, Third Grade Teacher on the Johnny Carson Show, Riceville, Iowa."

16. Letter to Jane Elliott, from Mrs. Loretta Ohrmann, July 13, 1968, Jane Elliott Papers, Women's Archives at the University of Iowa Libraries.

17. "Brown-Eyed Prejudice for Those with Blue," *Des Moines Register*, June 2, 1968, 1.

18. As late as 1984, *Time* magazine ranked the then-Cowles family-owned *Register* among the nation's top ten newspapers. The morning and afternoon editions reached into as many as 50 percent of Iowa homes in the 1960s. See William B. Friedricks, "The Newspaper That Captured a State: A History of the Des Moines Register, 1849–1985," *The Annals of Iowa* 54, no. 4 (1995): 303–37.

19. Examples include the *Albuquerque Journal*, *Arizona Daily Star* (page 1), *Baltimore Sun*, *Cedar Rapids Gazette* (page 1), *Davenport Times-Democrat*, *Fresno Bee*, *Oakland Tribune*, *Philadelphia Inquirer*, *Salt Lake Tribune*, *San Bernardino Sun-Telegram*, *St. Petersburg Times*, and *Spokane Spokesman-Review*. The AP moved several photographs to accompany the story. One photo showed Elliott's students reading; another showed students on playground swings; both images included students longingly looking in from the side. It's unclear when the photographs had been taken; school had been out for three weeks when the story moved, and the experiment had been concluded. The images were likely taken by Charlotte Button, a photographer and friend of Elliott. Button had contacted producers at *The Tonight Show* initially about the experiment. Button died in November 1972. Don Button, Charlotte's husband, who circulated the flyer around town that celebrated Elliott's invitation to appear on *The Tonight Show*, died in February 1977.

CHAPTER TEN: WHAT SOME OF THE KIDS SAID

1. Author interview, via email, with Kim Reynolds Huemann, July 13, 2004.

2. Author interview with Bruce Fox, January 25, 2019.

3. Author interview, via email, with Sharon Cummings Zobeck, June 9, 2004.

4. Author interview, via email, with Vickie Bill Roethler, February 13, 2019.

5. Author interview with Kay Worple, June 27, 2018.

6. Author interview with Pat Johnson, January 25, 2019.

7. Author interview, via email, with Alan Moss, July 21, 2004. Moss volunteered that his handwriting still is messy.

8. Author interview with Dorothy Wallace, July 19, 2004. Wallace died January 17, 2017.

9. Author interviews with Lavonne Moses, July 21, 2004, and October 31, 2018.

10. Author interview with Mary Lou Koschmeder, July 16, 2004. Koschmeder died August 21, 2016.

11. Author interview with Ruth Setka, July 19, 2004. Setka died July 13, 2020.

12. Author interview with Mary Myers, August 20, 2018. Myers died August 1, 2020.

13. Author interview with Carol Lou and Adolph Brunner, May 14, 2018. Their son, Dale Brunner, was killed in a motorcycle accident in the summer of 1976, just before he was to enter his senior year at Riceville High.

CHAPTER ELEVEN: ROTARIANS

1. Original mimeographed Rotary program, Jane Elliott Papers, Iowa Women's Archives at the University of Iowa Libraries.

2. Rotary membership was exclusively male until 1987, following the US Supreme Court ruling that Rotary Clubs could not exclude women from membership on the basis of gender. See Sarah Jones, "Celebrating 30 Years of Women in Rotary," *Rotary News Online*, May 2017, https://rotarynewsonline.org/celebrating-30-years-of -women-in-rotary/.

3. Kären Mason, "An Oral History Interview with Jane Elliott," November 4, 2009, Jane Elliott Papers, Iowa Women's Archives at the University of Iowa Libraries, 53.

4. In retrospect, the question arises: Was the brown-eyed latecomer to the Rotary luncheon a plant Elliott had arranged? Considering Elliott's protocol at other events where she tried out the experiment, it seems likely to assume yes. But there is no evidence to confirm this to be true or false.

5. Re-created from author interviews with Jane Elliott, September 24, 2003, and March 17, 2018, as well as from Jane Elliott, unpublished letter/manuscript, formatted as a remembrance to her children, November 1986, pp. 52–55, author's collection.

6. Original letter from Weston D. Birdsall on letterhead of Kurstenbach-Hauge & Associates, Inc. Agricultural Service, August 26, 1968, Jane Elliott Papers, Iowa Women's Archives at the University of Iowa Libraries.

CHAPTER TWELVE: "EYE OF THE STORM"

1. Author interview with Malinda Sunnes Whisenhunt, a former student in the class, June 21, 2004. Whisenhunt died January 22, 2018.

2. "Television Reviews: The Way It Is," *Variety*, October 16, 1968, 43; "Canadian Broadcasting System to Film Documentary in Riceville," *Riceville Recorder*, August 17, 1968, 1; "Riceville Experiment to Be Aired," *Waterloo Courier*, September 8, 1968, 16.

3. William Peters, *A Class Divided: Then and Now* (New Haven, CT: Yale University Press, 1987), 46. Elliott is referring not to the ABC documentary filmed two years later, but to this CBC program.

4. Peters, *A Class Divided*, 46.

5. The students in the 1968–69 class were Sue Aulman, Paul Bodensteiner, Todd Brandau, Mark Butterfield, Steve Cummings, David Graves, Gail Hoffman, Kristine Isaacson, Jeffrey Klein, Donna Jo Linkenmeyer, Steve Lubbert, Joseph Marr, Dale McCarthy, Debora Nath, Krystal Priebe, Brenda Rieken, Kevin Roske, Sandra Stark, Malinda Sunnes, Darrell Warburton, Robert Williamson, Joseph Winkels, and two unidentified children.

6. The exchange was culled from Peters, *A Class Divided*, and from "Obituary of Christopher Bodensteiner," *Mason City Globe-Gazette*, August 5, 1997, 9. Paul Bodensteiner's father, Christopher, was a one time Riceville school board member.

7. Author interview with Malinda Sunnes Whisenhunt, May 21, 2004.

8. Author interview with Dale McCarthy, June 22, 2004. McCarthy is a farmer in nearby McIntire.

9. Author interview with Malinda Sunnes Whisenhunt, May 21, 2004.

10. The *Variety* review of the CBC segment was glowing, saying it "has relevance everywhere. It should be seen in its entirety"; "Television Reviews: The Way It Is," *Variety*, October 16, 1968, 43.

11. Frank Penn, "Tiny Tim Gets Accolade," *Ottawa Citizen*, October 7, 1968, 21.

12. Jane Elliott, unpublished letter/manuscript, formatted as a remembrance to her children, November 1986, pp. 39–40, author's collection.

13. Elliott, letter/manuscript to her children, 47.

14. "Iowa Teacher of the Year to Be Chosen," *Hawarden Independent*, November 28, 1968, 9; "Teacher of the Year Is Named," *Quad City Times*, November 27, 1968, 11. Mrs. Leon Sharp was named the 1969 Teacher of the Year.

15. Letter to author sent by Jean Clausen, July 1, 2004.

16. Author interview with Brenda Church, June 1, 2018.

17. Jane Elliott's letter/manuscript to her children, 45.

18. Letter to *Reader's Digest*, July 22, 1968, Jane Elliott Papers, Iowa Women's Archives at the University of Iowa Libraries.

19. Letter from Loretta Marion, March 18, 1969, Jane Elliott Papers, Iowa Women's Archives at the University of Iowa Libraries.

20. "Exercise in Discrimination," *Scholastic Teacher*, April 18, 1969, 1315–16.

21. Copies of letters contained in Jane Elliott Papers, Iowa Women's Archives at the University of Iowa Libraries.

22. Letter from Bill Robinson, Iowa State Education Association, April 16, 1969, Jane Elliott Papers, Iowa Women's Archives at the University of Iowa Libraries. Letter from Marney Letts, Keokuk Rotary Club Ladies Night Committee chairman, May 23, 1969, Jane Elliott Papers, Iowa Women's Archives at the University of Iowa Libraries.

23. "Rotarians, Wives Learn Lesson on the Evils of Discrimination," undated clipping from unidentified newspaper, Jane Elliott Papers, Iowa Women's Archives at the University of Iowa Libraries.

24. Jane Elliott with Susan K. Golant, "Blinded by Color: A White Woman Challenges the Racial Status Quo in America," undated manuscript and book proposal, overview, chapter outline, p. 6, author's holdings.

25. Elliott, letter/manuscript to her children, 46.

26. Margalit Fox, "William Peters, 85, Journalist Who Examined Race in U.S., Dies," *New York Times*, May 24, 2007, 14; "William Peters, King-Era Journalist, Dies at 85," Associated Press, May 29, 2007.

27. The documentary would be produced, written, and directed by William Peters and his wife at the time, coproducer Muriel Neff Peters.

28. Elliott with Golant, "Blinded by Color," chapter outline, 5.

29. Author interview with a former Riceville resident who asked that her name not be used, May 24, 2018.

30. Elliott, letter/manuscript to her children, 46; Dinsmore Brandmill died on July 3, 1988, and was never interviewed for this book.

31. Elliott, letter/manuscript to her children, 69.

32. The classroom scene was re-created from Peters, *A Class Divided*, and the video of "Eye of the Storm," available online at "Eye of the Storm Jane Elliot 1970," Rick Silverman, April 23, 2017, video, 26:17, https://www.youtube.com/watch?v=6gi2ToZdKVc.

33. Author interviews with Sandi Dohlman Burke, July 9, 2004, and January 11, 2019.

34. See "Eye of the Storm Jane Elliot 1970."

35. "William Peters, 'Class Divided' Director, Has Died," *Weekend Edition*, National Public Radio, June 2, 2007.

36. NEA and ABC press releases, May 5, 1970, Jane Elliott Papers, Iowa Women's Archives at the University of Iowa Libraries.

37. Clarence Petersen, "Another Review by Mr. Agnew," *Chicago Tribune*, May 11, 1970, section 3, 13.

38. James Doussard, "'Eye of the Storm' is Simple, Touching," *Louisville Courier-Journal*, May 11, 1970, 21.

39. John Leonard, "The Eye of the Storm," *Life*, May 8, 1970, 16–18.

40. Terrence O'Flaherty, "The Eyes Have It," *San Francisco Chronicle*, May 11, 1970, 40.

41. Max Rafferty, "Educational Malfeasance in Iowa Race Experiment," *Sioux City Journal*, November 14, 1970, 4. Rafferty was reared in Sioux City, Iowa.

42. Letter from E. Mesa, undated, Jane Elliott Papers, the Iowa Women's Archives at the University of Iowa Libraries.

43. Letter to Dinsmore Brandmill from Dot Moyers, December 1, 1970, Jane Elliott Papers, the Iowa Women's Archives at the University of Iowa Libraries.

44. Letter from Jane Elliott to Susan T. Mitchell, July 6, 1970, Jane Elliott Papers, the Iowa Women's Archives at the University of Iowa Libraries.

45. Elliott, letter/manuscript to her children, 72–73.

46. Anonymous letter to Jane Elliott, May 29, 1970, Jane Elliott Papers, the Iowa Women's Archives at the University of Iowa Libraries; Jane Elliott response to a May 11, 1970, letter from Jerald Ruff, M.D., Bloomington, IN, Jane Elliott Papers, the Iowa Women's Archives at the University of Iowa Libraries.

47. To promote Peters's book, Doubleday, the book's publisher, sent Elliott and Peters on a round of national media events to drum up publicity. Elliott flew to New York and appeared with Peters on the nationally aired *Today Show*, touting the book and the experiment. The pair traveled to the Midwest to appear on the *Phil Donahue Show*. This was before Donahue had become a national television star; he was broadcasting a local talk show from his home state of Ohio, from Dayton, on station WLWD. Elliott was seated next to blue-eyed Peters, as blue-eyed Donahue, his trademark microphone in hand, roamed the studio audience. Whenever one of the audience members asked Elliott a question, Donahue would repeat and rephrase it. Then, when Elliott would start to answer, Peters would interrupt and take over, followed by Donahue, who had the habit of elaborating or distilling the question or answer. Finally, she exploded. "Look, blue eyes," Elliott said, pointing to both Peters and Donahue. "I can answer my own questions!" This recollection is contained in the Jane Elliott Papers, Iowa Women's Archives at the University of Iowa Libraries.

1. The decennial conferences were discontinued during the Reagan years and never resumed.

2. Memorandum to participate in the 1970 White House Conference on Children, Jane Elliott Papers, the Iowa Women's Archives at the University of Iowa Libraries. Stephen Hess, thirty-seven at the time, was a longtime Republican speechwriter who had worked for Eisenhower and Nixon. Contacted for this book at his office at the Brookings Institution in 2018, Hess said he had no recollection of Elliott's eye-color experiment at the conference.

3. As reported in Steve Clapp, "Aide Grapples with Youth Conferences," *San Antonio Express*, Washington Post News Service, September 19, 1970, 51.

4. In addition to Jane Elliott, members of Forum No. 18 were Jeanne Spurlock (chair), Ada Deer (vice-chair), Rabbi Alvin Fine, Melvin Ho, Robert Mendelsohn, Diane Oakley, K. Patrick Okura, Maurilio Ortiz, John Rasberry, Piri Thomas, and Rev. Robert Helm; "Report to the President: White House Conference on Children 1970," available at https://files.eric.ed.gov/fulltext/ED052828.pdf. Elliott was one of forty-two delegates from Iowa.

5. Printed program, White House Conference on Children 1970, Jane Elliott Papers, the Iowa Women's Archives at the University of Iowa Libraries.

6. Jane Elliott, unpublished letter/manuscript, formatted as a remembrance to her children, November 1986, p. 77, author's holdings.

7. Letter to "Cynthia," undated, Jane Elliott Papers, the Iowa Women's Archives at the University of Iowa Libraries.

8. Elliott, letter/manuscript to her children, 78.

9. The account of Forum 18's panel presented at the White House Conference on Children was re-created from various sources, including Jane Elliott with Susan K. Golant, "Blinded by Color: A White Woman Challenges the Racial Status Quo in America," undated manuscript and book proposal, chapter outline, pp. 8–10, author's collection; Elliott, letter/manuscript to her children; and Toni House, "Lesson in Prejudice," *Washington Evening Star*, December 14, 1970.

10. Piri Thomas was the author of the best-selling autobiography *Down These Mean Streets* (New York: Knopf, 1967), about growing up during the 1940s in New York's Spanish Harlem. He died in 2011. Kiyoski Patrick Okura served as a staff psychologist for Boys Town for seventeen years, then as executive assistant to the director of the National Institutes of Health. As a youth, Okura and his family were among the 120,000 Japanese-Americans forcibly removed and incarcerated in camps during World War II. He died in 2005.

11. Handwritten notes, undated, Jane Elliott Papers, the Iowa Women's Archives at the University of Iowa Libraries.

12. As quoted in House, "Lesson in Prejudice." *New York Times* reporter Nan Robertson (who was to go on to win a Pulitzer Prize in 1983 for her own chilling account about toxic shock syndrome) filed a story on the conference but had failed to gain access to the closed meeting room, and wrote only that "Mrs. Jane Elliott of Riceville, Iowa,

demonstrated how she taught her third-grade pupils about prejudice by eye color, with the forum acting out the blue eyes and the brown eyes [experiment]."

13. "Conference of Children Ends with Suggestions," *Waterloo Courier*, AP, December 18, 1970, 10.

14. "Conference on Children Stirs Local Delegates' Ire," *Waterloo Courier*, AP, December 22, 1970, 10.

CHAPTER FOURTEEN: TROUBLE

1. Letter from Wilda Wood to Jane Elliott, May 14, 1970, Jane Elliott Papers, the Iowa Women's Archives at the University of Iowa Libraries.

2. Jim Gibney, "... Now They Know How Segregation Hurts," *Boston Sunday Globe*, December 3, 1967, 100.

3. Gibney, "... Now They Know."

4. Letter from Mary Carroll to Jane Elliott, May 14, 1970, Jane Elliott Papers, the Iowa Women's Archives at the University of Iowa Libraries.

5. Roger Thorson, "Project Misery," *National Elementary Principal*, vol. 45, no. 4, February 1966, 38–40. The same article appeared in *Colorado School Journal*, vol. 81, no. 12, March 5, 1966, 27–28.

6. Wilda Wood, "Idea Exchange: Project Misery," *NEA Journal*, vol. 55, September 1966, 60; "Teaching Students about Discrimination: Give Them a Taste of It," *School Management*, January 1967, 27.

7. "Teaching Students about Discrimination," 27.

8. Wilda Wood died in 1999.

9. Leon Uris, *Mila 18* (New York: Doubleday, 1961).

10. Jane Elliott, unpublished letter/manuscript, formatted as a remembrance to her children, November 1986, p. 6, author's holdings.

11. Jane Elliott with Susan K. Golant, "Blinded by Color: A White Woman Challenges the Racial Status Quo in America," undated manuscript and book proposal, chapter 2, p. 6, author's holdings.

12. Robert Jay Lifton, *The Nazi Doctors: Medical Killing and the Psychology of Genocide* (New York: Basic, 1986); Gerald L. Posner and John Ware, *Mengele: The Complete Story* (London: Queen Anne Press, 1986).

13. From the German documentary *Blauäugig* (Blue Eyed), directed by Bertram Verhaag, 1996; "'Blue Eyed' Transcript," Internet Archive, https://web.archive.org/web/20150202090627/http://newsreel.org/transcripts/blueeyed.htm, accessed February 2021.

14. Jane Elliott email to Keith Salvas, September 4, 2018.

15. Author interviews with George Hanna, July 4, 2004, and February 4, 2019. Hanna recalled the last name of his teacher as either Peterson or Pederson, but no records today exist of any teacher at Erskine Elementary School in 1968 with that name.

16. Keith Salvas email to author, May 28, 2018.

17. Email from Jane Elliott to Keith Salvas, March 4, 2015.

18. Bruce Lambert, "Rachel D. DuBois, 101, Educator Who Promoted Value of Diversity," *New York Times*, April 1, 1993, 24.

19. "City Schools Map Tolerance Drive," *New York Times*, January 7, 1944, 19; "Dr. Latz Is Honored: Advocate of 'Springfield Plan' of Schooling Gets Citation," *New York Times*, April 10, 1946, 21; "School Plan to Decrease Bias," *New York Times*, September 16, 1945, 42.

20. See "200 Take Part in Anytown USA Parlay," *Los Angeles Times*, August 5, 1955, 32; "Leadership Youth Camp Draws 7 from Arizona," *Arizona Republic*, August 18, 1951, 3; "2 Brotherhood Scholars Named," *Honolulu Advertiser*, August 3, 1952, 5; "170 Can Go to Anytown's 4th Reunion," *Tucson Daily Citizen*, December 22, 1960, 21; "Camp Anytown USA Teaches Nevada Teens Tough Lessons," *Reno Gazette-Journal*, July 30, 1989, 1; Karen de Sá, "Camps That Push Teens to the Brink," *San Francisco Chronicle*, June 17, 2018, 1; author interview with director of Camp Anytown Phoenix, Richard Valenzuela, June 26, 2018.

21. Author interview with Dolores Steffen, July 15, 2004. Steffen died in 2013.

22. Author interview with Pat Johnson, January 25, 2019.

23. Author interview at Andy's Mini-Mart, Riceville, September 14, 2018. The man asked that his name not be disclosed.

CHAPTER FIFTEEN: BLACKBOARD JUNGLE

1. This and other incidents and descriptions involving Paul Richer are culled from George Mills, "Furor over Discharge of Teacher, 21," *Des Moines Register*, May 18, 1956, 1; "Would You Want This Man to Teach Your Children?" *Pageant*, September 1956, 62–71; "The Enthusiast," *Time*, April 9, 1956, 102; and author interview with Paul Richer, June 27, 2018.

2. Joseph Gaer, *How the Great Religions Began* (New York: Dodd, Mead, 1956).

3. Author interview with Paul Richer, June 27, 2018.

4. Mills, "Furor over Discharge of Teacher, 21."

5. "May Appeal Firing from Riceville Teaching Post," *Waterloo Courier*, March 20, 1956, 19.

6. Released in 1955 by Metro-Goldwyn-Mayer, *Blackboard Jungle* was directed by Richard Brooks, based on a 1954 novel by Evan Hunter. In addition to introducing Sidney Poitier, the film has two other marks of distinction: It was the first Hollywood movie to use the expression *rock 'n' roll*, starting with Bill Haley and his Comets' "Rock Around the Clock" as the film's theme, which helped rocket the song to fame. When the Glenn Ford character introduces himself to his students as Mr. Dadier, writing his name on a blackboard, a student throws a baseball at the blackboard, obliterating the letters *e* and *r*, leaving "Dadi." The students abbreviate the name to "Dadi-O," pronounced "Daddy-O," the moniker given Ford. The word gained widespread adoption with the success of the film.

7. *Blackboard Jungle*, 1955.

8. Mills, "Furor over Discharge of Teacher, 21," 1, 28.

9. Phyllis Fleming, "Paul Richer Says He Won't Quit Teaching," *Daily Iowan*, March 28, 1956, 1; Mills, "Furor over Discharge of Teacher, 21."

10. *Mason City Globe-Gazette*, March 27, 1956, 2.

11. Sinclair Lewis's classic novel *Main Street* focuses on the life of librarian Carol Milford Kennicott, who moves with her physician husband to his hometown of Gopher Prairie. She finds the community smug and uninviting. She is derided by nonstop gossip circulated by Gopher Prairie's catty cliques. Along with *Babbitt* and *Arrowsmith, Main Street* is considered Lewis's most enduring work. Lewis was awarded the Nobel Prize in Literature in 1930, the first time an American earned such recognition.

12. "Would You Want This Man to Teach Your Children?" 69.

13. As quoted in Casandra Leff, ed., *A History of Riceville Community School (1875–2012): Shining Brightly after 137 Years* (Riceville, IA: Riceville Recorder, 2012), 21, 22.

14. "The Enthusiast."

15. "Would You Want This Man to Teach Your Children?"

16. "Would You Want This Man to Teach Your Children?"

17. "Debate on Riceville Teacher," *Des Moines Register*, April 1, 1956, 17.

18. "One Like Him for Every County," letter to the editor from Mrs. T. V. Jacobson, *Des Moines Register*, March 25, 1956, 19.

19. As quoted in Bill Webb, "Riceville Finds Strength and Esteem in Its School Record," *Mason City Globe-Gazette*, April 13, 1956, 21.

20. After Richer left the Riceville School District, he was drafted in the army and served three years, mostly in West Germany. He then worked as a teacher in Nigeria, followed by his appointment as Midwest field director for the United World Federation. Amid controversy similar to what happened in Riceville, when he was thirty-one and head of the English Department at Kettle Moraine High School in Wales, Wisconsin, Richer assigned students to write an essay titled, "God Is Dead." The school administration received complaints, and the school board threatened not to renew his teaching contract. More than 250 students signed a petition protesting the board's action. Richer left to start a professional theater in a former Presbyterian church in Delafield, Wisconsin. Richer also taught drama and speech at Oconomowoc High School, Oconomowoc, Wisconsin. He was an administrator at the Lad Lake Center for Emotionally Disturbed Boys in Waukesha, Wisconsin, before leaving to teach in Guinea, West Africa. Today, he lives in Lakeland, Florida.

CHAPTER SIXTEEN: SPOONER

1. "Walkout on J. Crow Experiment," *Chicago Defender*, July 3, 1971, 6.

2. Author conversation with Darald Elliott, October 19, 2003; author interview with Sarah Elliott, Jane's older daughter, April 13, 2018.

3. When contacted by the author on July 13, 2004, former principal Crawford declined to discuss anything associated with Elliott or Riceville, saying, "I'm not

interested in getting involved in this." When pressed, Crawford responded, "What's the matter with you? Don't you understand the word 'no'?" before hanging up. When Steven Harnack took over the elementary and middle school in Riceville in 1977, Harnack recalled that all Crawford would allow about Jane was that "She's trouble!" Author interview with Harnack, November 19, 2018. Leonard Crawford died October 5, 2014.

4. Author interview with June Judge, June 18, 2018.

5. Author interview with Jerry Markham, August 10, 2018.

6. Author interview with Walt Gabelmann, July 13, 2004. Gabelmann died December 14, 2008.

7. Many persons reported such interactions with Elliott. Two accounts stand out. One woman who asked that her name not be used said that at a local gathering, she mentioned the issue of abortion to Elliott, admitting she was on the fence about the moral implications of the procedure, and Elliott "wouldn't hear anything else I could say. She started railing at me." Another person, Martha Dorow, who grew up in Osage, wrote the author in a May 8, 2018, email that she had been at a July Fourth barbecue during the 2016 presidential election year, when the issue of Iowa caucus candidates came up, and Elliott would not abide by anyone who didn't support her choice, Bernie Sanders. Dorow remembered being "shocked" at the "horrible things" she recalled that Elliott said. Dorow said she didn't remember specific assertions that Elliott allegedly made. Dorow's disapproval may very well be a reflection of regional, unspoken rules generally followed at social gatherings, even when politics are discussed.

8. Jane Elliott, unpublished letter/manuscript, formatted as a remembrance to her children, November 1986, pp. 73–74, author's collection.

9. Elliott, unpublished letter/manuscript, 10.

10. Elliott, unpublished letter/manuscript, 74.

11. Elliott, unpublished letter/manuscript, 76.

12. Elliott, unpublished letter/manuscript, 87–88.

13. Author interview with Sarah Elliott, March 17, 2018.

14. This observation was shared by fourteen persons with whom the author spoke.

15. This incident was relayed to the author by an Osage High School employee.

16. The recollections of growing up in Riceville and Osage are from the author's interview with Brian Elliott, April 7, 2018. The expression "hot LZ" came into the vernacular during the Vietnam War to identify where a helicopter would land. A "hot LZ" was a zone in which the Vietcong had a significant presence, and thus was dangerous for American soldiers. Since Vietnam, the term has come to mean a bad, rough, or uncomfortable situation.

17. Author interview with Brian Elliott, April 7, 2018.

18. Elliott, unpublished letter/manuscript, 75.

19. There are always at least two sides to every skirmish. One of Brian's fights that year apparently was with Tammy Bill, a fellow student at Riceville Elementary. Bill, from a family of fifteen brothers and sisters, recalled that Brian often justified fighting with other children by invoking his mother's name. "Every time, he'd push

someone down, he'd come back with, 'My mom, she's a teacher!'" Once, when Brian shoved two of Bill's younger siblings, she recalled, "I had had enough. So, I ran after him and he ran into his house. I was so angry that I went in and dragged him out and beat him up. I really hit him. His mother called my folks, and Mom told me, 'Just make sure he's not in his house when you hit him.'" Author interview with Tammy Bill Loecher, February 4, 2021.

20. Author interview with Tammy Bill Loecher, February 4, 2021.

21. Author interview with Rick Sletten, February 5, 2019. Sletten today is president of the Osage school board.

22. "Struck by Car, Osage Man Dies," *Waterloo Courier*, April 4, 1976, 20; "Osage Man Killed When Struck by Car," *Des Moines Register*, April 4, 1976, 15; "Two North Iowans among Weekend Traffic Fatalities," *Mason City Globe-Gazette*, April 5, 1976, 1; Gary Chrencik obituary, *Waterloo Courier*, April 5, 1976, 5; author interview with Brian Elliott, April 7, 2018.

23. Author interview with Mary Elliott Gasteiger, by email, March 11, 2018.

24. Author interview with Mark Elliott, October 26, 2004.

25. Author interview with Sarah Elliott, April 12, 2018.

26. Author interview with Brenda Church, June 1, 2018.

27. Author interview with Karen Schofield, January 17, 2019.

28. Author interview, October 10, 2018.

CHAPTER SEVENTEEN: A BLIND SPOT

1. These observations are based on author interviews with numerous former Riceville students and teachers conducted in 2018 and 2019, as well as with former Riceville Junior High School Principal Steven Harnack, October 21, 2004; November 9 and 19, 2018; and January 24, 2018.

2. Everett Berends died June 5, 1983; Helen Berends died June 30, 1999. These accounts were corroborated through author interviews with former teachers, administrators, and students.

3. News of the affairs was not a secret in Riceville, and many locals were aware of it, as shared with the author.

4. Author interview with Bruce Fox, January 25, 2019.

5. Such incidents weren't confined to Riceville. In nearby communities, similar incidents also would periodically occur. An administrator at Osage High School told the author in the winter of 2019: "These kids would jump a kid in the hall that's secluded. They would attack him, wrestle him down, someone would pull their pants down, they'd take a stick or a broom handle, and this happened several times. I think it's a jock thing."

6. The incidence of key parties certainly wasn't confined to Riceville. During the 1970s, such activities were prevalent in urban and rural settings alike. A businessman from nearby Osage said key parties were part of the bar culture there too during the same time period.

7. Gayda Hollnagel, "Pioneer Educator Speaks on Racism," *La Crosse Tribune*, May 27, 1999, 1.

8. Ashley Parrish, "Blueprints on Fighting Racism," *Tulsa World*, April 5, 2000, 9.

9. Author interview with Jane Elliott, September 12, 2004.

10. Author interview with Mitchell Laurren-Ring, July 29, 2004.

11. Author interview with Bill Blake, August 2, 2018.

12. Author interview with Merri Cross, June 21, 2004.

13. Author interviews with Aaron Dvorak, May 18, 2018, and March 21, 2021.

14. Author interview with Michael Blake, August 21, 2018.

15. Author interview with Jerry Markham, August 10, 2018.

CHAPTER EIGHTEEN: CLASS REUNION

1. Rodgers and Hammerstein, *South Pacific*, 1949. For a fascinating analysis of the provocative song, see Andrea Most, "'You've Got to Be Carefully Taught': The Politics of Race in Rodgers and Hammerstein's 'South Pacific,'" *Theatre Journal* 52, no. 3 (October 2000): 307–37.

2. Matthew 13:57–58 (Berean Study Bible).

3. Jane Elliott, unpublished letter/manuscript, formatted as a remembrance to her children, November 1986, pp. 99–100, author's collection.

4. Elliott, unpublished letter/manuscript, 102–7.

5. "A Class Divided," *Frontline*, March 25, 1985, available at https://www.pbs.org/wgbh/frontline/film/class-divided/.

6. William Peters, *A Class Divided: Then and Now* (New Haven, CT: Yale University Press, 1987), 117, 118, 121, 125.

7. Peters, *A Class Divided*, 128–29. These comments and those below were confined to Peters's book and were not included in the PBS *Frontline* video.

8. Peters, *A Class Divided*, 134.

9. Peters, *A Class Divided*, 135.

10. "A Class Divided," *Frontline*.

11. "A Class Divided," *Frontline*.

12. Author interview with Steven Harnack, November 19, 2018.

13. "A Class Divided," *Frontline*.

CHAPTER NINETEEN: THE OFFER

1. This exchange is based on author interviews with former Riceville Junior High School Principal Steven Harnack; former Riceville School Superintendent Norm Kolberg; an anonymous former school board member; former school board member Leo Jordan; and Jane Elliott, unpublished letter/manuscript, formatted as a remembrance to her children, November 1986, pp. 111–12, author's collection.

2. "Lytton Superintendent Is Hired at Riceville Schools," *Waterloo Courier*, April 10, 1977, 77.

3. Elliott, unpublished letter/manuscript, 112.

4. Elliott, unpublished letter/manuscript, 119.

5. Author interview with Norm Kolberg, July 13, 2004.

6. Author interviews with anonymous former school board member, July 7, 2004, and November 6, 2018.

7. Author interview with former school board member Leo Jordan, October 21, 2018.

8. Author interview with Steven Harnack, November 9, 2018.

CHAPTER TWENTY: UNBOUND

1. US West letter to Jane Elliott from Jan M. Fincher and R. Ann Welter, December 2, 1988. The phrase "pluralism training sessions" is contained in a decision from the United States Court of Appeals for the Tenth Circuit reversing an earlier order by the United States District Court for the District of Colorado, in a lawsuit filed against US West by Laurie Fitzgerald and Aaron Hazard, January 31, 1995. Laurie Fitzgerald and Aaron Hazard v. The Mountain States Telephone and Telegraph Company, d/b/a U.S. West Communications, Inc., 93–1142 (10th Cir. 1995).

2. David Olson, "Jane Elliott's 46-Year Fight against Bigotry," *Riverside Press-Enterprise*, February 7, 2014, https://www.pe.com/2014/02/07/menifee-jane-elliott8217s-46-year-fight-against-bigotry/.

3. Interview with Ann Jaramillo Welter, former US West manager–pluralism education, November 2, 2018.

4. Author interview with Mary Yager, April 12, 2018.

5. Jane Elliott, unpublished letter/manuscript, formatted as a remembrance to her children, November 1986, pp. 133–34, author's collection.

6. For a description of such retreats and workshops, see Selene Kumin Vega, "The Integration of Transformative Workshop Experiences," PhD diss., Saybrook University, November 2009.

7. Luke Rhinehart, *The Book of est* (New York: Holt, Rinehart and Winston, 1976).

8. Gregory Jay, with Sandra Elaine Jones, "Whiteness Studies and the Multicultural Literature Classroom," *MELUS* 30, no. 2 (Summer 2005): 99–121.

9. Author interview with former US West diversity trainer Judy Swinnerton, October 11, 2018.

10. Author interview with Judy Swinnerton, October 11, 2018.

11. Author interview with former US West employee Julie Pasicznyk, June 19, 2018.

12. Author interview with former US West employee Sandy Juettner, September 21, 2018.

13. Author interview with former US West employee Julie Pasicznyk, June 19, 2018. Elliott had employed such tactics back at Riceville Elementary decades earlier when she forced Julie Kleckner to kneel in Classroom No. 10.

14. Author interview with former US West Director Jan Fincher, October 9, 2018.

15. *Fitzgerald*, 93–1142. See note 16 below.

16. There's a postscript to Elliott's involvement with US West's pluralism workshops. Five months after Elliott was let go as a consultant, the company held a five-day seminar at its headquarters in Lakewood, Colorado, as a tryout for would-be facilitators, who, in part, would replace Elliott. Each of the twenty-five candidates was asked to relate an incident to show his or her commitment to diversity, and one participant, Laurie Fitzgerald, a white woman, talked about a romantic relationship with a Black man and how blowback from the Black community had torpedoed the couple. Fitzgerald was not hired by US West, she contended, because a Black female manager for US West told her, "You white bitches are always trying to take all the airtime, and I'm sick of it." A district federal jury awarded Fitzgerald $1.3 million; Fitzgerald's business partner was awarded $1.06 million. Two years later, though, a federal appeals court reversed the lower court's ruling, calling it "excessive" and "speculative." *Fitzgerald*, 93–1142.

17. US West letter to Jane Elliott from Jan M. Fincher and R. Ann Welter, December 2, 1988.

CHAPTER TWENTY-ONE: OPRAH

1. The quotes from Jane Elliott about her appearances on *The Oprah Winfrey Show* are culled from Jane Elliott, unpublished letter/manuscript, formatted as a remembrance to her children, November 1986, pp. 166–81, author's collection. Elliott first appeared on Winfrey's local talk show on June 20, 1986.

2. *The Oprah Winfrey Show* first aired nationally on September 8, 1986. Reviewing her first show, *Hollywood Reporter* critic Miles Beller wrote, "In a world run amok with pompous talk show pitchmen, Oprah Winfrey is something different"; Miles Beller, "'The Oprah Winfrey Show' First Episode: THR's 1986 Review," *Hollywood Reporter*, reposted Sept. 9, 2016, https://www.hollywoodreporter.com/review/oprah-winfrey-show-1986-first-926952.

3. All dialogue from the four *Oprah Winfrey Shows* upon which Elliott appeared as a guest is taken directly from the original episodes, as supplied to the author by the Oprah Winfrey Network.

4. Spoken by disgruntled and psychotic fictional newsman Howard Beale, played by actor Peter Finch in the 1976 film *Network*.

5. Welles's classic *War of the Worlds* radio broadcast on Halloween evening 1938, purportedly describing a Martian attack in New Jersey, was thought to be believed by tens of thousands of listeners, causing alarm and panic.

6. Jane Elliott's letter/manuscript, 171.

7. The Peters projection world map was created by historian and cartographer Arno Peters, and published in 1974. It seeks to show actual geographic masses; at its center is Africa, not the United States. The standard Mercator map was originally created in 1569.

8. Jane Elliott's letter/manuscript, 180.

9. Author interview with June Judge, June 18, 2018.

10. Email exchanges between Gemma Bauer and the author, November 7–8, 2018. When asked specifically about what Elliott had allegedly said to Winfrey at the conclusion of the show, Bauer responded, "We reached out to a producer who worked at Harpo at this time to verify the claim. The statement is not true, and we appreciate you discarding this information from the forthcoming book." She declined to elaborate.

CHAPTER TWENTY-TWO: THE GREATER GOOD

1. James M. Jones, *Prejudice and Racism*, 2nd ed. (New York: McGraw-Hill, 1997), 323–24.

2. Philip G. Zimbardo, in consultation with Floyd Leon Ruch, *Psychology and Life*, 1st ed. (Glenview, IL: Scott, Foresman and Company, 1975), 598–600.

3. The Coles quote has been cited numerous times in the popular press, but its origin is unclear. See Afterword.

4. ABC News, *Nightline*, May 23, 1996; *CBS Evening News with Dan Rather*, May 7, 1999; *ABC World News Tonight with Peter Jennings*, April 24, 1992.

5. NPR, *All Things Considered*, August 29, 2001.

6. Tracie L. Stewart et al., "Do the 'Eyes' Have It? A Program Evaluation of Jane Elliott's 'Blue-Eyes/Brown-Eyes' Diversity Training Exercise," *Journal of Applied Social Psychology* 33, no. 9 (2003): 1898–1921. A previous study was undertaken by Deborah A. Byrnes and Gary Kiger in 1990 to determine the efficacy of the blue-eyes, brown-eyes experiment. See Deborah A. Byrnes and Gary Kiger, "The Effect of a Prejudice-Reduction Simulation on Attitude Change," *Journal of Applied Social Psychology* 20, no. 4 (March 1990): 341–56. The Byrnes and Kiger study was undercut by several methodological considerations, including its abridged length and two prejudicial measures later seen as possibly undermining its accuracy. The experiment took place at Utah State University, and the two eye-color groups were made up almost entirely of female students belonging to the Church of Jesus Christ of Latter-day Saints. Byrnes and Kiger followed up with another article in 1992 assessing their evaluation; Deborah A. Byrnes and Gary Kiger, "Prejudice-Reduction Simulations: Ethics, Evaluations, and Theory into Practice," *Simulation and Gaming* 24, no. 4 (December 1992): 457–71.

7. Stewart et al., "Do the 'Eyes' Have It?" 1904.

8. Email exchange between Tracie Stewart and the author, July 31, 2018.

9. Email exchange between Tracie Stewart and the author, July 31, 2018.

10. Elizabeth Levy Paluck and Donald Green, "Prejudice Reduction: What Works? A Review and Assessment of Research and Practice," *Annual Review of Psychology* 60 (2009): 339–67.

11. Judith White, "Beloved Teacher Leaves Gift for the Gifted," *Saratogian*, July 1, 2005, https://www.saratogian.com/news/beloved-teacher-leaves-gift-for-the-gifted/article_7b288038–0a3c-5d02-a253-af9eb247db9f.html; "Phyllis Aldrich Gets Skidmore Post," *Glen Falls Post-Star*, March 20, 1973, 20. Watts was to marry in her second year of teaching at Saint Ann's, and took on the surname Aldrich.

12. Ariel Levy, "The Devil and Saint Ann's," *New York*, April 30, 2004, http://nymag.com/nymetro/news/people/features/n_10337/. In 2019, an internal investigation conducted by Saint Ann's revealed allegations of sexual misconduct at the school involving nineteen former administrators, faculty members, staff, and students that had taken place over a forty-year period, from the 1970s to 2017.

13. Author interview with Phyllis Watts Aldrich, July 25, 2019.

14. In William Golding's classic novel, *Lord of the Flies* (London: Faber and Faber, 1954), adolescent boys on a deserted island turn against one another based on the groups they choose to form, they believe, to survive.

15. Kate Gladstone's memory that the experiment lasted longer is shared by many other former students. When the author interviewed former students in Riceville, many recalled that the experiment lasted a week or more before each group traded its superior or inferior role. Malinda Sunnes Whisenhunt, who was in Elliott's class in 1968–69, remembered that the experiment "lasted much, much longer than two days. I think it was for three weeks, at least," she said. Author interview with Malinda Sunnes Whisenhunt, July 21, 2004.

16. Author interview with Kate Gladstone, May 16, 2018.

17. Author interview with Renee Gladstone, June 1, 2018.

18. Author interview with Jay McGovern, 2004.

19. For more information on the Iliff Preschool, Kindergarten, and School-Age Summer Camp, see http://iliffpreschool.com/about-us/. The school is known for its experiential learning. On its playground since 1971 has sat the body of a DC-7 aircraft known as *Charlie 21*.

20. Weberg said she doesn't do the experiment with all her kindergarten classes. "Each classroom is unique. The children I taught this past year were very young and unable to participate with the exercise. I knew who they were and what their social/emotional capabilities were. There was no reason to engage them at that level." Email exchange with the author, June 21, 2018.

21. Email exchanges between Mary Weberg and the author, June 11, 2018; June 21, 2018; September 6, 2019.

22. James's and Sapon-Shevin's comments were contained in Carolyn Thompson, "Schools Still Struggling with How to Teach about Slavery," Associated Press, July 6, 2019.

23. Author interview with Tammy Bill Loecher, February 4, 2021.

24. Beverly Daniel Tatum, *"Why Are All the Black Kids Sitting Together in the Cafeteria" and Other Conversations about Race* (New York: Basic, 1997), 202.

25. The episode originally aired on London's Channel 4 in 2009, hosted by Krishnan Guru-Murthy. "The Event: How Racist Are You? with Jane Elliott (Channel 4) (FULL)," Per Christian Frankplads, June 26, 2013, video, 47:27, https://www.youtube.com/watch?v=6MYHBrJIIFU.

26. Email exchange between Dominic Abrams and the author, August 22, 2018.

27. Andrew Anthony, "Jane Elliott, the American Schoolmarm Who Would Rid Us of Our Racism," *The Guardian*, October 17, 2009, https://www.theguardian.com/culture/2009/oct/18/racism-psychology-jane-elliott-4.

28. Author interview with Dick Woodruff, August 8, 2018.

CHAPTER TWENTY-THREE: THE DOGS BARK, BUT THE CARAVAN GOES ON

1. Author interview with Malinda Sunnes Whisenhunt, June 21, 2004.

2. Author interview with Jim Cross, April 13, 2018.

3. According to the Mitchell County, Iowa, Assessor's Office, February 2021.

4. According to Zillow.com, February 2021.

5. Merri Cross, ed., *History of Riceville, Iowa: A 150-Year History of Our Little Town along the Wapsi,* no further publishing information supplied. Cross, wife of Jim Cross, the former editor of the *Riceville Recorder* and current editor of the *Mitchell County Press News,* is a former student of Elliott. Other noteworthy Iowans include Mildred Wirt Benson, the original author of the Nancy Drew book series; Johnny Carson; opera singer Simon Estes; bandleader Glenn Miller; actor Ashton Kutcher; newspaper columnists Ann Landers and her sister, Abigail Van Buren; actresses Donna Reed, Sue Lyon, and Jean Seberg; John Wayne; composer Meredith Wilson; baseball pitcher Bob Feller; golfer Zach Johnson; artist Grant Wood; astronomer James Van Allen; politician and presidential candidate Henry A. Wallace; and the five Sullivan brothers, killed in action on the USS *Juneau* during World War II. US President Herbert Hoover was an Iowa native, but moved away to Oregon when he was eleven and rarely came back.

6. Author interview with Jim Cross, June 21, 2004.

7. Casandra Leff, ed., *A History of Riceville Community School (1875–2012): Shining Brightly after 137 Years* (Riceville, IA: Riceville Recorder, n.d.), 27.

8. Author interview with Bill Diederich, August 30, 2018. Diederich died September 26, 2019.

9. Author interview with Linda Ring Kinneman, August 24, 2018.

10. Murray Waldren, "She Shall Overcome," *The Weekend Australian*, November 22, 1997, 3, 4.

11. Author interview with Darald Elliott, October 19, 2003.

12. Darald Dean Elliott obituary, *Mitchell County Press News*, September 30, 2013.

13. "A Conversation on Race and Privilege with Angela Davis and Jane Elliott," University of Houston, Graduate College of Social Work, September 6, 2018.

14. Lloyd Jennison obituary, *Mason City Globe-Gazette*, July 6, 1990, 9; Gie Jennison obituary, *Mason City Globe-Gazette*, June 17, 2008, 10.

15. Author email exchange with Raymond Hansen, June 12, 2018.

16. Author email exchange with Rex Kozak, June 10, 2018.

17. The majority of these quotes come from a May 30, 2020, episode of the podcast, *The Last Outlaws*, hosted by Zack Leary; "Jane Elliott Interview: George Floyd Riots, Karens, and More . . ." *The Last Outlaws*, May 30, 2020, video, 26:49, https://www.youtube.com/watch?v=_26bpU7UgTs.

18. "Race Relations Expert Claims All U.S.-Born Whites Are Racists," *Los Angeles Sentinel*, October 14, 1993, A3.

19. Speaking fees culled from All American Entertainment, Speaker Booking Agency, the National Organization of Professional Athletes and Celebrities, and SMG Speakers Bureau.

20. Kären Mason, "An Oral History Interview with Jane Elliott," November 4, 2009, Jane Elliott Papers, Iowa Women's Archives at the University of Iowa Libraries, 60.

21. James Causey interview with Elliott on the Milwaukee PBS show, *Black Nouveau*; "Black Nouveau: Exclusive: Jane Elliott Interview, Part 1," Milwaukee PBS, November 2, 2017, video, 9:33, https://www.youtube.com/watch?v=4QJIu15VjQg.

22. "An Unfinished Crusade: An Interview with Jane Elliott," *Frontline*, December 19, 2002, posted January 1, 2003, https://www.pbs.org/wgbh/frontline/article/an-unfinished-crusade-an-interview-with-jane-elliott/; Mason, "An Oral History Interview," 59.

23. Author email exchanges with Robin DiAngelo, September 27 and 29, 2019.

24. "A Conversation on Race and Privilege with Angela Davis and Jane Elliott," University of Houston, Graduate College of Social Work, September 6, 2018.

25. *Red Table Talk*, hosted by Jada Pickett Smith, presented by Facebook Watch, November 12, 2018, https://www.facebook.com/538649879867825/posts/699300837136061/.

26. "An Unfinished Crusade."

27. Brian Cantor, "NBC Updates 'Tonight Show Starring Jimmy Fallon' Guest Lineups for June 1, 2, 3, 4 & 5 (Update)," *Headline Planet*, June 1, 2020, https://headlineplanet.com/home/2020/06/01/nbc-updates-tonight-show-starring-jimmy-fallon-guest-lineups-for-june-1-june-2/.

28. "Jane Elliott on Her 'Blue Eyes / Brown Eyes Exercise' and Fighting Racism," *The Tonight Show Starring Jimmy Fallon*, June 1, 2020, https://www.nbc.com/the-tonight-show/video/janeelliotton-herblue-eyesbrown-eyes-exerciseand-fighting-racism/4177870.

29. Alisha Haridasani Gupti, "A Teacher Held a Famous Racism Exercise in 1968. She's Still at It," *New York Times*, July 4, 2020, https://www.nytimes.com/2020/07/04/us/jane-elliott-anti-racism-blue-eyes-brown-eyes.html?action=click&module=RelatedLinks&pgtype=Article.

30. Brianna Holt, "The Return of Jane Elliott," *New York Times*, July 15, 2020, https://www.nytimes.com/2020/07/15/style/jane-elliott-anti-racism.html.

1. Jane Elliott, *A Collar in My Pocket: Blue-Eyes/Brown-Eyes Exercise* (Scotts Valley, CA: CreateSpace Independent Publishing Platform, 2016).

2. Judi Cunningham and Rozenia Cunningham, *Blue Eyes Brown Eyes* (Scotts Valley, CA: CreateSpace Independent Publishing Platform, 2018).

3. "The Stolen Eye," JaneElliott.com, https://janeelliott.com/video-store/the-stolen-eye.

4. "Blue Eyed: All in One," JaneElliott.com, https://janeelliott.com/video-store/blue-eyed-all-in-one.

5. "Indecently Exposed," JaneElliott.com, https://janeelliott.com/video-store/indecently-exposed; "Eye Opener," JaneElliott.com, https://janeelliott.com/video-store/eye-opener.

6. From the German documentary, *Blauäugig* (Blue Eyed) by Bertram Verhaag, 1996. The film's transcript may be found at "'Blue Eyed' Transcript," Internet Archive, https://web.archive.org/web/20150202090627/http://newsreel.org/transcripts/blueeyed.htm, accessed February 2021.

7. "Sarandon, Julia Roberts to Produce Film," *San Francisco Chronicle*, January 30, 1996, D6. A letter to Elliott, dated December 20, 1995, from Pliny Porter, president of production and development for Shoelace Productions, attests to the studio's interest, Jane Elliott Papers, University of Iowa Women's Archive at the University of Iowa.

8. The play, *Class*, written by a Madison, Wisconsin, playwright who goes by the name Coleman, is described as a dark comedy. This is *Class's* synopsis, as supplied by its author: "In this two-act fictional re-telling, following the introduction of her new lesson, the teacher is confronted by an angry parent and the school principal. They quickly succumb to the teacher's upside down logic as well as charm and learn her lesson with hilarious and tragic consequences." See "Coleman," New Play Exchange, https://newplayexchange.org/users/17426/coleman, accessed February 2021.

9. Author interview with Daniel Coles, October 21, 2019.

10. "'Beyond Rubies' Conference Is Slated," *Cedar Rapids Gazette*, January 27, 1985, 3B.

11. "Lesson in Racism Catapults Teacher to Forefront of Issue," *Hartford Courant*, November 22, 1985, C6.

12. "Sociology Students Open Sensitive Ears," *Wyckoff News*, January 18, 1990, 7; "Students Learn Tolerance at Workshop," *Sioux City Journal*, November 27, 1999, B8.

13. Aziz Gökdemir, "'Blue Eyes, Brown Eyes' Reveals Hidden Prejudice," *Daily Iowan*, January 22, 1991, 3A.

14. Alisha Dixon, "Race, Gender and Identity in the Workplace featuring Jane Elliott and Roland S. Martin," *Michigan Chronicle*, January 25, 2017, https://michiganchronicle.com/2017/01/25/race-gender-identity-in-the-workplace-featuring-jane-elliott-and-roland-s-martin-wctf-conference-free-keynote-address-registration/.

15. Those featured were Meenal Viz, Tamika Mallory, Riz Ahmed, Reni Eddo-Lodge, Yvette Williams, Patrick Hutchinson, Janet Mock, Angela Davis, Jane Elliott, Patrisse Cullors, Clara Amfo, Bernice A. King, Alice Wong, Jesse Williams,

Joan Smalls, Janaya Future Khan, Fiona Dwyer, and Brittany N. Packnett Cunningham, Marcus Rashford, and Adwoa Aboah.

16. Rutstein, journalist, author, educator, and founder of the Institute for the Healing of Racism, died May 22, 2006. The quote is cited in Carol Rutstein, ed., *From a Gnat to an Eagle: The Story of Nathan Rutstein* (Wilmette, IL: Baha'i Publishing, 2008), 187. Under Elliott's name on the sweatshirt, "#onerace #humanrace" is printed.

17. *Blauäugig* (Blue Eyed), by Bertram Verhaag, 1996.

18. Author interview with Brian Elliott, April 7, 2018.

19. Author interview with Sarah Elliott, April 12–13, 2018.

20. Kieron Johnson, "Jane Elliott, Creator of the 'Blue/Brown Eyes' Experiment, Says Racism Is Easy to Fix," *Oprah Magazine*, September 21, 2020, https://www.oprahmag.com/life/a33959630/jane-elliott-racism-2020-interview/.

CODA: ANDY'S AND THE VILLE

1. James Merchant and David Osterberg, "The Explosion of CAFOs in Iowa and Its Impact on Water Quality and Public Health," The Iowa Policy Project, January 2018, https://www.iowapolicyproject.org/2018docs/180125-CAFO.pdf; Bill Berry, "What Is Wisconsin Doing to Fend Off Negative Effects of CAFOs?" *Capital Times* (Madison, WI), July 22, 2019, https://madison.com/ct/opinion/column/bill-berry-what-is-wisconsin-doing-to-fend-off-negative-effects-of-cafos/article_d062a942-c160-58e9-bcb0-038715b448f6.html.

2. Quotes in this coda come from author interviews, September 14, 2018.

3. Two-time Cy Young winner Max Scherzer, a pitcher for the Washington Nationals, has a rare ocular condition known as heterochromia iridis. His right eye is blue and his left eye is brown.

INDEX

"Blue Eyed: All in One" (JaneElliott.com), 250n4

Blue Eyes, Brown Eyes, rhyming children's book, 205

blue eyes, brown eyes experiment: Associated Press story about, 87–88; at Bard College, 188–89; Carroll's accusation of Elliott's copying "Project Misery," 119–20, 238n4; Coles's "praise" for, 187; Darald's concerns, 49, 53, 64; *Des Moines Register* article about, 87; Elliott's concerns/doubts about, 53–54; Elliott's epiphany/origin/planning for, 46–50; on *The Event* (British tv documentary), 196–97; Iliff Preschool and Kindergarten, modified version, 185; impact on classrooms, universities, colleges, 187; impact on the students, 89–92; introduction/instructions to students, 54–61, 65–66; introduction of discrimination, prejudice, racism, 55–56; King's assassination as inspiration for, 45–46, 66; mentions of, in college textbooks, 187; naming as Discrimination Day, 66–67; national educators' praise of, 86–87; with the Osage Rotary Club, 93–95; previous iterations of, 122–24; "Project Misery" comparison, 120–21; reactions of other teachers, 61–63; responses of the students, 57, 63–65; *Riceville Recorder's* articles about, 67–69, 87; at Saint Ann"s School (Brooklyn, New York), 190–93; Stewart's gauging of the efficacy of, 188–89; student's descriptions of Negroes, 54–55; Thorson's complaint of Elliott's alleged misappropriation of "Project Misery," 120, 238n5; uncertainty of the students, 57; U.S./global use of, 189–90, 194; at US West, 166–72; as variation of a Nazi experiment, xi, xvi, 45–46, 97, 100, 102, 112, 121; Wood's suggestion of Elliott's misappropriation of "Project Misery," 118–22. *See also* Canadian Broadcasting Corporation (CBC), filming of blue eyes brown eyes experiment; "Eye of the Storm"; US West, blue eyes brown eyes experience

Blue Eyes Brown Eyes (Cunningham and Cunningham), 250n2

Bodenheim, Patty, 21, 225n5

Bodensteiner, Christopher, 234n6

Bodensteiner, Paul, 97–98, 234n5, 234n6

Bohi, William, 128

Boston College, 222

Brandau, Todd, 234n5

Brandmill, Dinsmore, 47, 54, 60–61, 71–73, 87, 96, 103, 108, 136–37, 229n2, 235n30, 236n43

Brando, Marlon, 26

Breitsprecher, Jean, 214, 215

Breitsprecher, Lee, 214, 215

"Brown-Eyed Prejudice for Those with Blue" *(Des Moines Register)*, 232n17

Brownie (Elliot family pony), 38

Brown University, 190

Brunner, Adolph, 23–24, 35, 233n13

Brunner, Carol Lou, 24, 92, 225n15, 233n13

Brunner, Dale, 66, 68, 229n2

Bucknell, Byron, 52, 229n2

Buls, Verla, 157

Burke, Sandi (née Dohlman), 33.105, 157, 227n24, 236n33

Butterfield, Mark, 234n5

Button, Charlotte, 73–74, 75, 106, 233n19

Button, Don, 75–76, 233n19

Byrnes, Deborah A., 246n6

CAFO (concentrated animal feeding operation), 212

Camp Anytown, 239n20

Canadian Broadcasting Corporation (CBC), filming of blue-eyes, brown-eyes experiment, 96–100; CBC's approach to Elliott, 96; Elliott's reluctance, 96–97; modifications from first experiment, 97; notices sent to parents, 96; public/viewer reaction, 99–100; student reactions, memories, 97–99

"Canadian Broadcasting System to Film Documentary in Riceville" *(Riceville Recorder)*, 234n2

Canadian Inuits, 96, 98

Capote, Truman, 3

Carroll, C. S., Rev., 20

Carroll, Mary, 119–20, 238n4

Doussard, James, 107
DuBois, Rachel Davis, 123, 239n18
Duke University, Center for Documentary Studies, 207
Duncomb, Margaret, 150
Dunn, LeRoy, 25, 43, 226n24
Dvorak, Aaron, 149–50, 243n13

"The Effect of a Prejudice-Reduction Simulation on Attitude Change" (Byrnes and Kiger) (*Journal of Applied Social Psychology*), 246n6
Elliott, Brian, 21n18, 26, 33, 37–39, 42, 139–43, 209, 241n16, 241n17, 241n19, 241n22, 251n18
Elliott, Darald Dean: background, 26; concerns about the experiment, 49, 53, 64; death from multiple system atrophy, 200; employment/memberships, 37, 142, 161; marriage/family with Elliott, 26–27, 37; purchase/ownership of Jennison Hotel, 138, 200; support for Elliott and family, 155, 200, 240n2; trip to New York for *Tonight Show* appearance, 71–80; victimization of the Elliot children, 139–44
Elliott, Jane: as ABC News "Person of the Week," 187; admiration for, 101, 113, 135, 155, 205; Alcorn's characterization of, 228–29n5; "Anatomy of Prejudice" lecture series, 190; Brunner's description of, 23–24; childhood/family background, 20–22; college years, 24–25; description of Dunn, 25; description of self/siblings, 24; direct personality of, 138; Elliott's children's thoughts about, 208–10; enjoyment of "black sheep" role, 42; firing of, by US West, 172, 244n1, 245n16; Gabelmann's comment about, xiii; high school years, 22–24; honoraria and speaking fees, 137, 201, 249n19; Iowa State Education Association presentation, 102, 130; lecturing in/out of the midwest, 148; letter from Wilda Wood, 119–25, 222; letter of resignation from teaching, 164–65; letters to Mickey Alcorn, 50–51, 64–65, 73, 77, 81, 228n5, 229n1; national educa-

tors' praise of, 86–87, 136; national media stories about, 135; negative reactions to *Tonight Show* appearance, 83–85; objection to the word "experiment," 108; offer to do onsite training for Mountain Bell, 162–65; participation in federal grant, 135; profiles of, by television journalists, 187; purchase/ownership of Jennison Hotel, 138, 200; racism/bias experiment, ix–xii; reaction to King's assassination, 43–45; *Reader's Digest* essay submission, 101; real estate holdings/value, 198; rhyming children's book, 205; Riceville citizens' opinions about, xii–xvi, 19, 70, 82–83, 91–92, 100, 112, 135, 137–39, 156, 212–17; Riceville school board's opinion of, 163–64; Richer's comparison with, 127–28, 131–34; run-ins with Harnack, 145–48, 151, 155; *Scholastic Teacher* essay submission, 101; training videos, 205; White House Conference on Children participation, 110–17
Elliott, Jane, teaching career: classroom pets, 31; cross-generational friendships projects, 31–32; first job (Randall, Iowa), 26; Hero of the Month unit, 36; invention of Pizzui (make-believe gremlin), 34; Iowa Teacher of the Year nomination, 100; letter of resignation, 164–65; Liberty Line trees project, 32; Magic Circle, 36, 64, 66–67, 105, 157, 192; math/economics classroom projects, 26–31; national endorsements, 86–87, 136; one-million counting project, 32; other teachers' reactions, 31, 35; participation in government grant, 135; polarized opinions about Elliott, 148–49, 148–50. *See also* Classroom No. 10; Riceville Elementary School; Riceville Junior High
Elliott, Mark, 143, 209, 242n24
Elliott, Sarah, 26, 37–39, 41, 85, 139–43, 201, 209–10, 228n1, 240n2, 241n13, 242n25, 261n19
Englert Theatre, xiii, 208
Erhard, Werner, 167
essays, by students, of Discrimination Day, 67–70

Leard, Dennis, 17, 224n10
Lemon, Don, 203
Leonard, George B., 101
Leonard, John, 107, 236n39
Letts, Marney, 235n22
Lewis, Danny, 52, 229n2
Lewis, Sinclair, 130, 240n11
LGBTQ community, 201
Life magazine, 107
Lifton, Robert Jay, 121
Linkenmeyer, Donna Jo, 98, 234n5
The Linkletter Show, 101
Loecher, Tammy Bill, 141, 196, 242n19–20, 247n23, cover
Look magazine, 101
Lord of the Flies (Golding), 247n14
"The Lottery" (Jackson), xvii, 223n10
Louisville Carrier-Journal, 107
Lubbert, Steve, 234n5
Lyon, Sue, 248n5

Machin, JoAnne, 84, 232n5
Maddix, William J., 228n24
Main Street (Lewis), 130, 240n11
Manly, Iowa, 25, 226n24
Marion, Loretta, 101, 151, 241n5, 243n15
Markham, Jerry, 137, 151, 241n5, 243n15
Marr, Joe, 98, 234n5
Martin, Cathy, 34, 35, 47, 237n26
Mason, Kären, 225n2, 227n17, 229n1, 230n1, 231n1, 234n3, 249n20
Mason City Globe-Gazette, 132, 240n19
May, Donna (née Reddel), 157
McCarthy, Dale, 98, 234n5, 234n8
McGovern, Jay, 194, 247n18
McLuhan, Marshall, 5
McMahon, Ed, 1–2, 5–6, 9, 78–79
Mendelsohn, Robert, 237n4
Mengele: The Complete Story (Posner and Ware), 121
Messersmith, M. E. (Smitty), 67–68, 70, 73–75, 80, 82, 87, 111, 138, 147, 162. *See also Riceville Recorder*
Meyer, Cinder, 229n2
Michigan State University, 207
Mila 18 (Uris), 45, 121, 206
Miller, Glenn, 248n5
Mills, George, 131, 239n1, 240n12

Mitchell County Press News, 198
The Moral Intelligence of Children (Coles), 207
The Moral Life of Children (Coles), 206
Morris, Gail Messersmith, 74, 231n7
Morrow, Donald H., 120
Moses, LaVonne, 91, 233n9
Mosher, Harvey, 214
Mosher, Jane, 214–15
Mosher's Dry Goods, 39
Moss, Alan, 64, 70, 91, 229n2, 233, n7
Moyers, Dot, 235n43
Murph's Tavern, 17, 154, 1147
Murphy, Lineq, 39
The Music Man (Wilson), xv
Myers, Mary, 92, 233n12

Nath, Debora, 234n5
National Brotherhood Week, 104–5
National Conference on Christians and Jews (NCCJ), 123–24
National Education Association (NEA): Committee on Professional Ethics, 120; endorsement of "Eye of the Storm," 106–7
National Elementary Principal, 120
Native Americans, 201
The Nazi Doctors: Medical Killing and the Psychology of Genocide (Lifton), 121
Nazis/Nazism: atrocities practiced by, 121; books written about, 121; as model for blue eyes, brown eyes experiment, xi, xvi, 45–46, 97, 100, 102, 112
NEA Journal, 120
Network film, 177
New York Times, 239n19
New York Times, stories on Elliot, 204
New York University, 190
Nixon, Richard M., 5, 73, 110–11, 237n2
Noble, Mary, 86, 232n11
Nold, Celiene, 87, 230n6
Northwestern University, 102

Oakley, Diane, 237n4
O'Flaherty, Terrence, 107
Okura, K. Patrick, 113–15, 237n4, 237n10
Oprah magazine, 210

Founded in 1893,
UNIVERSITY OF CALIFORNIA PRESS
publishes bold, progressive books and journals
on topics in the arts, humanities, social sciences,
and natural sciences—with a focus on social
justice issues—that inspire thought and action
among readers worldwide.

The UC PRESS FOUNDATION
raises funds to uphold the press's vital role
as an independent, nonprofit publisher, and
receives philanthropic support from a wide
range of individuals and institutions—and from
committed readers like you. To learn more, visit
ucpress.edu/supportus.